MANDALA THE ARCHITECTURE OF ENLIGHTENMENT

MANDALA

THE ARCHITECTURE OF ENLIGHTENMENT

DENISE PATRY LEIDY AND ROBERT A. F. THURMAN

ASIA SOCIETY GALLERIES, NEW YORK
TIBET HOUSE, NEW YORK
SHAMBHALA, BOSTON

This book has been published in conjunction with the exhibition "Mandala: The Architecture of Enlightenment," co-organized by the Asia Society Galleries and Tibet House.

Asia Society Galleries, New York
September 24, 1997–January 4, 1998

Mandala: The Architecture of Enlightenment and related programs are co-organized by the Asia Society and Tibet House. They have been funded in part by the National Endowment for the Arts, The Henry Luce Foundation, Mary Livingston Griggs and Mary Griggs Burke Foundation, The Woodcock Foundation, Ellen Bayard Weedon Foundation, Michael Marsh, and Frank and Lisina Hoch. Support for the Asia Society Galleries exhibitions and education programs has been provided by the Friends of Asian Arts, The Starr Foundation, The Armand G. Erpf Fund, and the Arthur Ross Foundation.

Cover/jacket: *Kalachakra Mandala*, Tibet, 17th century; ink and opaque watercolors on cloth, 47 1/8 x 30 7/8 inches (120.4 x 78.4 cm); Museum of Fine Arts, Boston, Frederick L. Jack Fund, 58.691 (catalogue no. 28).
Frontispiece: *Mandala of Jnanadakini* (detail), Tibet, Sakya order, late 14th–early 15th century; ink and opaque watercolors on cloth, 33 1/4 x 28 7/8 inches (84.5 x 73.3 cm); The Metropolitan Museum of Art, Purchase, Lita Annenberg Hazen Charitable Trust Gift, 1987.16 (catalogue no. 26).

Asia Society Galleries, 725 Park Avenue, New York, New York 10021 USA
Tibet House, 22 West 15th Street, New York, New York 10011 USA
Shambhala Publications, Inc., 300 Massachusetts Avenue, Boston, Massachusetts 02115 USA

Library of Congress Catalog Card Number: 97-74622

Printed in Singapore

ISBN 0-87848-088-9 (hardcover edition)
ISBN 1-57062-297-3 (softcover edition)

Photograph and illustration credits:

Photographs of originals and essay illustrations are courtesy of the owners unless otherwise noted.

American Committee for Southern Asian Art Color Slide Project - pages 16, 32 (figs. 22 and 23); Martin Brauen - page 152; Christopher Burke - page 105; Lynton Gardiner - pages 35, 51, 115 (cat. no. 39); Janice Glowski - page 34; Harvard College Library Photographic Services - pages 45 (fig. 41), 120, 121; Lisina Hoch - page 69; John C. Huntington - pages 19, 31, 32, 39 (figs. 33 and 34), 40; Brian Kistler - page 150; Janice Leoshko - page 34; Jürgen Liepe - page 24 (fig. 11); Carl Nardiello - pages 84, 97, 123; George Roos - pages 66, 67, 68, 82, 83, 102; John Bigelow Taylor - pages 20 (fig. 5), 43 (fig. 39), 56, 74, 75, 79, 80, 81, 108, 109, 111, 128; Robert A. F. Thurman - pages 126, 151; Graydon Wood - page 91; Doris Weiner - page 88; Katherine Wetzel - page 89; Bruce White - page 50

Chart on page 149 by Patrick Seymour
Chart on page 153 by Patrick Seymour and Michael Crumpton

Robert A. F. Thurman, *Mandala: The Architecture of Enlightenment* (essay). Copyright © by Robert A. F. Thurman.

Denise Patry Leidy, *Place and Process: Mandala Imagery in the Buddhist Art of Asia*. Copyright © by Denise Patry Leidy.

Excerpt from Barry Bryant, *The Wheel of Time Sand Mandala: Visual Scripture of Tibetan Buddhism*. Copyright © 1993 by Samaya Foundation. Reprinted by permission of the Samaya Foundation.

Matthieu Ricard, *Introduction to the Purpose and Symbolism of the Mandala in Tibetan Buddhism*. Copyright © by Matthieu Ricard. Reprinted by permission of the author.

Excerpt from Peter Gold, *Navajo & Tibetan Sacred Wisdom*. Published by Inner Traditions International, Rochester, VT 05767. Copyright © 1994 by Peter Gold. Reprinted by permission of Inner Traditions International.

Excerpt from C. G. Jung, *Mandala Symbolism*. Copyright © 1959, 1969, 1972 by Princeton University Press. Reprinted by permission of Princeton University Press.

CONTENTS

FOREWORD

Mandalas, the sacred cosmograms of the Hindu-Buddhist world in Asia, have captured the imagination of Westerners for over a century. The term *mandala* itself readily evokes an elaborate painterly or three-dimensional image of a sacred space filled with exquisitely rendered figures and objects. But the concepts behind this complex form and its varied manifestations throughout Asia are, as yet, not well understood.

We are delighted that the Asia Society and Tibet House could join forces in presenting this pan-Asian exhibition of mandalas to explicate the symbolic meanings of the form as well as highlight its artistic language. A distinctive feature of the exhibition is its attempt to open the discussion beyond the more familiar terrain of Tibetan and Nepali mandalas to include some very fine works from Japan and Southeast Asia. To present these wonderful images as religious symbols *and* superb artworks—and in doing so, to deepen the viewer's understanding of Buddhist art and ideas—has been a primary motive behind our collaboration.

Such a collaboration requires the participation of many colleagues at multiple levels. The idea for the exhibition began with a dinner conversation and soon blossomed into an exciting project, thanks to the cooperative efforts of the curators, Dr. Denise P. Leidy and Professor Robert A. F. Thurman. Now associate curator and administrator of the Metropolitan Museum's Department of Asian Art, Dr. Leidy initiated the project while still a member of the Asia Society staff. She valiantly continued with the laborious process of unearthing the treasures of museums and private collections around the country even as she began a demanding new job. Dr. Leidy has been a constant inspiration and an unflagging source of energy, encouragement, and thoughtful insight. Any success garnered by this exhibition is due in no small measure to her persistence and com-

mitment. Of course, staff members of both the Asia Society and Tibet House have worked tirelessly as well, and they are acknowledged in the introduction by Dr. Leidy and Professor Thurman.

Our very special thanks go to the Henry R. Luce Foundation for the original grant that underwrote the planning stages of the exhibition. Subsequently, the beleaguered but unbowed National Endowment for the Arts provided an indispensable enabling grant, supplemented by a generous grant from the Ellen Bayard Weedon Foundation for the accompanying educational programs. Our thanks to those institutions and to the Mary Livingston Griggs and Mary Griggs Burke Foundation, The Woodcock Foundation, Michael Marsh, and Frank and Lisina Hoch. Without the generosity of these donors, no exhibition would be possible.

Finally, we applaud and acknowledge the commitment of the lenders, who must believe in the vision of a particular show in order to give up, even temporarily, the joy of living with the beloved objects in their care. We are indebted and grateful to the institutions and individuals who have lent the beautiful objects in this exhibition.

Ultimately, the mandala represents an inner spiritual journey in visual form. We hope that the exhibition conveys this sense of the mandala, providing both spiritual inspiration and visual delight.

Vishakha N. Desai
Vice President for Cultural Programs and Director of the Galleries
Asia Society

Robert A. F. Thurman
Co-Founder and President
Tibet House

INTRODUCTION

We embarked upon this exhibition and study in order to explore the principles, methodology, and artistry of the mandala, a sacred space created in the process of transforming the universe from a realm of suffering to a realm of happiness.

Of course, mandalas as sacred spaces have always existed in every culture as the special natural place—cave, grove, mountaintop, island—or constructed temple wherein the almighty deity in control of the world resides or is remembered. In India, the term *mandala* initially referred to the chapters of orally preserved verses of the Vedas, in which the sacred vision of the gods and their world was articulated. But this mandala and other ancient mandalas were believed given as a fixed world-model by the all-powerful gods or god, as world-creation was considered their privilege and responsibility.

The humanistic revolution in India during the mid-first millennium BCE made it possible for freedom-seeking individuals such as Shakyamuni Buddha or Mahavira Jina to question the omnipotence of the gods and hence the fixity of the world-model. Their resulting breakthroughs in methodologies of human development and social amelioration allowed their legions of followers during succeeding centuries to discover the underlying mandala-principle, experiment with alternative world-models, and begin the "tantric" or artistic process of creating a profusion of mandalas—now blueprints for ideal worlds. It is our pleasure to present a select few of these mandalas in this exhibition and catalogue.

Mandalas are not yet well understood because of an underlying modern and Western prejudice that the spiritual traditions of the East were world-rejecting and inward-looking, legitimizing the social status quo and ignoring the environment. On the contrary, the sophisticated development of the art of mandalas, the systematic figural and architectural creation of exalting spaces for individuals and communities, reflects a longstanding commitment in both Hinduism and Buddhism to world transformation as well as individual liberation. This development parallels, in what we understand of the history of Buddhism, the emergence of the Mahayana or Universal Vehicle as well as significant social and cultural movements at the end of the first millennium BCE.

As Buddhism traveled from India to other parts of Asia, the mandala traditions migrated to the Himalayan world and flourished in the isolated and spiritually rich atmosphere of Tibet. Thus the greatest profusion of mandalas is based on still thriving—though currently endangered—Tibetan religious traditions. Represented here are a variety of Tibetan mandalas from different periods and traditions, including a colored sand-particle mandala created at the Asia Society Galleries by the monks of His Holiness the Dalai Lama's Namgyal monastery in Dharamsala.

But the great Ganges River of Buddhic visionary inspiration did not flow only out of India into Tibet. It also nourished the efforts and realizations of freedom-seeking individuals in Central Asia, China, Korea, Japan, and Southeast Asia as far as Indonesia. To suggest how widespread is the art of mandalas, we have included representative images from many of these cultures.

A secondary focus of our exhibition is to explore the relationship between the two-dimensional and three-dimensional mandala, how the former serves ultimately as a blueprint for the architecture, or catalyst for the vision, of the latter. We have therefore presented various renderings of three-dimensional models and a live creation of a sand mandala, considered the most powerful sort of vision-catalyst. Our hope is that the viewer will leave the exhibition with a strong sense of a mandala as a new way of feeling contained in an environment, an environment that nourishes and delights rather than a typical environment of scarcity and threat.

―――

This exhibition would not have been possible without the generosity of the funders and the lenders, as well as the dedication and skill of many individuals.

First we must thank Vishakha N. Desai, Asia Society Vice President for Cultural Programs and Director of the Galleries, for her keen grasp of the vision behind this exhibition and her determination to bring Tibet House and the Asia Society into harmonious and fruitful collaboration. William K. McKeever, Asia Society Director of Regional Center Coordination and Asian Activities, deserves sincere thanks for his thoughtful initiative in getting the project underway. Caron Smith, Curator and Associate Director of the Asia Society Galleries, administered the project with enthusiasm. At Tibet House, Nena v. S. Thurman, Treasurer, Jeffrey Jordan, Director of Exhibitions, and Leila Hadley Luce, Board member, were instrumental in mobilizing the support of their organization. We are grateful to Samuel Bercholz and his team at Shambhala Publications, in particular David O'Neal and Jonathan Green, for agreeing to publish this catalogue and for their participation in the editing process. We also thank Dr. Martin Brauen for the inspiration he provided through his wonderful German publication, *Das Mandala* (now available in English), which accompanied his exhibition on three-dimensional mandalas, especially the Kalachakra. Originally, we had planned to include elements of Dr. Brauen's exhibition in ours. Though this ultimately was not possible, we are delighted that he will participate in our symposium.

The late Venerable Pema Losang Chogyen was to have worked on this project in a very central capacity, designing an unprecedented three-dimensional Kalachakra mandala palace. Sadly, this aspect of the exhibition had to be postponed due to his untimely death, but his inspiration remained with us throughout.

It has been an enjoyable as well as enlightening experience to bring together the hard-working and dedicated staffs of the Asia Society Galleries and Tibet House in New York to collaborate on this exhibition and catalogue. At the Asia Society, we would like to thank Amy McEwen and Perry Hu for handling all of the logistics involved in borrowing and moving works of art and for carefully supervising the installation; Kathryn Selig Brown and Merantine Hens-Nolan, galleries associates, for all their painstaking work and wise advice on the details of the installation; Dan Schnur for his elegant and thoughtful exhibition design; Zack Zanolli for his skillful lighting design; and Jody Graff for design of the exhibition graphics.

We would also like to thank Susan Chun for her artful management of the book design, inspired collection of materials, and patient shepherding of authors. In producing this catalogue, she was supported by a team of dedicated professionals, including Kathryn Selig Brown, whose untiring collaboration improved both the publication and exhibition in countless ways; Bea Ferrigno and Philomena Mariani, the book's sensitive and careful editors; John Dibs, who created the index; Jean Wagner, who edited the notes; Pat Goley, who oversaw the color separations; and Patrick Seymour and Catarina Tsang, whose expert book design and typesetting made sense of wide-ranging and complicated material. We would also like to thank Linden Chubin, Anne Kirkup, and Rachel Cooper for their thoughtful work on the accompanying programs; Nancy Blume, who planned the educational programs for schools; and Alison Yu and Dawn Draayer, who raised the necessary funds for the mounting of the exhibition. The marketing and public relations departments, especially Karen Karp, Janet Gilman, and Heather Steliga Chen, applied their formidable skills to publicizing the exhibition. Mirza Burgos, Samantha Hoover, and Teresa Lai supported the work with humor and good cheer. Joseph Newland, Alexandra Johnson, Tucker Nichols, and Tran Ky Phuong all contributed to the exhibition or catalogue in their planning stages.

The staff of Tibet House collaborated on all aspects of the show, but their particular contribution to the creation of the sand mandala and to the preparation of other three-dimensional materials is gratefully acknowledged. We warmly thank Jeffrey Jordan for his unfailing help with all aspects of the project; Beata Tikos for her administration on the Tibet House side; and Annette Uhlfelder for her assistance in coordinating the exhibition in its later stages.

Denise Leidy would also like to thank several individuals for their help with her catalogue essay, including some of its early readers: Bob Thurman, Jane Casey Singer, and Steve Kossak, all of whom provided helpful comments; Elizabeth ten Grotenhuis, for sending her recent work on the Taima Mandara; and Deborah Klimburg, for a hurried but informative conversation about Tabo. Thanks also to Sondra Castile of the Asian Art Conservation Lab at the Metropolitan Museum of Art for her sound advice on the conservation of the works.

Above all, we are grateful to the curators and administrators of the lending institutions and to all the private collectors who have done so much to preserve the treasures of Tibetan and other Asian civilizations.

Denise Patry Leidy
Robert A. F. Thurman

LENDERS

The Asia Society Galleries

The Brooklyn Museum of Art

Mary Griggs Burke

The Cleveland Museum of Art

Mr. and Mrs. John Gilmore Ford

Dr. Wesley Halpert and Carolyn M. Halpert

Lisina and Frank Hoch

Michael J. and Beata McCormick

Memorial Art Gallery, Rochester, New York

The Metropolitan Museum of Art

Museum of Fine Arts, Boston

The Nelson-Atkins Museum of Art

Philadelphia Museum of Art

Private Collection (2)

Shelley Rubin and Donald Rubin

David Shapiro

Hiroshi Sugimoto

The Virginia Museum of Fine Arts

Zimmerman Family

NOTE TO THE READER

This book is designed for a general readership. As such, Tibetan, Sanskrit, Japanese, and Chinese names and words are transcribed in the Roman alphabet, without diacritical marks or silent letters, and in a manner corresponding to their phonetic pronunciation, for example, "Shakyamuni" rather than Śākyamuni, or "kamashastra" rather than kāmaśāstra. Diacritical marks appear for terms cited in the glossary. Standard transliteration systems are used only when foreign words are cited in conjunction with their romanized forms. In addition, terms have been standardized wherever possible. For instance, Buddhist terms are in Sanskrit rather than the language of the country of a work's origin, hence "Bodhisattva Avalokiteshvara" throughout, rather than "Kannon Bosatsu" for Japanese works.

Dimensions of paintings are given height by width, and do not include any mounts or frames. For most three-dimensional works, only height is stated. For sculptures, *right* and *left* should be interpreted from the sculpture's perspective. For paintings, directions are from the spectator's point of view.

Dates in the captions to the catalogue entries are by Denise Patry Leidy and Robert A. F. Thurman.

MONGOLIA

UZBEKISTAN

KYRGYZ
REPUBLIC

TURKMENISTAN

TAJIKISTAN

• *Dunhuang*

• *Yungang* • *Beijing*

IRAN

AFGHANISTAN

Hadda •
(GANDHARA)

Swat Valley

KASHMIR

• *Alchi*

Huang (Yellow) River

• *Longmen*

Indus River

PAKISTAN

TIBET

CHINA

H i m a l a y a s

• *Delhi*

NEPAL

• *Sakya s*

• *Lhasa*

Yangzi River

• *Shravasti*

• *Kathmandu*

BHUTAN

Ganga (Ganges) River

Banaras (Varanasi) •
• *Sarnath*

• *Nalanda*

BANGLADESH

• *Sanchi*

Bodhgaya •

INDIA

MYANMAR
(BURMA)

• *Hong Kong*

Ellora •
• *Aurangabad*

Calcutta •

Pagan •

Hanoi •

A R A B I A N   S E A

Irrawaddy River

LAOS

Mekong River

SOUTH CHINA SEA

*Yangon
(Rangoon)* •

B A Y   O F   B E N G A L

THAILAND

VIETNAM

Bangkok •

• *Angkor*

CAMBODIA

Phnom Penh •

*Ho Chi Minh City
(Saigon)* •

S R I   L A N K A

G U L F   O F   T H A I L A N D

BRUNEI

M A L A Y S I A

I N D I A N   O C E A N

SINGAPORE

KALIMANTAN
(BORNEO)

SUMATRA

Palembang •

I N D O N E

• *Jakarta*

JAVA

Borobudur •   • *Nganjuk*

BALI

SEA OF JAPAN

NORTH KOREA

•Pyongyang

•Seoul

JAPAN •Tokyo

•Mt. Hiei Kamakura

SOUTH KOREA

Kyoto•

•Nara

YELLOW SEA

anghai

MAP OF ASIA FEATURING
SELECTED BUDDHIST SITES

AIWAN

PHILIPPINES

PACIFIC OCEAN

IRIAN JAYA PAPUA
NEW GUINEA

SULAWESI
(CELEBES)

S I A

500 miles

316.8 km

PLACE AND PROCESS: MANDALA IMAGERY IN THE BUDDHIST ART OF ASIA

DENISE PATRY LEIDY

Mandalas are among the best known Buddhist icons in the world today, and their popularity is underscored by the use of the word *mandala* as a synonym for sacred space in Western scholarship[1] and by its presence in English-language dictionaries and encyclopedias. Both broadly define mandalas as geometric designs intended to symbolize the universe, and reference is made to their use in Buddhist and Hindu practices. The Sanskrit noun *mandala* means any circle or discoid object such as the sun or moon. In etymological studies, it is sometimes divided into *manda*—cream, best part, highest point—and *la*—signpost or completion. The combination is explained as a place or point which contains an essence. In the Vedic *Brahmanas*, some of India's earliest and most influential pre-Buddhist philosophical texts, *mandala* already signifies a sacred enclosure and is, at times, understood to mean a place created for the performance of a certain ritual or practice, or for the use of a great teacher or mystic.

Although mandalas have long been made in many materials—including sand, thread, and butter—the brightly colored and complex paintings of Tibet (and to a lesser extent Nepal) are most

familiar to contemporary viewers. These "palace-architecture" mandalas (figure 1) generally consist of an inner circle containing a principal deity (or deities), enclosed in a multilevel square palace with openings at the four cardinal directions. The palace is placed in a multitiered circle. Additional figures are generally found outside this large circle.

Mandalas are often described as cosmoplans in both the external sense, as diagrams of a cosmos; and in the internal sense, as guides to the psycho-physical practices of an adherent. Fundamentally, however, mandalas represent manifestations of a specific divinity *in* the cosmos and *as* the cosmos. As such, they are seen as sacred places which, by their very presence in the world, remind a viewer of the immanence of sanctity in the universe and its potential in himself. They thereby assist his progress toward enlightenment.

In Tibetan life, mandalas are used to decorate and sanctify temples and homes, in initiation rites for monks and rulers, as the focus of visualization by the clergy and of worship by lay followers, as well as in such specified roles as a support for the corpse in cremation. The complicated imagery of Tibetan mandalas is detailed in texts such as the *Sadhanamala* or *Nispannayogavali*, which contain chapters devoted to the arrangement of different types of mandalas and

opposite: view from the top level of Borobudur, Central Java, Indonesia

Figure 1. Mandala of Jnanadakini, Tibet, Sakya order, late 14th–early 15th century, ink and opaque watercolors on cloth, 33¼ x 28⅞ inches (84.5 x 73.3 cm) (catalogue no. 26)

their symbolism. They also describe the spiritual and mundane benefits obtained by creating, looking at, praying to, or meditating on these icons.

Texts such as these were brought to Tibet from the Pala kingdom (about eighth to twelfth centuries CE) of eastern India during the second major transmission of Buddhism in the late eleventh and early twelfth centuries. Palace-architecture mandalas, terrifying deities, and other iconographic types associated with these texts became prominent in the twelfth and thirteenth centuries, reflecting the spread of Unexcelled Yoga tantra during this period. Despite historic records of the transmission of these texts from India to Tibet, however, little visual evidence exists of palace-type mandalas prior to their first appearance in the Himalayas,[2] making it difficult to trace their evolution in the art of Asia. Nonetheless, mandalas of this type can be understood as a visual synthesis of several core concepts that underlie many forms of Buddhist imagery. These include the use of a sacred space for a spiritual process; the existence of innu-

merable buddhas, some of whom are not bound by time and space; the ability of these deities to create and maintain their own worlds; and the importance of mandalas as symbols of those worlds and the processes that occur within them. An understanding of the ways in which palace-architecture mandalas exemplify these ideas provides a paradigm for the development of Buddhist imagery in Asia and explicates the centrality of artistic representations of mandalas to broader religious traditions.

Place and Process in Buddhist History

The practice of making a spiritual journey in a sacred place lies at the heart of Buddhism, which was founded by Siddhartha Gautama (about 563–483 BCE) after he had spent some time wandering through India, studying and practicing with the noted religious teachers of his day. When they could not satisfy his existential questions, he sat under the Bodhi tree[3]—a place already sacred to India's seekers—and vowed not to move until he had reached enlightenment. Despite repeated attempts by the demon Mara and his hordes to interrupt Siddhartha's meditation, he was eventually successful and, having completed the process of enlightenment himself, decided to teach his understanding to others. Siddhartha is worshiped today as the Historical Buddha because he is the Buddha (one of many) who brought the path of Buddhism, its beliefs and practices, to this world (which is also one of many and will eventually self-destruct and be created again). He is also known as the Buddha Shakyamuni: *muni* means sage while Shakya is his family name.

Stupas and the Development of Buddhist Thought

Images of the Buddha in human form were not produced in India (or elsewhere in Asia) until the Kushana period (first to third centuries CE), six centuries after the foundation of Buddhism. A search for the beginnings of the place and process imagery that underlies later mandalas must therefore begin with monuments, such as the Great Stupa at Sanchi, which are among the earliest sources for the development of Buddhist art.[4] Stupas derive from pre-Buddhist traditions and were originally burial mounds marking the graves of religious or political leaders and reminding people of their power. They were incorporated into Buddhism after Shakyamuni's final passing (parinirvana) as symbols for his continuing presence in the world.

Also known as Stupa No. 1, the Great Stupa at Sanchi (figure 2) in Madhya Pradesh, central India, is one of the most revered

Figure 2. Stupa No. 1 (Great Stupa), Sanchi, Madhya Pradesh, India, 3rd century BCE–1st century CE

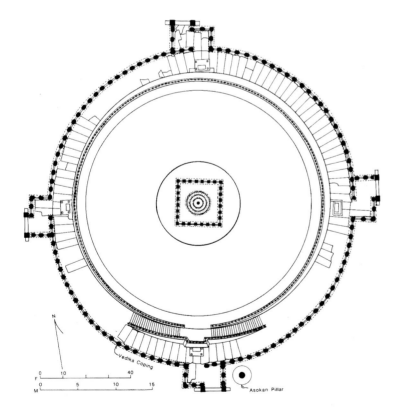

Figure 3. Plan of Stupa No. 1 (Great Stupa), Sanchi, Madhya Pradesh, India, 3rd century BCE–1st century CE

monuments in Buddhist art. It is called the Great Stupa because of its size, and is one of several stupas, among other buildings, found at Sanchi. The site was in use from at least the third century BCE to the eleventh century CE and many of its buildings, including the Great Stupa, were reconfigured over time.[5] The core of the Great Stupa dates from the third century BCE, but the structure as it appears today is generally dated to the second half of the first century CE.

As can be seen from its plan (figure 3), the Great Stupa consists of a domed hemisphere enclosed by two circular walkways and surrounded by a railing with elaborate gateways at the four cardinal points. The dome is capped by a square balcony in the center of which rises a pole covered by umbrellas. This pole extends through the center of the dome of the stupa (which is solid) and links the top of the stupa to the relics beneath. Variations on this structure underlie all stupas and their derivatives, such as the pagoda of East Asia (figure 4) or the chorten of Tibet (figure 5).

Because both actual monuments and miniatures were made over centuries throughout Asia, many different meanings have become associated with stupas. For example, their hemispherical shape is sometimes interpreted as a symbol of the cosmos or of the mythical Mount Meru, the center of a cosmos. Recent, more nuanced studies, however, point out that while such interpretations may be found in later stupas, the imagery of early examples, such as the Great Stupa at Sanchi, continues the royal symbolism associated with the earliest, pre-Buddhist examples.[6] This suggests that the Great Stupa and other earlier monuments should be understood primarily as memorials to the Buddha, and as reminders of his teachings intended to stimulate the good thoughts that lead to spiritual progress. Similarly, there is some argument about the meaning of the pole linking the top of the stupa to the relics beneath. Such a pole—found in most, but not all, stupas—can be understood to symbolize the *axis mundi* in later traditions, but in early monuments is most likely a reference to the pre-Buddhist cult of sacred trees. The incorporation of such pillars in stupas demonstrates the process by which sacred trees, such as the Bodhi tree, were replaced by stupas as symbols of enlightenment in Buddhist thought.[7]

The surface of the Great Stupa is undecorated, as are the surrounding railings. The gateways, however, are filled with carvings depicting the Buddha as a wheel, a footprint, a tree (figure 6), and even a stupa. These scenes illustrate the past lives and teaching

ous path, and, in particular, its stress on personal effort, is characteristic of early Buddhist thought and typifies the Buddhism generally known today as Hinayana or Theravada, or by more generic terms such as the monastic tradition or Individual Vehicle.

The construction of monuments such as the Great Stupa at Sanchi is usually understood to reflect profound changes in Buddhism that eventually resulted in the development of the Mahayana or Universal Vehicle. The basic tenets of this branch of Buddhism are found in certain sutras (texts) written over several hundred years, roughly from the second century BCE to the fifth century CE. In Universal Buddhism, enlightenment, while still a personal goal, is a cosmic process intended to benefit all sentient beings. In addition to Shakyamuni Buddha, the Universal branch accepts the existence of numerous buddhas both in our universe and in other worlds, and provides the devout with an expanded

Figure 4. Model of a pagoda, Japan, late 19th century, copper, cast iron, brass, and gold, height 50 inches (127 cm) (catalogue no. 7)

career of Shakyamuni and provide reference points for the practitioner, while the "presence" of the Buddha, signified by the stupa itself, indicates the ultimate goal. Thus the stupa is both a place where spiritual progress can occur and a symbol for that process. The four gateways surrounding the Great Stupa at Sanchi represent the ability of Buddhism to spread from this sacred site to other times and places.

Early stupas such as Sanchi illustrate a view of the universe as a single entity, and of enlightenment as a process that can occur during reincarnations within that sphere.[8] This austere, continu-

Figure 5. Miniature Stupa (Chorten), Tibet, Kadam order, 13th century, height 20 inches (50.8 cm) (catalogue no. 6)

pantheon including bodhisattvas, beings who reach the same point of spiritual development as buddhas but remain accessible to guide others on their path.

The northwestern and southern regions of India are believed to have fostered development of Universal Buddhism as they were both centers for important monk-scholars in that tradition. Northwest India and Kashmir, and the eastern regions of Orissa, Bangladesh, and West Bengal, however, are the primary sources for the third great branch which apparently developed between the fourth and eighth centuries and is known today as Vajrayana, Tantrayana, Tantric—or Esoteric—Buddhism, or the Apocalyptic Vehicle. Unlike the other branches, Esoteric Buddhism accepts that enlightenment is possible in one lifetime. Its pathway, characterized by elaborate rituals and a staggeringly complex pantheon, evolved to achieve that goal.

Esoteric Buddhism, based on texts known as tantra as well as the earlier sutras, is best known today as the religion of Tibet. Scholars of Tibetan Buddhist literature divide the tantras into four main groups: Action or Kriya tantras, many of which focus on Amitabha Buddha; Performance or Charya tantras featuring Vairochana Buddha in his one-faced form; Yoga tantras in which the four-faced Vairochana is prominent; and Anuttarayoga or Unexcelled Yoga tantras, further subdivided into male and female sets featuring Akshobhya Buddha and wrathful deities such as Chakrasamvara and Hevajra. The expanded pantheon associated with these forms of Buddhism is divided into three clans in the Action and Performance tantras, and into five in the Yoga and Unexcelled Yoga traditions.

It is generally accepted that many of the characteristic practices and beliefs of Unexcelled Yoga tantra derive from wandering ascetics (male and female) who chose not to practice in monasteries but gathered instead at obscure or unorthodox locations such as cemeteries. The importance of female and wrathful deities and certain types of sexual symbolism are thought to stem from the practices of these seekers.[9] The paucity of written or visual material pertaining to the earliest phases of Esoteric Buddhism is often linked to the disdain of earlier practitioners for the monastic life and to their emphasis on oral transmission. Thus, it is difficult to reconstruct the early history and development of Esoteric Buddhism. Nonetheless, certain visual traditions from India, Central Asia, and China provide some preliminary evidence for the evolution of this branch during the sixth to the eighth centuries and for its contribution to later Buddhist art.

Figure 6. Detail from a gateway, Sanchi, Madhya Pradesh, India, c. 1st century CE

Cosmic Buddhas

An interest in multiple universes is shared by Universal and Esoteric Buddhism. This belief can be traced back in some part to the preaching career of Buddha Shakyamuni and an event known popularly as the miracle at Shravasti. Literary biographies such as the *Divyavadana* or the *Jatakamala* record that Shakyamuni, when challenged by unbelievers, demonstrated his spiritual accomplishment by performing miracles such as rising into the air while issuing flames and water from his body. In another version,

sculptures in cave 16 at Yungang (figure 7) exemplifies the use of the 1,000-buddha motif in early Chinese Buddhist art: the smaller seated images illustrate the motif as symbolizing the existence of innumerable buddhas inhabiting myriad universes; while the larger images, which manifest from within the Buddhist cosmoses, represent specific deities or illustrate familiar events in the life of Shakyamuni.

One of the earliest images of a colossal buddha as a symbol of the cosmos (figure 8) is found in cave 18 at Yungang. The robe of the central image—a monumental standing buddha—is filled with images of smaller buddhas seated in meditation. The standing buddha is attended by two bodhisattvas, ten disciples, and two worshipers set against a background of the 1,000-buddha motif. The identity of this colossal buddha has rarely been discussed,[11] but it seems likely that he represents Shakyamuni in the form of Vairochana (resplendent one), a role specifically attributed to Shakyamuni in the *Avatamsaka* or *Flower Garland Sutra*. This text,

Figure 7. Detail of south wall, cave 16, Yungang, Shanxi Province, China, Northern Wei period, c. 460–467

Shakyamuni produced a mango tree and caused it to rise into the heavens, then sat under the tree and multiplied himself. Sutras of the Universal Vehicle often mention a group of 1,000 buddhas, an expression understood to represent an infinity of buddhas appearing simultaneously in a myriad of cosmic spheres throughout all time.

Cosmic or multiple buddhas, which are occasionally identified in the visual arts of the subcontinent, became important icons in the early Buddhist art of Central Asia and China. Numerous images of the 1,000 buddhas are found in sites such as the cave-temples at Dunhuang[10] in Gansu, Yungang in Shanxi, and Longmen in Henan Province, which date from the late fifth through eighth centuries. A detail of the wonderful reliefs and

Figure 8. Colossal Buddha (probably Vairochana), cave 18, Yungang, Shanxi Province, China, Northern Wei period, c. 460–467

Figure 9. Vairochana Buddha, China, Northern Qi period, c. 560–580, limestone, height 69¼ inches (173.1 cm), Freer Gallery of Art, Washington, D.C.

probably assembled into its current form in India during the late second and early third centuries, was first translated into Chinese by Buddhabhadra between 408 and 410 CE. It gives a very detailed account of Shakyamuni/Vairochana's quest for enlightenment, and offers the view that existence is the combination of individual identity and interdependence, a crucial theme in the development of Indian Buddhist thought. The *Flower Garland Sutra* became influential in the late sixth and seventh centuries through the works of monks such as Fashun (557–640 CE) and Zhiyen (602–668 CE), and later was the central text of the semiesoteric Huayen order in China, which is known as Kegon in Japan.

Cave 18 is part of a set of five caves (numbers 16–20), each of which contains a colossus. The construction of these caves between 460 and 467 CE is attributed to the influence of the monk Tanyao and to the revival of Buddhism after a period of persecution from 446 to 452 CE. The study of Yungang has focused on the development of a stylistic sequence for the sculptures in the caves

rather than on the iconographic identification of the various deities. The five colossi in caves 16–20, which are among the earliest cave-temples excavated there, have generally been interpreted as "portraits" showing the lineage (beginning with Daowu Huangdi) of the Northern Wei rulers responsible for the construction of this site. However, the representation of five buddhas and identification of the central icon as Vairochana can also be understood to illustrate the five principal families of Buddhism, each headed by a different buddha.

According to this system, which is important to the development of Yoga and Unexcelled Yoga tantra, all Buddhist deities are assembled into clans headed by five transcendent buddhas: Vairochana, Ratnasambhava, Amitabha, Amoghasiddhi, and Akshobhya. Each clan exemplifies a type of wisdom and is associated with a certain personality type or mental habit, as well as specific types of rituals. The clans are often distinguished from one another by their association with either one of the four cardinal directions or the zenith, and each is symbolized by a certain color. As discussed above, Vairochana (blue or white) heads the buddha clan and is the central buddha in the Performance and Yoga tantra traditions, while Akshobhya (also blue or white), the lord of the vajra clan, is prominent in Unexcelled Yoga tantra. (See the glossary for further information.)

The representation of Vairochana at the center of the five buddha families at Yungang would mark the first known depiction of this concept in the visual arts. With this in mind, it is interesting to note that Tanyao was a student of the Kashmiri master Shixian. As is often the case with early Buddhist monks in China, both Shixian and Tanyao were as revered for their magical skills as for their more scholarly understanding of Buddhist thought. Such skills, coupled with Shixian's ties to Kashmir, a region known to have fostered the development of Esoteric Buddhism, suggest possible links between this tradition and some of China's earliest Buddhist art.

Additional images of Buddha as the cosmos were produced in China in the second half of the sixth century and again in the late seventh century, and in Central Asia particularly from the fourth to the sixth century.[12] These include sculptural works such as a large standing buddha in the collection of the Freer Gallery of Art (figure 9), datable to the third quarter of the sixth century; paintings such as examples from cave 428 at Dunhuang from the same period;[13] and the seated Vairochana in the Fengxian caves at Longmen from the late seventh century (figure 10). Central Asian examples include a large painted figure from cave 13 at Kizil (figure 11), and the famous wall painting from Balawaste, now in the National Museum, New Delhi.[14] In addition, the now-lost colossal eighth-century buddha of Todai-ji temple in Nara, Japan, seated on a lotus pedestal with each petal symbolizing a different universe—as does its possible proto-type at Longmen—was also a representation of Vairochana as the cosmos.[15]

There is some reluctance to identify the fifth- and sixth-century Chinese cosmic buddhas as Vairochana largely because it is believed that Esoteric Buddhism did not flourish in China until the eighth century, at which point it was transmitted to Japan and almost immediately disappeared from the mainland.[16] While it is clear that court support for Esoteric Buddhism was strongest in the eighth and first half of the ninth century, ideas associated with this form of Buddhism have a much longer and more complicated history in China than is generally understood. For example, the magical spells known as *dharani*, found in the Chinese Buddhist canon from at least the third century onward, play an important role in esoteric practice. In addition, some of the earliest instruc-tions for the creation of a mandala, for building a fire altar, and for other practices associated with early East Asian esoterism, are pre-served in an obscure text translated in southern China between 502 and 557 CE.[17] It should also be pointed out that in the late fifth and late sixth centuries—the two periods marked by the appear-ance of cosmic buddhas—China renewed ties with the Buddhist traditions of Central Asia and Northwest India and may then have

Figure 11. Vairochana Buddha, cave 13, Kizil, Turfan, 4th–6th cen-tury, height 62⅜ inches (156 cm), Museum für Indisches Kunst, Berlin

Figure 10. Vairochana Buddha, Fengxian, Longmen, Henan Province, China, Tang period, c. 650–675

been more open to new ideas, such as those associated with the development of Esoteric Buddhism. The interest in groups of four directional buddhas and the organization of cosmic spaces, illus-trated in the four-sided stele and funerary pagodas produced throughout the north in the second half of the sixth century,[18] may be examples of this because of the importance of the four cardinal points in later cosmic spaces such as mandalas.

Figure 12. Amitabha Buddha seated in his Western Paradise, China, Sui period, 593, gilt bronze, height 30½ inches (76.25 cm), Museum of Fine Arts, Boston

Pure Lands and the Case of the Taima Mandara

The development of a recognizable iconography for the pure land of Amitabha Buddha in the late sixth century also provides evidence for the evolution of mandalalike perfected spaces in early Chinese Buddhist art. As the belief in multiple buddhas and bodhisattvas evolved, it was assumed that each divinity occupied his own personal buddha-field (*kshetra),* known as a pure land or paradise. This land, which was the result of the buddha's (or bodhisattva's) actions, and which he created and maintained, was a perfect place with conditions conducive to the pursuit of enlightenment.

Textual sources for the pure land of Amitabha, known as Sukhavati or the Western Paradise, were produced in Northwest India around the second century CE. There is some evidence for visual representations of this pure land in Northwest India around the same time.[19] It was not until the sixth century in China, however, that paintings and sculptures of the pure land became popular. By the seventh century, belief in Sukhavati and desire for rebirth in paradise evolved into a distinct East Asian order generally known today as Pure Land Buddhism.

A famous bronze sculpture in the collection of the Museum of Fine Arts, Boston (figure 12), characterizes the earliest Chinese versions of this important theme. Dated 593, it shows Amitabha Buddha seated on a jeweled throne beneath two ornamented trees. He is attended by the bodhisattvas Avalokiteshvara and Mahasthamaprapta and two lay figures. Two guardians and two lions protect the pure land. Directly beneath the seated Buddha, a caryatid lifts a lotus bud. The small seated figure in the center of that flower represents the souls who will soon be reborn in Amitabha's paradise. Desire for rebirth in the pure land and faith in that possibility are important elements in this type of Buddhist practice.

The relationship between pure lands and mandalas, both places where deities manifest themselves to aid adherents, are illustrated by images known in Japan as Taima Mandaras, the latter being the Japanese pronunciation of Sanskrit *mandala.* Their name derives from the Taima-dera, a small temple south of Nara, which housed the original Taima Mandara tapestry, imported to Japan from China in the eighth century. Mandalas of this type became important from the thirteenth through seventeenth centuries as objects of devotion and exposition used by the Jodo sect of Pure Land Buddhism developed by the monk Genku Honen (1133–1212 CE).[20] The textual basis for this icon is the *Amitabhadhyana Sutra* or *Sutra on the Meditation on the Buddha of Infinite Light*, probably translated into Chinese in 424 CE from a Sanskrit original, now lost, and a later commentary on it by the Chinese monk Shandao (613–681 CE).

A Japanese painting dated to about 1300 in the collection of the Metropolitan Museum of Art (figure 13) illustrates the basic composition of a Taima Mandara. The core of the painting, in which Amitabha, accompanied by Avalokiteshvara and Mahasthamaprapta, is seated before an elaborate palace, derives from

Figure 13. Pure Land of Amitabha Buddha, Japan, Kamakura period, 13th century, color and gold on silk, 36 1/8 x 28 5/8 inches (91.8 x 72.7 cm) (catalogue no. 8)

earlier representations of Sukhavati. Both bodhisattvas are attended by their own assemblies, and other groups are found to the right and left in the foreground of the painting. A lotus pond filled with souls in varying degrees of rebirth—according to the merit they may or may not have acquired in their past lives—fills the center of the foreground, which also has scenes of musicians and dancers entertaining the assembled multitudes.

The narrative scenes depicted in the borders around the left, right, and bottom of the painting illustrate a way to reach the paradise at its core. Reading from bottom to top, the scenes to the left of the central image tell the story of Queen Vaidehi and King Bimbisara who were imprisoned, and almost murdered, by their son Prince Ajatashatru. Heartbroken, Vaidehi prayed to Shakyamuni Buddha, who responded by granting her a vision of the paradises of the ten directions. She chose to focus her devotion on the western pure land of Amitabha and Shakyamuni gave her a series of sixteen meditations to help her. Thirteen of these are represented—from top

to bottom—in the right-hand border. The remaining three, subdivided into the nine possible degrees of rebirth, are shown in the lower border on either side of a long standardized inscription explaining the rediscovery of the original Taima Mandara in Japan and its importance to the Jodo order.

Eighth-century Chinese examples pairing Amitabha's pure land with sixteen meditations are found in several murals in the cave-temples at Dunhuang and other sites.[21] As has already been mentioned, Esoteric Buddhism flourished in China during the eighth century; it is interesting that an icon showing both a place as the goal of meditation and the actual process of reaching it can be traced to this period. It should be noted, however, that the goal of a devotee of a Pure Land sect is rebirth in a paradise which can then lead to enlightenment in a later reincarnation, rather than enlightenment in this lifetime, the goal of Esoteric Buddhism.

Mandala of the Eight Bodhisattvas

Groups of eight bodhisattvas assembled around a seated buddha, identified by certain texts as the mandala of the Eight Great Bodhisattvas, are among the earliest and most widespread examples of mandala imagery in Asia. Lists of eight great bodhisattvas occur in some of the earliest sutras of Universal Buddhism, such as the *Astabhuddhaka Sutra,*[22] where they are described as protectors of the faithful and providers of mundane blessings—such as the fulfillment of wishes—and are linked to a group of eight buddhas whose pure lands are protected by the four heavenly kings who guard the cardinal directions. This sutra, in which the Eight Great Bodhisattvas greet souls of the newly deceased as they enter the pure lands, also provides an interesting parallel to the East Asian tradition mentioned above which produced painted and sculpted images of Amitabha descending to earth and accompanying souls to his pure land. Another list is found in the *Mahavairochana-abhisambhodhi Sutra,* translated by Amoghavajra between 746 and 774 CE, which identifies the eight bodhisattvas as Maitreya, Akasagarbha, Samantabhadra, Padmapani, Vajrapani, Manjushri, Kshitigarbha, and Sarvanivaranavishkambhin. Slightly different lists of eight are also found in later texts such as the *Sadhanamala* and the *Nispannayogavali.*

The earliest textual evidence for the mandala of the Eight Great Bodhisattvas (as opposed to a simple list) is the *Ashtamahabodhisattvamandala Sutra,* translated into Chinese by Subhakarasimha in 725 CE. References to an earlier version, however, are found in the Chinese biography of the monk Punyodaya, who brought a copy to

Figure 14. Mandala of the Eight Great Bodhisattvas, possibly Uttar Pradesh, India, 6th century, terra cotta, height 4¾ inches (11.9 cm), The Metropolitan Museum of Art, New York

the Chinese court in 655 CE and may also have taken the text with him to Cambodia on a later journey.[23]

The extensive visual evidence for this type of mandala[24] (whose central buddha is identified as Shakyamuni, Amitabha, or Vairochana), illustrates its popularity from the sixth through the tenth centuries. Sixth-century representations include an unusual gilt bronze Chinese plaque in the collection of the Museo Nationale d'Arte Orientale in Rome[25] and a small Indian terra-cotta plaque in the Metropolitan Museum of Art (figure 14). Both mandalas show a central buddha seated in meditation with his hands in a preaching gesture, surrounded by eight bodhisattvas. Eighth-century examples include a group of individual bodhisattvas found along the interior walls of cave 11 at Ellora,[26] a distinctive ninefold arrangement from cave 12 at the same site, the exterior reliefs of Chandi Mendut in Indonesia,[27] and a large mural in cave 25 from the Yulin grottoes in Gansu Province, China (figure 15).[28] Ninth-century examples are found in the interior sanctuaries of the Indonesian monuments at Chandi Sari and Chandi Pawon and among the recently rediscov-

ered images at Denma Drak in the Chamdo district of Tibet.[29] Ninth- and tenth-century examples were used as bases during the Pala period[30] and a tenth-century representation is also known from Ratnagiri in Orissa.[31] An eleventh-century composition is found in the wall paintings of the Dukhang, or Assembly Hall, of Dranang monastery in the Dranang Valley of Tibet.[32] Sets of eight bodhisattvas are associated with the buddhas of the Three Ages (Shakyamuni, his immediate predecessor Prabhutaratna, and successor Maitreya) in early Tibetan temples such as Drolma Lhakhang, Drepung, and other sites.[33] A Japanese variant, the Sonsho Mandara, was known and used by the esoteric Tendai order.[34]

A widely published and rare example of a portable wood altarpiece, now in the collection of the Nelson-Atkins Museum of Art (figure 16), illustrates one of the variants of this mandala and provides evidence for one means by which images of this type could have spread throughout Asia.[35] The altarpiece, dated to the late eighth or early ninth century, is divided into three sections and can be closed, presumably to be carried, by turning the sides in toward the center. In the center of the altarpiece, a seated buddha holding his hands in a gesture of meditation is attended by eight bodhisattvas, ranged in two groups to his right and left. Two additional bodhisattvas and a lay devotee are carved in the lower part of the central panel. The side panels are both divided into three sections and have nearly identical iconographies: the top areas show seated buddhas with kneeling attendants; the guardian kings of the four directions are shown in the middle; and ferocious four-armed protectors are carved into the lower sections.

Figure 15. Mandala of the Eight Great Bodhisattvas, cave 25, Yulin, Gansu Province, China, Tang period, 8th–9th century

Figure 16. Mandala of the Eight Great Bodhisattvas, Xinjiang Autonomous Region (Turfan area), China, late 8th–early 9th century, height 12 inches (30.5 cm), The Nelson-Atkins Museum of Art, Kansas City, Missouri

The two additional bodhisattvas in the center section are connected to the lay devotee rather than to the other divinities. One figure touches the head of the worshiper, while the other holds a circular object, possibly a gourd. It has been suggested that these three figures represent an initiation ceremony, or *abhisheka*. In the context of Esoteric Buddhism, such ceremonies, derived from the consecrations of Indian rulers, were important ritual introductions to the practices associated with a particular mandala. The depiction of such a scene on this wooden altarpiece suggests that such esoteric practices were known in Asia in the eighth and ninth centuries.

Representations of the mandala of the Eight Great Bodhisattvas fall into three basic types: those, such as the Nelson Gallery shrine, in which the eight bodhisattvas are ranged in two sets of four to either side of the central buddha; those in which the eight bodhisattvas encircle the central buddha; and less common examples, such as the work in the Metropolitan Museum of Art or the larger image in cave 12 at Ellora, in which the nine figures in the mandala are ranged in groups of three placed one above the other. Of these, the circular arrangements—which provide prototypes for the inner sections of other mandalas, including the palace-architecture type—are the most influential in later Buddhist art.

The Diamond and Womb World Mandalas

The best documented and most thoroughly studied examples of early Buddhist mandalas are the Diamond Matrix World and Womb Matrix World mandalas of the Shingon order in Japan.[36] Both have structural parallels to variants of the mandala of the Eight Great Bodhisattvas discussed above: a buddha surrounded by eight bodhisattvas forms the core of the Womb World mandala, and a ninefold arrangement is repeated in the structure of the Diamond World mandala.

Examples of both mandalas are said to have been brought to Japan from China in the early ninth century by Kukai (774–835

Figure 17. Inner precinct of the Golden Hall, Kanshin-ji, Osaka, Japan

Figure 18. *Mandala of the Womb World, Japan, Muromachi period, 15th–16th century, ink and colors on paper, 76 x 39½ inches (193 x 100.3 cm), Memorial Art Gallery, Rochester, New York*

Figure 19. *Mandala of the Diamond World, Japan, Muromachi period, 15th–16th century, ink and colors on paper, 76 x 39½ inches (193 x 100.3 cm), Memorial Art Gallery, Rochester, New York*

CE). With the exception, however, of an eighth-century Diamond World mandala incised into the tops, sides, and back of a funerary casket, unearthed during the excavation of an underground chamber at the Famensi monastery near Xian in the early 1980s,[37] no Chinese prototypes are extant.

Also known as Kobo Daishi, Kukai is revered today as the founder of the Shingon order in Japan, and the practices and imagery of this school are well documented in contemporary scholarship. In this tradition, the Womb and Diamond World mandalas are shown as a pair and placed to the east and west of an altar in the inner precinct of a temple (figure 17). The Womb World symbolizes the possibility of buddhahood in the phenomenal world as it is perceived by a practitioner, while the Diamond World is a guide to the spiritual practice that leads to enlightenment. Each mandala is based (to some degree) on a different text: the Womb World derives from the version of the *Mahavairochana*

Sutra translated from Sanskrit into Chinese by Subhakarasimha (637–735 CE) in the eighth century; the Diamond World is based on the *Sarvatathagatatattvasamgraha Sutra* translated by Amoghavajra (705–774 CE) during the same period. Together with Vajrabodhi (669–741 CE), these monks are revered as the founders of Esoteric Buddhism in China. Their journeys throughout South, Southeast, and Central Asia illustrate the international nature of Buddhist culture during the seventh through ninth centuries, and exemplify the transmission of Yoga tantra at that time

The earliest extant Japanese versions of these mandalas, known as the Takao Mandaras,[38] are preserved in the Jingo-ji temple in Kyoto. Executed in gold and silver pigments on a purple-dyed damask, these two paintings are believed to have been made by Kukai at the request of Emperor Junna (reigned 823–834 CE). Two similar paintings from the second half of the ninth century in the To-ji temple in Kyoto, said to be copies of those made in China

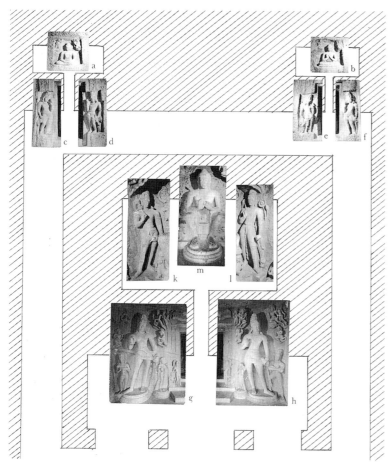

Figure 20. Iconographic sketch, cave 6, Aurangabad, Maharashtra, India, mid-6th century: (a) Buddha displaying dharmachakramudra, *(b) Buddha in* dhyanamudra, *(c) Padmapani, (d) Vajrapani, (e) Padmapani, (f) Vajrapani, (g) Padmapani, (h) Vajrapani, (k) Padmapani, (l) Vajrapani, (m) Buddha displaying* dharmachakrapravartanamudra

at the request of Emperor Montoku (reigned 850–858 CE), provide further evidence for the longevity of this pair of mandalas in Japan. Numerous later examples, such as a late thirteenth- or early fourteenth-century pair in the Brooklyn Museum (see catalogue nos. 41 and 42) or a Muromachi-period pair in the Memorial Art Gallery (figures 18 and 19), as well as iconographic drawings detailing various images from the two mandalas, are also known.

Vairochana Buddha, shown with one face and two hands, is the central deity of both mandalas. The Womb World mandala is composed of twelve precincts or courts containing 414 deities. The central court, known as the "court of eight petals," shows Vairochana sitting at the center of an open lotus flower whose eight petals contain seated buddha images at the cardinal points of

the compass and seated bodhisattvas at the intermediate points. The court to the right of this central image is known as the "vajra-holders court," while that to the left is called the "lotus-holders court." The vajra-holders symbolize the power of the intellect to destroy human passions, while the lotus-holders illustrate the purity of all human beings. These three central courts can also be seen as symbols of the three main families of divinities worshiped in early Esoteric Buddhism, the buddha, lotus, and vajra families. It has recently been suggested that this division into three main families is at the core of the iconography of sculptures produced in Orissa, a region noted for its contribution to the development of esoteric thought.[39] This area has also yielded images of some of the vajra deities associated with the Diamond World mandala, as well as figures, such as Hevajra and Chakrasamvara, which later became popular in Tibet with the spread of Unexcelled Yoga tantra.

The Diamond World mandala contains 1,461 deities. The central court is divided into five circles and is known as the "attainment of buddhahood assembly." Vairochana is surrounded by four bodhisattvas in the middle circle. Four additional circles, each containing a buddha and four bodhisattvas, are placed at the cardinal points of this court, while smaller individual images fill the intermediate zones. A large circle, surrounded by four guardian figures, encloses the five smaller circles. The arrangement of this court is the most common in the Diamond World mandala and is also found in the six courts that form its two bottom sections.

The three courts at the top of the mandala are all quite distinctive. The court at the right, known as the "assembly of four hand signs," consists of a large circle filled with five buddha images. The central court, known as the "assembly of a single hand sign," depicts a large image of Vairochana holding his hands in the wisdom-fist gesture, in which the right hand encloses the index finger of the left, representing the union of divine wisdom with the deluded knowledge of mankind. Images based on this part of the mandala are often found as independent icons in Japan. The overall composition of the Diamond World mandala is repeated in the ninefold arrangement of the left court, the "two-conduct assembly," in which Vairochana in the form of Vajrasattva is attended by male and female bodhisattvas.

The long history of the Womb and Diamond World mandalas in Japan has spurred scholars to seek other examples of these images in the Buddhist art of Asia. For example, it has been suggested that some figures in cave 6 at Aurangabad can be understood to symbolize the mandalas of the Womb and Diamond

Figure 21. Mandala of the Eight Great Bodhisattvas, antechamber to the central shrine, cave 12, Ellora, Maharashtra, India, late 7th–early 8th century

Worlds.[40] This site, generally dated to the mid to late sixth century, is one a group of caves in western India that are sometimes associated with the development of Esoteric Buddhism because their iconography often includes female deities, figures with multiple heads and limbs, and mandalas, or compositions which can be seen as prototypes for mandalas.

Cave 6 at Aurangabad is a square room with two smaller antechambers to the right and left (figure 20). The central figure in the cave is a large buddha seated with pendant legs; his hands are held in a preaching gesture. The bodhisattvas Padmapani (lotus-holder) and Vajrapani (vajra-holder) stand to the right and left respectively of the seated buddha. The triad can be seen as an image of the three main buddha families of early Esoteric Buddhism, as discussed above. The principal buddhas in the two rear chambers are both seated in postures of meditation. The figure at the right holds his hands in the gesture of turning the wheel of the law *(dharmachakramudra),* the same one used by Vairochana in the Womb World mandala. The buddha in the chamber to the left holds his hands in the gesture of meditation *(dhyanamudra),* used by the central Vairochana in the Diamond World mandala. Both antechambers are flanked by images of the

bodhisattvas Padmapani and Vajrapani, an arrangement that parallels both the structure of the main chamber and the inner structure of the Womb World mandala as it is known in Japanese Esoteric Buddhism. In addition, two mandalas that may illustrate the Diamond World (figure 21) are found in cave 12 at Ellora, which dates to the late seventh and early eighth centuries. Later examples of the Womb and Diamond World mandalas are found in the monastery at Tabo near Spiti in Ladakh and in cave 3 at Yulin in Gansu Province near Dunhuang, which will be discussed in greater detail later in this essay.

Borobudur

The importance of the Diamond World mandala in early Esoteric Buddhism has led many to associate this tradition with Borobudur[41] in central Java, one of the most magnificent and intriguing monuments in the Buddhist world (figures 22 and 23). Built around the late eighth or early ninth century, Borobudur has been defined as a stupa, a mandala, neither, or both. This enormous monument consists of a large basement-level terrace surmounted by five stepped terraces in the shape of articulated squares; three graduated rows of seventy-two stupas, each containing a single buddha; and a single stupa with a buddha at the topmost level. An additional 108 buddha images are found in the niches along the outer walls of the five terraces. These are distinguished from one another by their placement on the north, south, east, or west walls and by their different hand gestures. There has been much discussion regarding the precise identity of each of the four groups of twenty-seven buddhas and many attempts have been made to identify them as groups of four directional buddhas.

It is not possible to define Borobudur completely in terms of the Diamond World tradition as it is preserved today, nor to link this fantastic building with any other known texts. Nonetheless, the delineation of path and process in its structure and iconography, and the precise arrangement of the stupas at its apex, indicate that at least the top part, if not the entire structure, should be identified as a type of mandala. Esoteric Buddhism was known in Indonesia when Borobudur was constructed.[42] One of the most famous centers for its study was in Sumatra. Monks from around the world, including Amoghavajra and Atisha (982–1054 CE), a seminal figure in the development and spread of Buddhism in Tibet, studied there. As has already been mentioned, their travels and those of many other monks contributed to the international nature of Buddhism in the seventh, eighth, and ninth centuries.

Figure 22. Borobudur, Central Java, Indonesia, late 8th century

Figure 23. Detail of stupas on the top gallery, Borobudur, Central Java, Indonesia, late 8th century

The patrons of Borobudur would have been aware of prevailing currents in Buddhist thought and would most likely have incorporated the most up-to-date interpretation into the program of the monument.

Mandalas are also known to have been produced in Java after the construction of Borobudur. Two examples of three-dimensional mandalas consisting of smaller figures have been associated, albeit loosely, with the tradition of the Diamond World mandala: a well-known late tenth- to early eleventh-century group from

Nganjuk (figure 24) discovered in the village of Chandi Reja in 1913; and a slightly earlier version found more recently at Surocolo.[43] In addition, it has been suggested that the complicated and syncretic blending of Buddhist and Shaivite iconography found in late thirteenth-century works at Chandi Jago may also represent a distinctly Indonesian variant of the interest in place and process that underlies the mandala.[44]

Furthermore, the narrative imagery on the platform and terraces of Borobudur is linked to esoteric thought. The basement and lower terraces illustrate scenes from the biography of Buddha Shakyamuni, particularly as found in the *Lalitavistara;* stories from his past lives, found in the *Jataka;* and legendary tales, known as *avadana.* The upper two terraces and part of the third depict sections of the *Gandavyuha,* an important part of the *Avatamsaka Sutra,* which follows the young pilgrim Sudhana as he journeys through cosmic India in his quest for enlightenment.[45] The *Lalitavistara* is the version of Shakyamuni's biography associated with the Sarvastivadin sect that flourished in Northwest India at the turn of the first millennium. The beliefs of this sect are often cited as a primary source for the later development of Esoteric Buddhism. The visionary *Avatamsaka Sutra* has already been discussed as one of the most important of a group of very influential texts written between 200 BCE and 200 CE that played a formative role in Buddhist thought. The prominence given the story of Sudhana in the imagery of Borobudur links this monument to the traditions of China and Japan, where representations of his journey are common.

Figure 24. Four deities from a Diamond World mandala, Nganjuk, East Java, Indonesia, late 10th–early 11th century, bronze, height each 3 ½ inches (8.9 cm) (catalogue no. 40)

Finally, it is interesting that the imagery of Borobudur can be read as a history of Buddhism.[46] The stories of Shakyamuni's life on the lower levels represent the formative phases of the religion, the pilgrimage of Sudhana symbolizes later developments found in the Universal Vehicle, and the arrangement of the mysterious multiple buddhas on the upper terraces represents Esoteric Buddhism. Scenes from the Buddha's biography and Sudhana's pilgrimage are combined with mandalas in the eleventh-century murals of the Dukhang, or Assembly Hall, in the great Tabo monastery in Spiti in Ladakh.[47] Iconographic programs linking various traditions within Buddhism must have been important to the development of Esoteric Buddhism as it moved from the ascetic world of the yogis and yoginis into a more monastic and structured tradition. Both Borobudur and Tabo were constructed during a formative period in the history of Buddhism, one which saw the final development of Esoteric Buddhism and the flowering of the tradition now known as Unexcelled Yoga. It is not surprising that both record an interest in structuring Buddhist history to coordinate early traditions with more current practices.

The Problem of Pala

Several impediments exist to developing a full picture of Buddhism in Asia during the period just before and after the construction of Borobudur. The obvious problem is that the few texts and images remaining from this era are survivors of what was once a flourishing Buddhist culture. Two major persecutions of Buddhism occurred in the ninth century, one in China and another in Tibet, and were doubtless responsible for the loss of much written and visual material. Further losses occurred due to Muslim invasions that ravaged northeastern India beginning in the late twelfth century.

Our imperfect understanding of the art and imagery fostered by the Pala and Sena rulers in Bihar, West Bengal, and Bangladesh[48] also contributes to this issue. As has already been mentioned, this region of India, home to famous monasteries such as Nalanda and Vikramashila and a center for monks and pilgrims from around the world, played a formative role in the second great transmission of Buddhism which brought most of the texts of the Yoga tantra and Anuttarayoga tantra traditions, as well as prototypes for painting and sculpture, to Tibet.

The most numerous Buddhist icons from the Pala period are stone stelae depicting Shakyamuni seated in meditation surrounded by smaller images of standing or seated buddhas that symbolize

Figure 25. Eight Scenes from the Life of Shakyamuni Buddha, Sarnath, Uttar Pradesh, India, c. 8th century, sandstone, height 38 inches (96.5 cm), Sarnath Site Museum, India

moments from his life and teaching career.[49] This stress on the Historical Buddha has often been interpreted as a reflection of the conservative nature of Buddhism in northeastern India during the Pala and Sena periods because such scenes are among the most long-lasting and prevalent images in Buddhist art.

However, a quick survey of representations of Shakyamuni's life, from their inception to the Pala period, illustrates subtle changes in this perennial theme which reflect transitions in Buddhist thought. Early depictions of the Buddha, either as a symbol—such as the example mentioned on the Great Stupa at Sanchi earlier in this essay—or in the human form found in relief panels and sculptures from the Kushana period, are primarily narrative. They record moments from Shakyamuni's life and often are part of larger sequential groupings. By the Gupta period (about fourth to

Figure 26. Shakyamuni Buddha with Scenes from His Life, Jagdispur, Bihar, India, Pala period, late 10th century, height 120 inches (300 cm)

sixth century), these representations had become iconic images in which seated and standing buddhas, signifying key moments in Shakyamuni's life, are grouped together and distinguished by their postures, gestures, and relationships to one another.[50] These changes, which occur during the same period as the production of mandalas such as that of the Eight Great Bodhisattvas, illustrate the use of Shakyamuni's biography as a paradigm for the process of spiritual development and enlightenment as well as a record of one's specific personal success in that quest.

By the eighth century, a group of eight events—four from the life of the Buddha prior to his enlightenment, and four from his teaching career—had become standardized. The figures in an important example in the Sarnath Museum (figure 25), read clockwise from lower right to lower left, illustrate Shakyamuni's birth

and first bath, the monkey's gift of honey to the Buddha, Shakyamuni's descent from the heaven of the thirty-three gods (where he preached to his mother), his first sermon, his parinirvana, the great miracle at Shravasti where Shakyamuni multiplied himself, the taming of the wild elephant Nalagiri sent by his evil cousin to kill him, and the assault of Mara. Two of these scenes, the monkey's gift of honey and the taming of the wild elephant, became common in visual treatments of Shakyamuni's biography only after the eighth century and were incorporated into the ubiqui-tous Pala-period representations of Shakyamuni and scenes from his life.

The largest (nearly seven feet tall) and possibly earliest example of these classic Pala-period icons is a magnificent work from Jagdispur near Nalanda (figure 26).[51] Shakyamuni seated in meditation with his hands in the gesture of calling the earth to witness (*bhumisparshamudra*) is the major figure in the Jagdispur stele. His gesture is a reference to Siddhartha's quest when, as he was meditating under the Bodhi tree, the demon Mara challenged his right to seek enlightenment. The Buddha touched the earth, validating his right to undertake the search, and Mara was vanquished. Reading clockwise from lower right to lower left, the smaller buddha figures represent Shakyamuni receiving the offering of honey, the first sermon at Sarnath, his descent from the heaven of the thirty-three gods, his parinirvana, the taming of the mad elephant Nalagiri, the miracle at Shravasti, and his birth.

The lack of chronological precision in the presentation of these scenes is typical of Pala-period representations in which moments from Shakyamuni's biography had become multivalent symbols. On the one hand, these events, all of which happened in different places, represent eight sacred sites which were the focus of pilgrimages beginning in the eighth century. On the other hand, they represent the overall process of journey any devotee takes in his quest for enlightenment. In addition, individual events can be interpreted as symbols for specific processes. For example, the taming of the elephant Nalagiri is often understood as a symbol for individual internal and external obstacles that must be overcome on the path to enlightenment.[52]

Several subsidiary elements in the iconography of the Jagdispur stele illustrate the juxtaposition of imagery associated with Esoteric Buddhism and scenes from the life of the Buddha. The top of the stele, which is now missing, once depicted the five transcendent buddhas that head the five buddha-clans in Yoga and Unexcelled Yoga tantra.[53] Two goddesses associated with Esoteric

Figure 27. *Crowned Buddha Shakyamuni, Bihar, India, Pala period, 11th century, height 27¾ inches (70.5 cm), The Asia Society Galleries, New York*

later thought and ceremonial practices—during initiations, monks were crowned to signify their attainment of certain levels of spiritual development.

Only one two-dimensional mandala has been found that can be dated to the Pala period. This is a mandala dedicated to Jambhala that was incised on the back of a sculpture of this deity excavated at Ratnagiri.[55] Published only as a rubbing and difficult to read, the Jambhala mandala is not of the palace-architecture

Figure 28. *Namasamgiti Manjuvajra in a Stupa Mandala, Bihar, India, Pala period, 11th–12th century, schist, 50¾ x 23¾ inches (128.9 x 60.3 cm) (catalogue no. 3)*

Buddhism, Marichi and an unidentified multiarmed deity, are found to either side of the central Buddha's seat. Finally, two groups of four bodhisattvas each are found to the right and left of the base of the Jagdispur stele. These figures, which symbolize the mandala of the Eight Great Bodhisattvas, place the biography of Shakyamuni and the processes it symbolizes within a sacred enclosure not unlike the palaces and other structures in later Tibetan mandalas.[54]

The crown and other adornments worn by the central buddha in a stele in the collection of the Asia Society, which are symbols of Shakyamuni's status as a teacher and universal ruler, also represent esoteric additions to traditional icons (figure 27). Found in the art of Kashmir and Central Asia in the eighth century and in Pala works from the eleventh century onward, such jewelry illustrates the belief in the transcendence of the Buddha that characterizes

type, but consists of an eight-petalled lotus in a central circle surrounded by other circles, all of which contain syllables that refer to deities. Additional information for Pala-period mandala imagery is found in three-dimensional mandalas such as the one dedicated to Manjuvajra, an esoteric form of Manjushri, the Bodhisattva of Wisdom (figure 28) in the Metropolitan Museum of Art.

In this sculpture, Manjuvajra has three faces and six arms. Four stupas and a stupa-temple, each containing another manifestation of Manjuvajra, are found at the top of the sculpture, while minuscule images of practitioners and other devotees appear on the base. This striking sculpture is a visual reinterpretation of works such as *Hymn of the Names of Manjushri* or the first chapter of the *Nispannayogavali,* two important texts which include descriptions of a Manjuvajra mandala, although, as is often the case, details differ both between the texts and between the texts and the visual interpretations.[56]

Manjuvajra is an emanation of Vajrasattva Buddha represented in the stupa-temple at the top of the sculpture. He is attended by the buddhas of the four cardinal directions who are distinguished by their attributes: Vairochana (sword, lotus, diamond), in the lower stupa to the right, marks the north; Ratnasambhava (emerald), the south; Amitabha (lotus), the west; and Amoghasiddhi (sword, wheel, gold, and lotus), the east. These buddhas symbolize the five buddha families and illustrate Manjuvajra's creation of a cosmos and manifestation within that sphere. Manjushri/Manjuvajra's gesture, known as *prajnalinganabhinaya,* indicates that he is embracing a

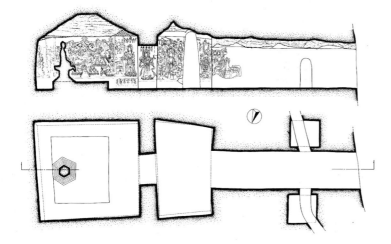

Figure 29. Plan, cave 25, Yulin, Gansu Province, China, late 8th century

missing female partner and places this image in the Unexcelled Yoga tradition in which the pairing of male and female partners, a type commonly known by its Tibetan name *yab-yum* (father-mother), has a crucial role.

Evidence from the Tibetan Periphery: Alchi and the Yulin Grottoes

Evidence for the development of several types of mandalas, as well as for the ways in which these images were incorporated into Buddhist iconography, is preserved in sites such as the Yulin cave-temples near Anxi, Gansu Province, China, and the complex at Alchi in Ladakh. The Yulin site contains about forty cave-temples constructed during various periods under the control of different peoples between the eighth and the fourteenth centuries. This fascinating site, located east of Dunhuang, was first recorded by Sir Aurel Stein and subsequently visited by a group from Harvard in 1925.[57] The recent publication of a monograph on this site by Chinese and Japanese scholars will hopefully lead to future work on the Yulin caves, whose murals illustrate changes in Buddhist thought from the eighth through the twelfth centuries and a distinctive form of Buddhism which combines Chinese and Tibetan tradition.[58]

The mandala of the Eight Great Bodhisattvas in cave 25 (mentioned earlier; see figure 15) covers most of its east wall, the most important in this west-facing grotto. Dated to the late eighth century when Yulin (like Dunhuang) was under Tibetan control, cave 25 is square with a pillar (derived from the Indian stupa) at its center (figure 29). Representations of Manjushri and Samantabhadra are painted at either side of the entryway, helping to identify the buddha seated on the pillar in the center of this cave as Vairochana because these two bodhisattvas are his attendants in the *Flower Garland Sutra.*

Amitabha's paradise, with scenes of the sixteen meditations at the right and of souls in different stages of rebirth at the left, dominates the south wall (figure 30), while Maitreya's paradise is depicted on the north wall. The iconographic program of this cave, which includes paradise scenes, a mandala of the Eight Great Bodhisattvas, and Vairochana Buddha, both illustrates important Buddhist currents found in Gansu in the late eighth century, and gives a summary of the images and ideas suggested as conceptual prototypes for mandalas throughout this essay.

Mandalas are prominent in caves constructed during the Xixia or Western Xia (1032–1227 CE) period, when the Yulin caves were

Figure 30. Detail of Amitabha's Western Paradise, south wall, cave 25, Yulin, Gansu Province, China, late 8th century

tiful representations of Manjushri and Samantabhadra (figure 33), which also show these bodhisattvas and their retinues in our world.

Unlike the mandala of the Eight Great Bodhisattvas in cave 25, the mandalas painted on the north and south walls and the unidentified mandala on the ceiling of cave 3 are all of the palace-architecture type. The prominence of this type in the Xixia-period caves at Yulin reflects ties between the Tanguts and the Tibetans and helps to date the flowering of this type of mandala to the eleventh to twelfth centuries, while the overall iconography in caves such as number 3, in which the major deities manifest in the phenomenal world, may help explain the prominence of this type of mandala in later Buddhist art. The structure of these mandalas and their cardinal orientations, together with the landscapes and

Figure 31. Interior view, cave 3, Yulin, Gansu Province, China, Xixia period (1032–1227)

under the control of the Tanguts, a people of Tibetan stock.[59] For instance, the west-facing square cave 3 is filled with sculptures and covered with murals (figure 31) unmistakably illustrating a world in which the mundane interacts easily with manifestations of the divine. Manjushri and Samantabhadra guard the entryway, suggesting once again that the central buddha represents Vairochana. A Womb World mandala (figure 32), an image of Sukhavati with the sixteen meditations, and a mandala dedicated to the Bodhisattva Avalokiteshvara are painted on the south wall. A Diamond World mandala, a scene from the *Devata Sutra*,[60] and a five-buddha mandala grace the north wall. An 11-headed, 1,000-armed Avalokiteshvara is painted on the north side of the east wall, and a 51-headed, 1,000-armed version of this bodhisattva is depicted to the south. They surround a scene of Shakyamuni's final passing. Great care has been taken to illustrate Avalokiteshvara's manifestation in the phenomenal world and both forms of this bodhisattva are surrounded by charming scenes of threshing, winnowing, acrobatics, and other daily events. A similar interest is found in the beau-

Figure 32. Mandala of the Womb World, south wall, cave 3, Yulin, Gansu Province, China, Xixia period (1032–1227)

genre scenes found in cave 3, ground the mandala deities in the everyday world and make the accessibility of enlightenment unmistakable.

Further information about the development of Buddhist art in the twelfth and thirteenth centuries is provided by the magnificent murals in temples such as those at Alchi in the district of Ladakh, which spans the borders of Jammu and Kashmir in northern India.[61] The temples in this area, which was at various times part of the Tibetan cultural sphere, illustrate Buddhism as practiced by Tibetans after its second wave of propagation. This wave has historically been associated with the pious King Yeshe O, who ruled

the region of Ngari in western Tibet in the early tenth century. An ardent follower of Buddhism, he rebuilt damaged temples, constructed new monasteries, and sent monk-translators and others to India and Kashmir to regain lost texts and images. Three of the buildings at Alchi—the Dukhang or Assembly Hall, the Sumstek or Three-Storied Building, and the Lhakhang Soma or New Temple—are decorated with elaborate murals which have been the subject of several recent studies.

The Assembly Hall is a single-storied building with an entryway through a courtyard. The primary sculpture in this building, a large seated sculpture of Vairochana, is placed in a niche on the back wall. Additional sculptures and murals decorate the side and entryway walls, as well as those in the courtyard. These include

Figure 33. Samantabhadra Bodhisattva, west wall, cave 3, Yulin, Gansu Province, China, Xixia period (1032–1227)

Figure 34. *1,000-buddha images with detail of a colossal figure of Avalokiteshvara Bodhisattva, interior of the Three-Storied Building, Alchi (Ladakh region), Kashmir, 12th or early 13th century*

Figure 35. *Mandala of Sarvavid-Vairochana, interior of the Assembly Hall, Alchi (Ladakh region), Kashmir, 12th or early 13th century*

narratives, representations of various deities, and mandalas. The lower story of the Sumstek, or Three-Storied Building, is dominated by colossal sculptures of the bodhisattvas Avalokiteshvara, Maitreya, and Manjushri, with colorful scenes painted into their clothing. These principal figures are attended by smaller sculptures set against a background of small seated buddhas in the 1,000-buddha motif. Large-scale mandalas are painted on the walls of the second and third stories.

The paintings in the Assembly Hall and Three-Storied Building are dated to the twelfth or early thirteenth centuries. Stylistically, these works derive from the artistic traditions of Kashmir. Iconographically, these paintings and sculptures show several parallels to the earlier works at Yungang in China, for example, in the use of colossal figures or the prominence awarded to the 1,000-buddha motif (figure 34), again linking these icons to Buddhist traditions found in Northwest India and Kashmir, regions that, as was previously noted, have been associated with the early development of Esoteric Buddhism.

However, the paintings in the New Temple, which are dated to the latter part of the thirteenth century, reflect the introduction of new styles and iconographies to the art of Alchi. The style of the paintings has been linked to traditions from the easternmost regions of Central Asia and western parts of China, possibly areas such as Karakhoto that were under the control of the Tanguts. The imagery, in particular the prominence given to figures in the father-mother or *yab-yum* pose, and to deities of the vajra family such as Hevajra and Chakrasamvara, illustrates the spread of Unexcelled Yoga tantra in Tibet in the thirteenth century.

Palace-architecture mandalas are prevalent in the iconographic programs at Alchi. Their importance is reflected in their careful placement in the upper registers of floors of the buildings, which suggests, as at Borobudur, that they illustrate the attainment of different levels of spiritual reality.[62] Some of these mandalas, such as an example from the second story of the Sumstek (figure 36), are divided into the ninefold composition first seen in the mandala of the Eight Great Bodhisattvas and best preserved in the Diamond

Figure 36. Detail from a Vajradhatu Mandala, interior of the Three-Storied Building, Alchi (Ladakh region), Kashmir, 12th or early 13th century

World tradition of Japan. Others, such as the mandala of the Sarvavid-Vairochana in the Assembly Hall (figure 35),[63] continue the use of an eightfold center that is among the most common forms of the mandala. In general, the mandalas at Alchi contain more figures and have more elaborate decoration than do those found in the Yulin grottoes, illustrating trends in the development of mandala imagery that will continue in Tibet for several centuries.

Mandalas in Tibet

A Hevajra mandala dating from the late twelfth or early thirteenth century (figure 37) illustrates the basic composition of a Tibetan mandala.[64] The Hevajra (Laughing Vajra) in the center of the mandala has a light blue body, four legs, sixteen hands—each holding a skull cup—and he embraces his partner Nairatmya, "she who is without ego." This form of Hevajra is based on the eighth chapter of the *Nispannayogavali* and is known as Hevajra Kapaladhara, or the one who holds the skull cup. The skull cups in his right hands contain animals, while those in his left hands hold divinities symbolic of the elements and other forces such as death and wealth. Hevajra is naked except for garlands of skulls and severed heads. He tramples on the backs of four supine figures (known as Maras) that symbolize basic hindrances to enlightenment.

Hevajra and Nairatmya embrace in the center of an eight-petalled lotus flower inhabited by female adepts known as yogini, each associated with a directional point. The lotus is in the center of the mandala palace, a square structure with elaborate gateways to the four cardinal directions. This compasslike orientation is reiterated by the use of different colors for the four sections of the palace interior. Initiation vases are located in the four corners of the palace and an additional set is placed in the entryways to the gates. These vases, which are filled with pure water and medicinal and nutritious substances, play an important role in rituals and initiations and symbolize the nature of the adherent and the internal bounds he must break in his practices. The palace, divided into interior and exterior courts, is enclosed by a large circle of lotus petals symbolic of rebirth and purity, which marks the transition from the mundane to the sacred.

Additional manifestations of Hevajra and Nairatmya are found in the outer four corners of the painting. They symbolize the buddhas of the four cardinal directions just as the central image represents the primary buddha of the five families as they are organized in this particular combination of text and image. Yamantaka, a fierce form of the Bodhisattva Manjushri who signifies triumph over death, together with five monks and a four-armed version of Hevajra with Nairatmya, are depicted in the lower border. The upper border provides a Kagyu order lineage consisting of a Guhyasamaja father-mother (one of the most important in Tibetan practice), Vajradhara, the adepts Tilopa and Naropa, three monks of the Kagyu order, and a Chakrasamvara father-mother pair. The somewhat mystical Kagyu order, founded by Marpa, Milarepa, and Gampopa, traces its origins to Tilopa and Naropa, presumably sources of the imagery and practices depicted in this painting.

Fascinating scenes of adepts, practitioners, and world-gods (semidivinities often incorporated into Buddhism from other reli-

Figure 37. Hevajra Mandala, Tibet, Sakya order, early 13th century, ink and opaque watercolors on cloth, 14 x 13 inches (35.6 x 33 cm) (catalogue no. 15)

tual process. Each plays many roles during rites and visualizations which presumes a constant dialogue between the deity at the heart of the mandala (and in its various components) and the practitioner who moves, at least metaphorically, from outside the mandala to its core. On this journey he encounters the various forces radiating from the inside out, identifies with the central deity, apprehends all manifestations as parts of a single whole, and moves closer to the goal of perfect understanding or enlightenment.

The sheer difficulty inherent in the more complex practices associated with mandalas is illustrated by the creation and use of mandalas in series. A group of fifteenth-century paintings illustrating a text known as the *Vajravali* exemplifies the astonishing iconographic and compositional complexity that underlies these works and the practices they illustrate. At least fourteen paintings are extant from the best known *Vajravali* series. (See catalogue no. 21

Figure 38. Four Mandalas from a Vajravali Series, Tibet, Sakya order, 1430s–1440s, ink and opaque watercolors on cloth, 32 1/2 x 29 inches (82.6 x 73.7 cm) (catalogue no. 22)

gious traditions) are found in the eight death-grounds (each with its own stupa, mountain, river, and tree) between the outer edges of the mandala and its inner circle. These charnel grounds are associated with the eight cardinal points as well as with specific sites where Indian ascetics assembled for meditations. They are also sometimes understood as the eight aggregates of human consciousness that must be overcome to escape ties to the phenomenal world. Cremation grounds are most commonly found in mandalas of wrathful deities such as Hevajra. Mandalas representing these deities are among the most commonly preserved in the Tibetan tradition and may have been made more frequently because they are among the first divinities introduced to initiates.

Each figure in a mandala has several purposes, functioning as a specific deity, as a manifestation of the central deity's power, as a focus of visualization and meditation, and as a signpost for a spiri-

Figure 39. Indrabhuti Vajradakini Mandala, Tibet, Kagyu order, late 17th–early 18th century, ink and opaque watercolors on cloth, 16⅛ x 13¼ inches (41 x 33.7 cm) (catalogue no. 32)

research shows that each of the works in this set contains one mandala, which gives the series its name (in this case the Vairochana mandala from the *Vajravali*) and three from the *Collection of Rites* by Darpanacharya.

The development of mandala series and the interest in preserving and codifying traditions may be linked to the prominence of the monastic Sakya order[66] from the fourteenth through sixteenth centuries. This order traces its origins to the founding of the Sakya monastery by Khon Konchok Gyalpo (1034–1102 CE) in 1073. Noted for their scholarship, rigorous curriculum, and interest in the preservation, transmission, and amalgamation of texts, members of this order often trace their theological lineage to the Vikramashila monastery in northeastern India. Sakya monasteries such as Ngor in central Tibet were also renowned artistic centers noted for their distinctive blending of Nepali traditions with the Kashmiri and Pala strains found in earlier works. The global interests of monks from this order are also reflected in their roles as spiritual mentors to Khubilai Khan and other Mongol rulers of China during the Yuan dynasty (1279–1368 CE).

Figure 40. Chamunda Fierce Fire Offering Symbol Mandala, Tibet, Geluk order, 17th–18th century, ink and opaque watercolors on cloth, 24 x 18½ inches (61 x 47 cm) (catalogue no. 36)

for the Philadelphia example.) They were commissioned by the monk Ngorchen Kunga Zangpo (1382–1456 CE) in honor of his teacher Sazang Pakpa.[65] A member of the Sakya order, Sazang Pakpa taught poetics to Tsong Khapa (1357–1419 CE). One of the most influential monks in Tibetan Buddhism, Tsong Khapa developed a monastic curriculum and is now worshiped as one of the three great Tibetan incarnations of the Bodhisattva Manjushri.

Each of the paintings in the *Vajravali* series contains four individual mandalas and a background of additional images that can be read as a fifth mandala. For example, the four mandalas in a work in a private collection (figure 38) include a Marichi mandala (lower right), one dedicated to Bhutadamara Vajrapani (lower left), a Dharmadhatu Vairochana mandala (upper left), and a mandala of Shakyamuni (upper right). An inscription at the top of the painting indicates it is the thirteenth in the series. Recent

Figure 41. Star Mandala (detail), Kyongsang Province, South Korea, 18th century

Figure 42. Star Mandala, Japan, Edo period, 17th century, gold and colors on wood, diameter 21½ inches (54.6 cm) (catalogue no. 47)

Mandalas, and other paintings produced after the sixteenth century, are often distinguished from earlier works by the more prevalent inclusion of naturalistic landscape backgrounds, as seen in an eighteenth-century mandala (figure 39) of the goddess Indrabhuti Vajradakini. Landscapes are frequently interpreted as a reflection of the influence of Chinese art on that of Tibet. They may, however, also have an iconographic explanation as manifestations of the divine and the powers of a divinity in the phenomenal world. The inclusion of landscape settings helps to place these manifestations firmly in the world perceived by the viewer of the painting. The interest in a more concrete background for this mandala must also reflect the rising prominence of the Geluk order from the sixteenth century onward. Noted for its comprehensiveness and synthesis of a vast array of Buddhist teachings, this order helped to place Esoteric Buddhism into all aspects of Tibetan life and culture.

A distinctive mandala in the Zimmerman family collection (figure 40) provides another example of innovations found in the development of this icon in Tibet during the seventeenth through nineteenth centuries.[67] Dating to the seventeenth or eighteenth century, this mandala consists of an inverted triangle within a larg-

er triangle, both containing symbols rather than deities. The triangles are placed in a circle that fills the center of the mandala palace, which is itself filled with bones, skulls, and fragments of skeletons. The palace is placed within a human figure—or possibly on its flayed skin—floating in a sea of abstract red forms that may be intended to symbolize blood. It is enclosed in another triangular wall and surrounded by flames.

No text has been identified as the basis for this mandala, but it may have been made as a model for the preparation of a fire hearth used for offerings to Chamunda, consort of Yama, the Lord of Death. The flames of the background show that Chamunda's mansion is thought to exist in the center of the heart of Agni, the fire god. Like the more gentle landscapes discussed above, this symbolic mandala represents an interest in making abstract internal concepts and practices visually concrete.

East Asian Mandalas: Later Traditions

A striking eighteenth-century mandala[68] (the only known Korean example) recently discovered in the Yongmun-sa temple in northern Kyongsang Province in South Korea (figure 41) reveals a tantalizing new aspect of the study of mandalas in East Asia. A preaching

Vairochana Buddha, attended by two bodhisattvas and two monks, is seated in the center of the mandala. His assembly is encircled by ten additional seated buddhas and a host of other images, many tentatively identified as astrological symbols.

Astrology played a prominent role in Tang-period Buddhism, and Yijing, the famous seventh-century Chinese disciple of Amoghavajra, was as renowned for his skill as an astrologer as for his study of Buddhism. Paintings depicting the planets, stars, and Big Dipper are known in some number from Korea and Japan, particularly from the twelfth through fourteenth centuries. Amitabha Buddha is the central figure in an unusual seventeenth-century Japanese example, painted on wood, in the Philadelphia Museum of Art (figure 42). He is surrounded by twenty-eight bodhisattvas, each shown with a particular constellation representing one of the twenty-eight lunar mansions, or *xiu,* of early Chinese astrology. The thirty-six guardians, also known as the thirty-six auspicious stellar gods, are depicted at the outer edges of the mandala. Many of these works are believed to preserve lost Chinese traditions, and the rise of astrological imagery in Chinese Buddhism is attributed to the blending of Sinitic and Indic beliefs and to the influence of early esoteric thought.

Japan, whose crucial role in preserving many esoteric traditions has already been discussed, also contributed several distinctive innovations to the development of mandala imagery in Asia. Some of the most intriguing are mandalas of sites such as the Kasuga shrine in Nara, the Sanno shrine on Mount Hiei (northeast of Kyoto), or the Kumano cult from the southern tip of the Kii Peninsula in eastern Japan. In these mandalas, native gods known as *kami* are understood as manifestations of imported Buddhist deities in a system called *honji-suijaku,* or "true-nature manifestation."[69]

Worship of these famous sites and the divinities associated with them has a long history in Japan and played an important role in the development of Buddhism there. The paralleling of native and Buddhist deities flourished with the growth of *shugendo,* or way of mystical practice, in the Heian period (794–1185 CE). Adherents of this practice generally retreated to isolated mountains to meditate and practice austerities and—in their openness to multiple beliefs—helped to further solidify an appreciation for nature as a manifestation of divinity, as well as the practice of identifying various deities as manifestations of each other. By the twelfth century, many of their practices had been incorporated into the esoteric Tendai and Shingon orders and expressed as mandalas.

Several images associated with the Kasuga cult are elegantly depicted in a painting dating from around 1300, now in a private collection (figure 43). The temple in the foreground is the Kofuku-ji, built as the family temple for the powerful Fujiwaras in the eighth century and reconstructed many times. A path leads from this Buddhist temple through the wooded Kasuga plain to the Kasuga shrine, the Shinto center of this region. It is worshiped for its mountain and agricultural divinities and as the locus of the Fujiwara family gods. Deer, sacred to the Kasuga cult, walk through the woods. The conical Mount Mikasa and the heavily wooded Mount Kasuga are shown in the background. Above them, two angel-like beings lift a mirror, a potent political and religious symbol, that reflects the five Buddhist deities of the Kasuga cult. The central buddha is Shakyamuni as a form of the principal local deity, Takamikazuchi no Mikoto. He is accompanied by Bhaishajyaguru (Futsunushi no Mikoto); Kshitigarbha (Ame no Koyane no Mikoto); Avalokiteshvara in his eleven-headed form (Himegami); and Manjushri, the Buddhist form of the local *wakamiya* (a young god worshiped as the actual child of the principal deity).

The same buddhas are seated above the Kasuga and Mikasa mountains in the background of a Kasuga cult painting of the sacred deer of that site (figure 44). The deer carries a branch of the *sakaki* tree, a longstanding Shinto emblem of prosperity, which in turn bears a mirror. In this example the deer, a symbol for the entire site, seems far removed from the Buddhism of India and Tibet. Nonetheless, this uniquely Japanese painting illustrates some of the core beliefs and practices of Buddhism: it shows a place whose sanctity is enhanced by deities, their presence inspiring the faithful to set out on a path (symbolized by the passage from Kofuku-ji to the Kasuga shrine) which—long or short, straight or crooked, real or imaginary—reminds them of their own power to seek enlightenment and guide others to the same goal. As such, the sacred Shinto deer of Kasuga may not be so far removed from the animals who heard Shakyamuni's first preaching at Sarnath, for they both remind us of the ability of Buddhist deities to manifest in our world and guide us to their greater reality.

Figure 43. Kasuga Shrine Mandala, Japan, Kamakura period, c. 1300, colors on silk, 31 x 11 inches (78.7 x 27.9 cm) (catalogue no. 44)

Figure 44. Kasuga Deer Mandala, Japan, Muromachi period, 15th century, colors on silk (catalogue no. 45)

1. See, for example, Peter Gold, *Navajo & Tibetan Sacred Wisdom: The Circle of the Spirit* (Rochester, Vt.: Inner Traditions, 1994).

2. A possible prototype for the palace-architecture structure is inserted into an eleventh-century *Prajnaparamita* manuscript. See Pratapaditya Pal and Julia Meech-Pekarik, *Buddhist Book Illuminations* (New York: Ravi Kumar, 1998), fig. 19.

3. Odette Viennot, *Le culte de l'arbre dans l'Inde ancienne: Textes et monuments brahmaniques et bouddhiques* (Paris: Presses Universitaires de France, 1954).

4. Literature on stupas and their role in Buddhist art and practice is voluminous. A good overview is provided by Anna Libera Dahmen-Dallapiccola and Stephanie Zingel-Avé Lallemant, eds., *The Stúpa: Its Religious, Historical, and Archaeological Significance* (Wiesbaden: Steiner, 1980).

5. See the India-based periodical *Marg* 47, no. 3 (1996), an issue dedicated to Sanchi.

6. Gerard Fussman, "Symbolism of the Buddhist Stupa," *Journal of the International Association of Buddhist Studies* 9, no. 2 (1986), pp. 37–54.

7. Peter Harvey, "The Symbolism of the Early Stupa," *Journal of the International Association of Buddhist Studies* 7, no. 2 (1984), pp. 67–93.

8. Randy Kloetzli, *Buddhist Cosmology from Single World System to Pure Land: Science and Theology in the Images of Motion and Light* (Delhi: Motilal Banarsidass, 1983).

9. The most comprehensive survey of Esoteric Buddhism to date is David L. Snellgrove, *Indo-Tibetan Buddhism: Indian Buddhists and Their Tibetan Successors* (Boston: Shambhala, 1987).

10. These sites remain poorly published particularly in Western languages. One good source for information is a Japanese series entitled *Chugoku Sekkutsu* (The Grotto Art of China), which details several of the more famous cave-temples. For an English-language study of Yungang, see James O. Caswell, *Written and Unwritten: A New History of the Buddhist Caves at Yungang* (Vancouver: University of British Columbia Press, 1988).

11. A notable exception is John C. Huntington, "The Iconography and Iconology of the 'Tan Yao' Caves at Yungang," *Oriental Art* 32 (Summer 1986), pp. 142–60.

12. For a study of this material, see Angela Falco Howard, *The Imagery of the Cosmological Buddha* (Leiden: Brill, 1986), which is also a source for images of many of the works discussed in this part of the essay.

13. See ibid., fig. 16.

14. See Jacques Gies and Monique Cohen, *Serinde, terre de Bouddha: Dix siècles d'art sur la Route de la Soie* (exh. cat., Paris: Galeries Nationales du Grand Palais, 1995), pl. 271.

15. For an overview of this sculpture and related pieces, see Takeshi Kobayashi, *Nara Buddhist Art, Todai-ji*, translated and adapted by Richard L. Gage, Heibonsha Survey of Japanese Art, vol. 5 (New York: Weatherhill; Tokyo: Heibonsha, 1975).

16. Charles D. Orzech, "Seeing Chen-yen Buddhism: Traditional Scholarship and the Vajrayana in China," *History of Religions* 29 (1989), pp. 86–114.

17. This sutra is preserved in the *Taisho Shinsho Daizokyo* ([Tokyo: Taisho Issaikyo Kaukokai, 1924–34], sutra no. 1005a), a 100-volume edition of the Chinese version of the Buddhist *Tripitaka*, compiled by Takakusu Junjiro et al.

18. Wai-kam Ho, "Notes on Chinese Sculpture from Northern Ch'i to Sui, Part I: Two Seated Stone Buddhas in the Cleveland Museum," *Archives of Asian Art* 22 (1968–69), pp. 6–55.

19. John C. Huntington, "A Gandharan Image of Amitayus' Sukhavati," *Annali dell' Istituto Orientale di Napoli* 30 (1980), pp. 651–72.

20. See Elizabeth ten Grotenhuis, "Rebirth of an Icon: The Taima Mandala in Medieval Japan," *Archives of Asian Art* 36 (1983), pp. 59–87, which also includes additional images of this type of mandala.

21. Elizabeth ten Grotenhuis, "Nine Places of Birth in Amida's Western Pure Land," in *Bukkyo bijutsushi kenkyo ni okeru "zuzo to yoshiki"/"Iconography and Style" in Buddhist Art Historical Studies*, 14th International Symposium on Art Historical Studies (Kobe: Kokusai Koryo Bijutsushi Kenkyokai, 1996).

22. See *Taisho Shinsho Daizokyo*, sutra no. 427. It was translated into Chinese by Zhijien.

23. Lin Li-Kouang, "Punyodaya (Na-t'i), un propagateur du Tantrisme en Chine et au Cambodge à l'époque de Hiuan-tsang," *Journal Asiatique* 227 (1935), pp. 83–100.

24. Pratapaditya Pal, "A Note on the Mandala of the Eight Bodhisattvas," *Archives of Asian Art* 26 (1972–73), pp. 71–73; Hiram W. Woodward, Jr., "Southeast Asian Traces of Buddhist Pilgrims," *Muse*, no. 22 (1988), pp. 75–91.

25. Pal, "Mandala of the Eight Bodhisattvas," fig. 3.

26. For a recent study of this site emphasizing its esoteric connections, see Geri Hockfield Malandra, *Unfolding a Mandala: The Buddhist Cave Temples at Ellora* (Albany: State University of New York Press, 1993).

27. For images of the Indonesian sites, see August J. Bernet Kempers, *Ancient Indonesian Art* (Amsterdam: Van der Peet, 1959).

28. See *Ansei Yurinkutsu/The Yulinku Grottoes* (Tokyo: Heibonsha, 1990), part of the *Chugoku Sekkutsu* series.

29. Amy Heller, "Early Ninth Century Images of Vairochana from Eastern Tibet," *Orientations* 25 (June 1994), pp. 74–79.

30. Radha Banerjee, *Ashtamahabodhisattva: The Eight Great Bodhisattvas in Art and Literature* (New Delhi: Abha Prakashan), pls. 30–32.

31. Heller, "Early Ninth Century Images of Vairochana," fig. 7.

32. Michael Henss, "A Unique Treasure of Early Tibetan Art: The Eleventh Century Wall Paintings of Drathang Gonpa," *Orientations* 25 (June 1994), pp. 48–53.

33. Giuseppe Tucci, *To Lhasa and Beyond: Diary of the Expedition to Tibet in the Year MCMXLVIII*, translated by Mario Carelli (Rome: Istituto Poligrafico dello Stato, 1956), pp. 65, 70, 105.

34. For an example, see *Zaigai Nihon no Shiho* (Tokyo: Mainichi Shinbunsha, 1980), vol. 1, pls. 38, 39.

35. Phyllis Granoff, "A Portable Buddhist Shrine from Central Asia," *Archives of Asian Art* 22 (1968–69), pp. 81–95.

36. Two English-language works on this school are Minoru Kiyota, *Shingon Buddhism: Theory and Practice* (Los Angeles: Buddhist Books, Int., 1978), and Taiko Yamasaki, *Shingon: Japanese Esoteric Buddhism*, translated and adapted by Richard Peterson and Cynthia Peterson; edited by Yasuyoshi Morimoto and David Kidd; foreword by Carmen Blacker (Boston: Shambhala, 1988).

37. The first publications on this important site include two reports by the Famensi Archaeological Team, "Fufeng Famensi ta Tangdai digong fajue jianbao" (Brief Report on the Excavation of the Tang Dynasty Underground Treasury at Famen Monastery Pagoda in Fufeng), *Wenwu*, no. 10 (1988), pp. 1–28, and "Fufeng Famensi Tangdai digong fajue jianbao" (Brief Report on the Excavation of the Tang Underground Treasury at Famen Temple, Fufeng), *Kaogu yu Wenwu*, no. 2 (1988), pp. 94–106. *Wenwu*, no. 10 (1988) also contains several other articles concerning Fufeng, and one of them, Su Bai et al., "Famensi ta digong chutu wenwu bitan" (Exchange of Letters on the Cultural Relics Excavated from the Underground Treasury of the Famensi Pagoda), pp. 29–43, first suggests that the casket may represent the Diamond World mandala. For English-language materials, see Zhu Qixin,

"Buddhist Treasures from Famensi: The Recent Excavation of a Tang Underground Palace," *Orientations* 21 (May 1990), pp. 77–83; and Roderick Whitfield, "Esoteric Buddhist Elements in the Famensi Reliquary Deposit," *Asiatische Studien/Études Asiatiques* 44 (1990), pp. 247–66.

38. Osamu Takata, Terukazu Akiyama, and Taka Yanagisawa, *Takao mandara: Bijutsu Kenyojo hokoku* (Report of the Institute of Art Research: The Oldest Mandala Paintings of Esoteric Buddhism in Japan) (Tokyo: Yoshikawa Kobunkan, 1967).

39. Nancy Hock, "Buddhist Ideology and the Sculpture of Ratnagiri, Seventh through Thirteenth Centuries" (Ph.D. dissertation, University of California, Berkeley, 1987); Yoritomo Motohiro, *Mandara no kansho kiso chishiki* (An Intellectual Foundation for Appreciating Mandalas) (Tokyo: Shibundo, 1991).

40. John C. Huntington, "Cave Six at Aurangabad: A Tantrayana Monument?" in *Kalodaroana: American Studies in the Art of India*, edited by Joanna G. Williams, pp. 45–55 (Leiden: Brill, 1981).

41. Again there is a great deal of material on this site. For a good overview, see Luís O. Gomez and Hiram W. Woodward, Jr., eds., *Barabudur: History and Significance of a Buddhist Monument*, papers originally presented at the International Conference on Borobudur, University of Michigan, May 16–17, 1974 (Berkeley and Los Angeles: University of California Press, 1981).

42. For some suggestions regarding the nature of early esoteric practice in Southeast Asia, see Denise Patry Leidy, "Bodhisattva Maitreya, Prakhon Chai, and the Practice of Buddhism in Southeast Asia," in *Buddha of the Future: An Early Maitreya from Thailand*, by Nandana Chutiwongs and Denise Patry Leidy (exh. cat., New York: The Asia Society Galleries, 1994). For a different interpretation, see Marijke J. Klobbe, "Borobudur, a Mandala: A Contextual Approach to Function and Meaning," *International Institute for Asian Studies Yearbook* (1995), pp. 191–219.

43. Jan Fontein, *The Sculpture of Indonesia*, with essays by R. Soekmono and Edi Sedyawati (exh. cat., Washington, D.C.: National Gallery of Art, 1990), pp. 223–33.

44. Kathleen O'Brien, "Chandi Jago as a Mandala: Symbolism of Its Narratives," *Review of Indonesian and Malayan Affairs* 22 (1988), pp. 1–61.

45. Jan Fontein, *The Pilgrimage of Sudhana: A Study of Gandavyuha Illustrations in China, Japan, and Java* (The Hague: Mouton, 1966).

46. Lokesh Chandra, "Borobudur: A New Interpretation," in Dahmen-Dallapiccola and Zingel-Avé Lallemant, *Stúpa*, pp. 301–19.

47. This site is reasonably well published. For a recent monograph, see O. C. Handa, *Tabo Monastery and Buddhism in the Trans-Himalaya: Thousand Years of Existence of the Tabo Chos-Khor* (New Delhi: Indus, 1994).

48. Susan L. Huntington and John C. Huntington, *Leaves from the Bodhi Tree: The Art of Pala India (8th–12th Centuries) and Its International Legacy* (exh. cat., Dayton, Ohio: Dayton Art Institute, 1990).

49. For a discussion of more obviously esoteric images, see Robert Linrothe, "Compassionate Malevolence: Wrathful Deities in Esoteric Buddhist Art" (Ph.D. diss., University of Chicago, 1992).

50. Joanna Williams, "Sarnath Gupta Steles of the Buddha's Life," *Ars Orientalia* 10 (1975), pp. 171–92.

51. Janice Leoshko, "Scenes of the Buddha's Life in Pala-Period Art," *Silk Road Art and Archeology* 3 (1994), pp. 251–76.

52. John C. Huntington, "Pilgrimage as Image: The Cult of the Astamahapratiharya, Part II," *Orientations* 18 (August 1987), pp. 56–68.

53. G. Bhattacharya, "Buddha Shakyamuni and Panca-Tathagatas: Dilemma in Bihar-Bengal," *South Asian Archaeology* (1985), pp. 350–71.

54. See Pal, "Mandala of the Eight Bodhisattvas," for another example showing the pairing of scenes from Shakyamuni's life with the mandala of Eight Great Bodhisattvas.

55. Debala Mitra, "Jambhala-Mandalas in Sculpture," *Journal of the Asiatic Society of Bengal, Letters* 3, no. 1 (1961), pp. 39–41.

56. Jane Casey Singer, "Manjuvajra Mandala: A Medieval Sculpture from Eastern India" (typescript, n.d.). For an additional example of a Pala-period stone mandala, see Janice Leoshko, "An Eleventh Century Jambhala Mandala of the Pala Period," *Orientations* 27 (July–August 1996), pp. 35–37.

57. See *Ansei Yurinkutsu/Yulinku Grottoes* for the most recent monograph on this site. Additional information is available in Langdon Warner, *Buddhist Wall-Paintings: A Study of a Ninth-Century Grotto at Wan Fo Hsia* (Cambridge, Mass.: Harvard University Press, 1938).

58. For a preliminary attempt to describe this tradition, see Mikhail Piotrovsky, ed., *Lost Empire of the Silk Road: Buddhist Art from Khara Khoto (X–XIIIth Century)* (exh. cat., Lugano: Fondazione Thyssen-Bornemisza, Villa Favorita, 1993), and Robert

Linrothe, "Peripheral Visions: On Recent Finds of Tangut Buddhist Art," *Monumenta Serica* 43 (1995), pp. 235–62.

59. The April 1996 issue of *Orientations* was dedicated to the study of art produced under Xixia rule.

60. *Taisho Shinsho Daizokyo*, sutra no. 592.

61. David L. Snellgrove and Tadeusz Skorupski, *The Cultural Heritage of Ladakh*, 2 vols. (Warminster: Aris and Phillips, 1980); Pratapaditya Pal, *A Buddhist Paradise: The Murals of Alchi, Western Himalayas*, photographs by Lionel Fournier (Hong Kong: Kumar, 1982); Roger Goepper and Jaroslav Poncar, *Alchi: Ladakh's Hidden Buddhist Sanctuary* (Boston: Shambhala, 1996).

62. See Robert Linrothe's discussion in Goepper, *Alchi*.

63. Pal, *Buddhist Paradise*, pl. 21.

64. This discussion has benefited from Marie-Thérèse de Mallmann, *Introduction à l'iconographie du tântrisme bouddhique* (Paris, 1975), and Alex Wayman, *The Buddhist Tantras: Light on Indo-Tibetan Esotericism* (Delhi: Motilal Banarsidass, 1973).

65. David P. Jackson, *A History of Tibetan Painting: The Great Tibetan Painters and Their Traditions* (Vienna: Verlag der Österreichischen Akademie der Wissenschaften, 1996), p. 82, n. 182.

66. Good sources on Tibetan painting and its evolution include Pratapaditya Pal, *Art of Tibet: A Catalogue of the Los Angeles County Museum of Art Collections* (Los Angeles: Los Angeles County Museum of Art, 1983); Pratapaditya Pal, *Tibetan Painting: A Study of Tibetan Thangkas, Eleventh to Nineteenth Centuries* (Basel: Ravi Kumar, 1984); and Marilyn Rhie and Robert A. F. Thurman, *Wisdom and Compassion: The Sacred Art of Tibet* (exh. cat., San Francisco: Asian Art Museum; New York: Tibet House, 1991).

67. Pratapaditya Pal, *Art of the Himalayas: Treasures from Nepal and Tibet*, contributions by Ian Alsop, Heather Stoddard, and Valrae Reynolds (exh. cat., New York: American Federation of Arts, 1991), nos. 111, 112.

68. I am indebted to Dr. Kang Woo Bang of the National Museum in Seoul for sending me a photograph of this mandala and a copy of his preliminary study of this painting.

69. Haruki Kageyama, *The Arts of Shinto*, translated and adapted by Christine Guth (New York: Weatherhill, 1973); Haruki Kageyama and Christine Guth Kanda, *Shinto Arts: Nature, Gods, and Man in Japan* (exh. cat., New York: Japan House Gallery, 1976).

SPACE AND SANCTITY
IN BUDDHIST ART

The prominence awarded mandalas in later Buddhist art reflects religious developments at the core of Esoteric Buddhist thought. One such development was the stress on the possibility of achieving enlightenment in a single lifetime (as opposed to several). The concepts underlying this art form, however, can be traced to early religious and philosophical traditions that have played an enduring role in Indian art and architecture.

The practice of creating a circle or other space for use in personal devotions or by a great teacher is found in the Vedic Brahmanas, some of India's earliest and most influential texts. It is also at the heart of Buddhism. Shakyamuni's choice of the Bodhi tree at Bodhgaya as the site of his enlightenment was based to some extent on the perennial belief that the tree and the area surrounding it were sacred, imbued with the knowledge and powers of others who had used the site for their own spiritual quests.

Indian religious buildings are carefully structured as earthly homes for deities and as bases from which they can generate goodwill and spiritual understanding to guide and teach others. Miniature versions of temples, stupas, and other buildings—such

as the examples in this section of the exhibition—function both as reminders of sacred sites and as symbols of the presence of the divine and the enlightened in our world.

Stupas, the earliest Buddhist monuments preserved in India, began as solid hemispherical domes that were used to mark the remains of a great leader or teacher. They were incorporated into early Buddhist art as symbols of the continuing presence of Shakyamuni Buddha after his parinirvana (or final transcendence), and as reminders of the path he defined for his followers. The models of stupas in this exhibition include Indian examples as well as a Tibetan chorten and a Japanese pagoda, which show how this architectural form was redefined in other parts of Asia.

Two objects exhibited here are based on actual buildings. The first, a small soapstone piece from India, is a model of the famous temple at Bodhgaya that marks the site of Shakyamuni's enlightenment. The second, a large copper pagoda, is a copy of the famous five-storied structure at the Todai-ji temple in Nara. Like the painted mandalas that are the focus of this exhibition, representations of both specific buildings and generic types exemplify spaces that have been sanctified over time by the deities who inhabit them and the practitioners who visit them.

opposite: detail of catalogue no. 5

1

Miniature Stupa

❀

Pakistan, Gandhara, about
4th century

Bronze

Height 22 ¾ inches (57.8 cm)

The Metropolitan Museum of Art,
Gift of Mr. and Mrs. Donald J.
Bruckman, 1985.387

The stupa symbolizes the Buddha's mind, while the scripture represents his speech, and the image (sculpture or painting) his body. In the Pali *Ultimate Nirvana Scripture,* Shakyamuni Buddha decreed that a buddha's ashes and relics should be gathered and placed in a cairn or stupa more magnificent than that of a world emperor. The stupa would serve to turn people's awareness of death away from admiration of the worldly toward impermanence and enlightenment. Looking at this small, remarkably solid, yet ethereal stupa, we note that the four smaller stupas on the corners, just above the animal heads supporting the main platform, make it into a cluster of stupas, creating a mandalalike space. The square base symbolizes the earth element; the rounded dome, water; the rising spire, fire; the umbrellas, wind; and the tiny spire at the top represents the space element. The whole is suffused with buddha-mind, mind being the sixth element. Small, portable stupas such as this were made for individual devotees and were intended to commemorate a loved one, a revered teacher, or a departed family member.

2

Shakyamuni Buddha with Two Stupas

✸

India, Bihar, Pala period, late 9th–
early 10th century

Schist

Height 28 ¾ inches (73 cm)

The Asia Society Galleries, 1979.37

This powerful Shakyamuni is flanked
by two bodhisattvas, identified as
Maitreya and Avalokiteshvara by the
two different lotuses that they hold.
There are two stupas above them,
and two figures (identified as the
earth goddess and the donor of the
stupa) below. These figures and the
Bodhi tree foliage above evoke the
subliminal mandalas emanating from
the Buddha's very presence. Icons of
this type are among the most common images produced in Northeast
India during the Pala period, a seminal era in the development of Tantric
Buddhism. As is often the case, the
motifs represented on these sculptures can be understood on many
levels. For example, the two stupas
above the Buddha's head, which symbolize eternity, may also signify the
locations of two of the eight miraculous events in his lifetime or serve as
reminders of the immanence of the
past buddhas and the coming presence of future buddhas.

SPACE AND SANCTITY IN BUDDHIST ART

3
Namasamgiti Manjuvajra in a Stupa Mandala

India, Bihar, Pala period,
11th–12th century

Schist

50 ¾ x 23 ¾ inches
(128.9 x 60.3 cm)

The Metropolitan Museum of Art,
Bequest of Cora Timken Burnett,
57.51.6

The central icon of this sculpture is the Bodhisattva of Wisdom, Manjushri, in his manifestation as the tantric Manjuvajra. This image is a two-dimensional representation of Manjuvajra as the central figure in the famous *Hymn of the Names of Manjushri*, although this image has six arms, as in the Guhyasamaja Manjuvajra, instead of the more usual eight. He is shown at the center of a mandala within a great stupa, clearly a reference to the great stupa of Amaravati in South India, despite the Bengali architectural form. His mandala is believed to be the primordial source of all mandalas, located at the foundation of the great stupa, in legend the site of the major tantric revelation bestowed by Shakyamuni Buddha. Manjuvajra's mandala is considered the foundational mandala universe from which arises the world of the Kalachakra Buddha, and all other archetype-deity buddha-forms. He holds a vajra scepter and bell in his two front hands, would have held a bow and arrow in his second pair, and the sword and flower with a missing text of the *Transcendent Wisdom Scripture* in the last pair. His three faces represent the three passions transmuted into the three wisdoms, the three visions of the subtle mind, or the three channels of the yogic nervous system. The five smaller Manjuvajra images in the stupas above his head (see detail) are the Manjuvajra forms of the heads

of the other buddha-clans, located in the four directions and the zenith in a three-dimensional mandala. The crisp, elegant carving of this sculpture exemplifies the art of the Pala kingdom in Northeast India from the late ninth to twelfth centuries. The buddhas, their stupas, and the floral ornamentation are precisely carved and finished. All of the buddhas have broad shoulders and chests, articulated waists, and long, powerful legs. Their faces are full and almost square, with long, thin features. This Pala-period style traveled from India to Nepal and Tibet, where it became one of the major sculptural and painting traditions.

4
Model of the Bodhgaya Temple
✤

India, Bihar, 10th–11th century

Soapstone

Height 5 ⅙ inches (13.5 cm)

Museum of Fine Arts, Boston, Gift of
Benjamin Rowland in memory of
Ananda K. Coomaraswamy, 47.1343

Models of temples, like those of stupas, functioned as reminders of the presence of the buddhas and bodhisattvas in the universe. This particular model depicts the temple built by the emperor Ashoka (reigned about 272–231 BCE) at the holy site of the Bodhi tree, where the Buddha attained supreme enlightenment. Known as Bodhgaya, this sacred site, a small village located on the bank of the Phalgu River in Bihar Province, is one of the most famous sacred sites of Buddhism. The tree under which Shakyamuni attained enlightenment and the throne upon which he sat are represented in Indian art as early as the second to first centuries BCE. There may also have been a temple at the site even at this early date. The current Bodhgaya, or Mahabodhi, temple is a modern restoration. Small-scale models such as this one, which record the Pala-period temple, show that it had an opening portal leading to a rectangular sanctuary covered by one large and four smaller towers. The surface of the temple was decorated with lively illustrations of Shakyamuni's life as well as different buddhas and bodhisattvas. This model, representing the sanctity of this famous site and the process of the Buddha's enlightenment, is typical of pilgrimage souvenirs that were carried through Asia and may have inspired the construction of similar temples in Burma, Thailand, and other lands.

5

Miniature Stupa

✻

Eastern India, Bangladesh,
or Himalayan region, about
12th century

Copper alloy with semiprecious
stones

Height 11 ½ inches (29.2 cm)

Cleveland Museum of Art,
John L. Severance Fund, 82.132

Stupas began in pre-Buddhist India as hemispherical burial mounds that marked the remains of temporal rulers. At an early stage in the development of Buddhist art, they became symbols of the Buddha's continuing immanence as well as representations of his mind. Both architectural monuments and miniature forms, such as this example, play an important role in the practices of Buddhist Asia. This exquisitely refined stupa takes a form common among small- and large-scale stupas from Pala-period India. It has a reticulated square base, bulbous dome with four shrine portals, and a tapering spire topped by a flaming jewel. The base, the area between the base and the dome, and the exteriors of the shrine portals are decorated with precisely carved floral motifs. A lion lounges at each corner of the base. Four buddhas are seated in the shrine portals: Vajrasattva, holding a vajra in his right hand and the stem of a flower in his left; Shakyamuni to his left, with his right arm in earth-witness gesture (seen in the photograph); Prajnaparamita to his right, her hands in the teaching gesture; and Maitreya on the opposite side of the stupa. The fourteen rings around the spire are all that remain of the royal umbrellas often found in stupas such as the earlier example in this exhibition. They symbolize the fourteen stages traversed in the attainment of buddhahood; the four tantric stages added to the ten bodhisattva stages make this a stupa with clear tantric references. As the crystals and gemstones decorating the surface of this miniature stupa are more in keeping with Himalayan traditions than with those of Pala-period India, it is difficult to ascertain the provenance of this lovely work.

6

Miniature Stupa (Chorten)

❈

Tibet, Kadam order, 13th century

Brass

Height 20 inches (50.8 cm)

The Zimmerman Family Collection

Chortens are the Tibetan versions of the ubiquitous Buddhist stupas. This example is wonderfully ornate, with a lotus earth base, a bell-shaped dome of water element, a tier of fire element, a turquoise-studded upper umbrella holding the wind element, surmounted by a large moon-disc of space element and a shining *bindu* (drop) of enlightened consciousness. It is an example of the Kadam style named after the order founded in 1056 by Dromton Gyalway Jungnay (1004–1064), the chief disciple of Atisha, the Indian master. Atisha (982–1054), a Bengali prince who became a great monk, scholar, and adept, visited Tibet during the last twelve years of his life. The Kadam order is noted for creating the most viable synthesis of the monastic, messianic, and apocalyptic trends which Tibetan Buddhism received from India. Its curriculum was adopted in the main by the founders of each of the other three major orders, the Nyingma, Sakya, and Kagyu, and integrated with each one's distinctive historical and con-templative traditions.

7
Model of a Pagoda
❋

Japan, late 19th century

Copper, cast iron, brass, and gold

Height 50 inches (127 cm)

The Metropolitan Museum of Art,
Gift of the estate of
Mrs. E. Harriman through
Louise Cochran, 34.45

Pagodas are the East Asian variants of the Indian stupa. Their towerlike structure, use of the post-and-lintel system, and elaborate roofs derive from early Chinese wooden architecture. Pagodas play a pivotal role in East Asian monastic complexes and are generally placed at the heart of a compound. In addition, individual examples are sometimes erected at important locations either for religious or nationalistic purposes. Like their Indian prototypes, full-size pagodas often have a sublevel at their center, used to store relics and other valuables. Similar items can also be stored inside smaller examples. This one opens on the lower level to reveal two seated buddhas and is a model of one of the pagodas built at Todai-ji in Nara, established in the late eighth century.

PURE LANDS AND OTHER PERFECTED WORLDS

Buddhist thought accepts the existence of multiple buddhas (and other deities) in our world and others. Each of these divinities has the ability to disseminate his or her understanding and compassion throughout these multiple worlds. Each can use his or her abilities to create a paradiselike perfected or pure land, similar to that generated by the central deity of a mandala. Pure lands, however, are not intended to represent the immediate attainment of enlightenment, unlike mandalas, which simulate the exalting experience of enlightenment, allowing an individual practitioner to identify with the buddha-deity at their core. Pure lands provide an environment in which conditions are conducive to a spiritual quest. They are way stations on the path, desirable locations in which to be reborn, but not the ultimate goal of Buddhist practice.

All buddhas generate their own pure lands. However, certain of these paradises became the focus of specific practices and were therefore more commonly depicted in the visual arts. One example is the pure land of the Buddha Amitabha, known as Sukhavati or the Land of Bliss. Also called the Western Paradise because of

Amitabha's position in that quadrant of the universe, this pure land was universally important in Mahayana Buddhist countries, and remains widespread in the art and religious practices of Tibet, China, Korea, and Japan. The Japanese painting in this section of the exhibition defines Amitabha's pure land as an elegant multi-tiered, many-chambered golden palace set in a jeweled, gardenlike world. In the Tibetan work, on the other hand, the Buddha and his attendant bodhisattvas dominate the composition, with the many inhabitants of Sukhavati involved in solitary or group practices arrayed along the four borders.

The painting of the Tibetan monk Tsong Khapa, descending from the Tushita Heaven, illustrates the mutual interpenetrability of a Buddhist pure land and our phenomenal world. The Tushita (or Joyful) Heaven contains the pure land of Maitreya, who will be the teaching buddha of the future after the world we currently inhabit is destroyed and recreated. Maitreya and others—shown living and practicing in an idyllic landscape—await the coming of this new age when his descent will herald a paradise on earth. Tsong Khapa, like others who are spiritually evolved, is believed to dwell in the Tushita Heaven, waiting to bring needed teachings to those living in the current imperfect and difficult world.

opposite: detail of catalogue no. 10

8

Pure Land of Amitabha Buddha (Taima Mandara)

❀

Japan, Kamakura period, 13th century

Color and gold on silk

36 ⅛ x 28 ⅝ inches (91.8 x 72.7 cm)

The Metropolitan Museum of Art, Rogers Fund, 57.156.6

Desire for rebirth in Amitabha's pure land (Sukhavati) was an important component of Buddhism in East Asia, and the focus of certain orders. Paintings such as this one, which combines images of Sukhavati with narrative scenes in the borders, are known as Taima Mandaras (mandalas) because the first icon of this type (which was made in China) is preserved in the Taima-dera temple in Japan. The painting depicts Amitabha (see detail) and his attendant bodhisattvas seated on elaborate thrones on a platform in the center of a golden lotus pond. Other buddhas and their retinues grace platforms to the right and left of musicians in the foreground. Faithful souls, reborn in Sukhavati, sit or kneel on the calyxes of lotus flowers, float in boats, or reside in the background houses. The figures, architecture, and other elements in this painting are elegantly drawn with black ink outlines filled with colors and covered in gold (see detail). The hint of roundness in the figures distinguishes this thirteenth-century painting from those of the fourteenth, when forms became broader and flatter. The narrative scenes in the side borders illustrate a series of sixteen meditations that can lead to rebirth in this paradise (see detail), while those at the bottom show the nine degrees of rebirth possible in the pure land.

detail of no. 8

PURE LANDS AND OTHER PERFECTED WORLDS

detail of no. 8

9

Pure Land of Buddha Amitayus

Tibet, 15th century

Ink, opaque watercolors, and gold
on cloth

26 x 22 inches (66 x 55.8 cm)

Michael J. and Beata McCormick
Collection

The belief in multiple buddhas includes an acceptance of the fact that each buddha dwells in a pure land or paradise which he creates through his enlightened compassion. This idea plays an important role in the development of mandala imagery because mandalas are also pure lands, although they presume a more active role and presence on the part of the practitioner. This painting depicts the pure land or buddha-universe of Amitayus, who sits flanked by the powerful bodhisattvas Avalokiteshvara and Mahasthama-prapta. Amitayus (Measureless Life) Buddha is an alternative form of Amitabha (Measureless Light) Buddha, who presides over the pure land called Sukhavati, the blissful. Amitayus holds the vase of the nectar of immortality (one of his more consistent symbols) surmounted by a small blazing sun of life-energy.

Buddhists believe that all souls who have faith in the Buddha Amitayus/Amitabha are reborn in the pure land of Sukhavati, where they are installed in lotuses and absorb pure energy from the environment while receiving all the teachings they need until they attain their own enlightenment. The composition of this painting, with a large central triad surrounded by several loosely placed smaller scenes, reflects traditions commonly associated with western Tibet, as are the full lower face and pronounced ushnisha of the buddha. The small palaces in the four corners probably represent the heavenly abodes of the Dharma kings of Tibet and suggest the physical presence of Sukhavati within Tibet.

10

Green Tara

❀

Tibet, 17th century

Ink and opaque watercolors on cloth

$60\frac{1}{2}$ x $38\frac{1}{2}$ inches (153.7 x 97.8 cm)

Shelley Rubin and Donald Rubin
Collection

The Bodhisattva Tara appears in her dynamic emerald form surrounded by 1,024 little Green Taras, with a small Shakyamuni above her halo and a small fierce red Kurukulla guarding her throne. Her emerald color represents the wonder-working wisdom powered by the wisdom-transmuted energy of jealousy. This is a painting that reaches out and surrounds the beholder, as atomic Taras engulf one within her field of lifesaving goodness. The combination of Tara's long, elegant proportions and the sense of volume in this painting help date it to the seventeenth century. Tara wears a green skirt and gold and red scarves, is firmly seated on her throne, and is surrounded by a jeweled mandorla that matches her crown. The flowers encircling her halo and the lotus petals supporting her throne are depicted as full, lush blooms bursting with vitality. Great care has been taken to distinguish each flower and petal and they are skillfully modeled to suggest variety and growth.

11

Tsong Khapa Emerging from the Tushita Heaven

Tibet, 18th century

Ink and opaque watercolors on cloth

18 x 13 inches (45.7 x 33 cm)

Shelley Rubin and Donald Rubin Collection

Tsong Khapa (1357–1419), master scholar, saint, and adept, sits with his two main disciples, Gyalsabjey and Kedrupjey, in a visionary tableau on a cloud emanating from the heart of the future Buddha Maitreya, shown seated on his throne in the Tushita Heaven, depicted in this painting as an elegant tree-filled arcadia housing monks and students all committed to the teaching and practice of Buddhism (see details). Beneath him stand three fierce protector deities (left to right): Yama Dharmaraja, Mahakala, and Shri Devi. The vision illustrated in this painting is central to the faith of adherents of the Geluk order, who see Tsong Khapa's ministry as coming from the mercy of Maitreya, providing access to the future Buddha's liberative teaching millennia ahead of his own descent to earth. In the meanwhile, the devotee can aspire at death to leave this planet in its difficult age and gain rebirth at the feet of Maitreya in his pure land.

detail of no. 11

detail of no. 11

PURE LANDS AND OTHER PERFECTED WORLDS

12

Portable Mani Shrine

❊

Bhutan, 18th–19th century

Painted and gilded wood with
terra-cotta figures

Height 29½ inches (74.9 cm)

Private Collection

This kind of portable stupa or shrine
is used by wandering lamas or adepts
to teach Buddhism to the common
folk. It is popularly called a Mani
shrine, as the mantra of great compassion, OM MANI PADME HUM, is the
one most often taught to villagers.
Atop the stupalike dome is a figure of
Padmasambhava, a noted Indian
master who was invited to Tibet in
the eighth century to help tame the
demons that plagued it. His mission
to Tibet has been compared to that
of St. Patrick to Ireland. He is worshiped now as a buddha and an emanation of Hayagriva, the fierce counterpart of Avalokiteshvara. Other
practitioners may be taught the
mantra OM AH HUM VAJRA GURU
PADMA SIDDHI HUM and might, therefore, identify the shrine as representing his Copper Mountain mandala
paradise.

DIVERSITY IN MANDALAS FROM NEPAL AND TIBET

The brilliantly colored, intricate paintings of Tibet (and to a lesser extent Nepal) are the best preserved and most widely known examples of mandalas today. A majority of these paintings are structured in the "palace-architecture" composition. A central deity is housed in a circle or flower-shaped center placed within a square, multiwalled palace with elaborate gateways to the four cardinal directions. This building is surrounded by a large, multi-tiered circle. Additional deities are sometimes presented outside of this circle, along with famous practitioners and monks.

Mandalas of this type became prominent in Tibet during the twelfth and thirteenth centuries, paralleling the development of Unexcelled Yoga tantra, a form of Esoteric Buddhism. Erotic figures in the "father-mother" (sexual union) pose, and terrifying deities such as Hevajra and Chakrashamvara, are also prominent in the art associated with Unexcelled Yoga tantra, which is noted for its evolved pantheon and elaborate practices which aim at direct encounter with the practitioner's deepest energies.

The dating of Tibetan mandalas (or any other aspect of Tibetan art) is controversial. The ornamentation of the architectural structure is generally less complicated in paintings produced during the twelfth through early fourteenth centuries, with fewer figures in the sides and borders. Mandalas dating to the fourteenth and fifteenth centuries are characterized by more complex architectural configurations, as well as more figures enlivening them. In addition, during this period mandalas were sometimes produced in sets or series. Some examples—such as the two *Vajravali* series in this exhibition—feature multiple mandalas grouped into one painting. This greater complexity is often attributed to the growth of monasticism in Tibet, which led to the development of new texts and practices and the need for more elaborate visual images.

Sixteenth-century mandalas can often be distinguished from earlier works by the inclusion of landscape backgrounds and a greater variety of iconographic types and compositions. Examples in this exhibition include both mandalas composed of symbols rather than (or in addition to) figures of deities, and those which are designed as symbolic maps of the cosmos.

Differences in style, composition, and iconography also reflect the traditions of the four main orders of Tibetan Buddhism, each of which has its own practices and favored deities. Generally, however, mandalas dedicated to quintessentially fierce buddha-deities such as Hevajra or Paramasukha-Chakrashamvara are more common than those featuring other buddhas and bodhisattvas, which reflects their importance in Unexcelled Yoga tantra. Because these fierce guardians are the first to be introduced to a practitioner, they are frequently the central images in mandalas and paintings.

opposite: detail of catalogue no. 13

13

Paramasukha Chakrasamvara Mandala

✻

Nepal, about 1100

Ink and opaque watercolors on cloth

26 ⅞ x 19 ⅞ inches (68.2 x 50.5 cm)

The Metropolitan Museum of Art,
Rogers Fund, 1995.233

This is a superb and rare example of a relatively early Nepalese Chakrasamvara (Supreme Bliss Wheel) mandala. The rich palette of this painting, dominated by red and yellow, and the elongated proportions and animation of the figures are characteristic of contemporaneous illustrated manuscripts. Their rounded faces are typical of early Nepali works. The placement of the eight graveyards (standard in the iconography of the Chakrasamvara mandala) in the outer edges of the painting as well as the attention to detail and humor in these scenes are also characteristic of earlier paintings. The careful treatment of details throughout the painting—the jewelry worn by Vajravarahi and Chakrasamvara, the delicate crossed vajras that fill the outer edges of the central circle, the many jewels and other elements that decorate the mandala palace—exemplify the best of Nepali painting and foreshadow the influence of this artistic tradition in Tibet during the fourteenth through sixteenth centuries. The central couple is surrounded by six deities, rather than the usual four or eight. There are hundreds of forms of the Chakrasamvara mandala because it is considered the chief of all Mother tantras of the Unexcelled Yoga tantra class. This one is remarkable for the medley of varied figures in the charnel grounds just outside the circle (see detail) and for the variety of their movements and actions. These death areas represent the Supreme Bliss Wheel vision of the ordinary life cycle, where pleasures are ephemeral and constant dying is the rule. In stark contrast stands the pure land or buddha-world of the mandala, where an inconceivably supreme, transorgasmic bliss is reliable, even foundational for everything else.

14
Mandala of Surya, the Sun God
❀

Nepal, by Kitaharasa, dated
about 1379

Ink and opaque watercolors on cloth

36 ¼ x 21 inches (92.1 x 53.3 cm)

The Zimmerman Family Collection

Worship of planetary deities was
important in Nepali Buddhism in the
fourteenth through sixteen centuries and appears to have declined
thereafter. The central figure in this
mandala is the sun god, Surya, who
holds two lotuses and rides a chariot
pulled by seven horses, accompanied
by four consorts. The eight planetary
deities surround the chariot in a
circle, again surrounded by a larger
circle containing twenty-eight figures—representing the main constellations and astral mansions—around
the ecliptic. The twelve signs of the
zodiac are represented in the four
corners. Beneath sit a yogin donor on
the left (see detail), the five
Pancharaksha goddesses, and two
women donors on the right. The
absence of a group of five buddhas at
the top of the painting suggests that
this particular work may have been
intended for use in a Hindu, rather
than Buddhist, context. Little is
known about Kitaharasa, one of the
few Nepali artists whose name is preserved. His careful draftsmanship is
evident in the outlines of all the figures and in the exquisite detail. These
characteristics epitomize Nepali
painting and persist in works created
by Nepali artists at Tibetan monasteries or by their Tibetan students.

15

Hevajra Mandala

Tibet, Sakya order, early 13th century

Ink and opaque watercolors on cloth

14 x 13 inches (35.6 x 33 cm)

Michael J. and Beata McCormick Collection

This exquisite mandala of Hevajra (Laughing Diamond-Thunderbolt) Buddha presents in delicate clarity the dynamic realm of this archetype-deity form. The volume and power in the main icon and other figures, and the simplicity of the composition date this painting to the early thirteenth century, as does the abbreviated lineage at the top of the painting. The careful detailing of the gateways and the small starlike dots found between the inner circle and the mandala palace indicate ties to Nepali painting. This Hevajra is based on the eighth mandala listed in Abhayakara's *Garland of Perfection Yogas (Nispannayogavali)* and is known as the skull bowl–bearing Hevajra (Raghu Vira and Lokesh Chandra 1995, pp. 40–41). The central Hevajra has a light blue body (dark blue under a layer of crematorium ash), and embraces his consort Vajranairatmya (Diamond Selflessness). The couple is surrounded by eight female dakini attendants. The skull bowls in his right hands contain animals, symbolizing his various powers, and those in his left hands hold deities symbolic of elements and forces such as death and wealth. Directional forms of Hevajra occupy the corners of the central section of the painting, dividing the scenes from the eight death-grounds depicted outside the ring of diamond flames. The upper border has eight niches, containing representations, left to right, of Guhyasamaja Buddha father-mother, Vajradhara, Tilopa, Naropa, three lay lamas (probably the Nepali Pamting brothers and the translator Drogmi), and Paramasukha Chakrasamvara father-mother. The lower border has seven niches, containing the Lone Hero Yamantaka, five lamas, two laymen and three monks, and a four-armed Mahamaya Buddha father-mother. The *Hevajra Tantra* is an important Mother tantra of the Unexcelled Yoga class, considered foundational in the central tantric yoga of burning the inner fury-fire *(gtum mo)* from the navel center of the yogin, to melt the innermost subtle drops of awareness which then flow down to suffuse the throat and heart with bliss.

16

Mahashri Heruka Mandala

Central Tibet, Nyingma order,*
late 12th–early 13th century

Opaque watercolors on cloth

38 x 32 inches (96.5 x 81.3 cm)

Michael J. and Beata McCormick
Collection

This striking painting is perhaps the earliest known Nyingma order mandala, depicting the central deity Mahashri Heruka father-mother (see detail). He has three faces and six arms, while she is one-faced and two-armed, embracing him from the side instead of frontally in full sexual union as is more common in later Tibetan representations of father-mother archetype-deities. On the eight outer petals of his inner circle stand the fierce deities of his realm, four fierce directional father-mother deities like himself, and four guardianesses with animal heads in the four quarters. His central lotus is surrounded by eight smaller lotuses occupied by the eight main archetype-deities of the Mahayoga category of Unexcelled Yoga tantra. Additional mother-father deities, buddhas, lamas, and other deities and protectors fill the upper part and sides of the painting. The Crow-faced

Mahakala in the center of the bottom row, combined with the three other forms of Mahakala, yellow Jambhala, and two forms of Shri Devi, suggests that this Nyingma order work was affiliated with the Kagyu order, possibly the Drigung or Taglung branches, in some fashion in its practice lineage. The style of the painting also relates to works associated with the Kagyu order and, in particular, with art from the monastery at Taglung. The power and volume of the figures, the use of large areas of bold colors, the clear composition, and details such as the use of variously colored lotus petals to frame the mandala parallel features found in paintings associated with this monastery.

* Identification of the iconography of this painting has benefitted from discussions between Bob Thurman and Nyingma Ganteng Kensur Gyurme Dorje.

DIVERSITY IN MANDALAS FROM NEPAL AND TIBET

17
Vajravarahi

Tibet, 13th century

Gilt bronze with inlay

Height 11 inches (27.9 cm)

Michael J. and Beata McCormick
Collection

This exquisite dancing sculpture of Vajravarahi (Diamond Sow) Buddha, identified by the small sow's head emerging from her coif, has a monumentality that belies its size. Her elegant, slightly elongated proportions and well-articulated waist reflect Pala-period influence on early Tibetan sculpture, while the turquoise inlays are typically Tibetan. Vajravarahi is a form of the buddha as Supreme Mother, equivalent to Paramasukha Chakrasamvara in the male or Heruka form, as archetype-deity of the Mother tantras of Unexcelled Yoga. She stands with one foot atop the demon of ignorance, who lies in the center of her distinctive mandala, two interlocking triangles that form a Seal of Solomon (see detail). She brandishes her diamond chopper, a flaying knife symbolizing critical wisdom that dissects the world of falsely appearing substantial selves and things. In her left hand she holds the skull bowl of the blood and guts of ordinary life transmuted by her wisdom into the elixir of enlightenment. She wears a garland of shrunken heads that symbolize her conquest of all negative emotional states. In the crook of her left arm should stand the missing staff *(khatvanga)* that represents her mastery of the Three Bodies of Buddhahood, as well as the three nerve-channels of the central yogic life-energy system. She is the three-dimensional representation of the central deity of mandala no. 33 in this exhibition.

18

Dharmadhatu Vagishvara Manjuvajra Mandala

❁

Tibet, Sakya order, 14th century

Ink and opaque watercolors on cloth

28 x 26 ½ inches (71.1 x 67.3 cm)

Shelley and Donald Rubin
Foundation

This mandala closely follows the pattern of the twenty-first mandala described in Abhayakara's *Diamond Garland* (Raghu Vira and Lokesh Chandra 1995, pp. 68–72), the main difference being the roundness of the outermost of the four mansions. At the heart of the mandala is a golden Manjushri with four faces and eight arms, here identified with the Buddha Vairochana in the Sarvavid form. In this cosmic mandala, Manjushri is identified as the Ultimate Realm Lord of the Word, a divine being who rests in the absolute, yet inexhaustibly articulates the structure of the relative world for the sake of beings who need to evolve to their own ultimately fulfilled condition. Around him in the four man-

sions are 219 deities, listed by name in the sources. There is a top register with fifteen different forms of Manjushri, and the deities in the little medallions around the sides and bottom also seem to be different forms of Manjushri, except for the six deities at the very bottom. Inscriptions on the back are for consecratory purposes and give little information (see detail). A cursive inscription on the bottom edge is too effaced to decipher. The boldness of the drawing and colors in this mandala connect it to murals and other works at the great stupa at Gyantse, which also include floral backgrounds and other details characteristic of central Tibetan painting. Their directness and immediacy in this work, however, are unusual.

19

Mandala of Amitabha and the Eight Bodhisattvas

Tibet, 13th–14th century

Bronze

Height 9 ⅞ inches (25.1 cm)

Dr. Wesley Halpert and Carolyn M. Halpert Collection

The earliest mandalas for which both texts and visual examples are available are known as mandalas of the eight bodhisattvas and consist, as does this example, of a buddha surrounded by other divinities. This structure often forms the inner circle of the more complicated painted mandalas seen in this exhibition. The central buddha in this example can be identified as Amitayus because he holds a vase containing the elixir of immortality. Groupings such as this one are invoked in rituals and contemplations intended to remove obstacles to one's lifespan, to assure a full life for the practice of the dharma. The powerful yet somewhat elongated physique of Amitabha and his attendants reflect artistic influences from the Pala kingdom in India. Their slightly stiff postures and the style of their jewelry, particularly the crowns and long necklaces, however, are typical of early Tibetan art.

20
Paramasukha Chakrasamvara Mandala

Tibet, 14th century

Ink and opaque watercolors on cloth

21 ¾ x 22 ¼ inches (55.2 x 56.5 cm)

Collection of Mr. and Mrs. John Gilmore Ford

This elegant mandala is the five-deity Gandhapa arrangement of the Supreme Bliss father-mother buddha. The main archetype-buddha stands in the center in sexual union, surrounded by Dakini in the east (below), Lama in the north (to the right), Khandaroha in the west (above), and Rupini in the south (to the left). The four vases of elixir in the four quarter directions are unusually large. The eight charnel grounds are done in fine detail within a ring outside the ring of vajra flames, the style indicating strong Nepali influence. The lack of additional deities or lineage lamas around the painting indicates that it was made for initiations, to be laid flat in a small mansionlike altar as the center of a ceremony.

21

Four Chakrasamvara Mandalas from a Vajravali Set

✳

Tibet, Sakya order, Ngor monastery, early to mid-15th century

Ink and opaque watercolors on cloth

32 ½ x 29 inches (82.6 x 73.7 cm)

Philadelphia Museum of Art: Stella Kramrisch Collection, 1994-148-636

This is a similar arrangement of four mandalas in a single thang ka, presumably from the Ngor tradition of the Sakya order. Both paintings are characterized by strong, flat, carefully applied but dramatic colors in bold shades. Fastidious attention has been paid to the modeling of figures and the treatment of details, notably in the backgrounds of the central sections, which each have dense floral scrolls curving in endless patterns. These intricate patterns, together with the delicate rendering of gateways, their ornaments, and other details, produce a distinctive jewel-like quality that belies the lack of movement in the paintings. The scrolling background and elegant details were introduced to Tibet by Nepali artists, but Tibetan works are noted for their intensive use of these elements. Judging from the way in which the charnel grounds are represented in the spaces between the mandalas, outside the fire rings, this work may be a little earlier than no. 22 in this exhibition, perhaps from a different set. Or it could be from the same set, but by a different Nepali artist working on the Unexcelled Yoga tantras, which have the charnel ground setting. No inscriptions remain on the borders. The upper left of the four mandalas is the Sixty-two-Deity Luyipa-system Chakrasamvara, *Diamond Garland* no. 12 (bSodnams rGyamtsho 1991, no. 62), with a cen-

tral father-mother buddha-archetype, he dark blue, with four faces and twelve arms; she bright red, with one face and two arms. They are surrounded by four circles: an inner bliss circle with four dakini goddesses and four skull cauldrons; a second circle with the eight blue mind-hero/heroine couples; a third with the eight red speech-hero couples; and a fourth with the eight white body-hero couples. The eight fierce female protectors guard the doors and corners. The other three mandalas also follow the basic Chakrasamvara pattern, varying

the central buddha-couple (variations mentioned in the *Diamond Garland*). The one in the lower left has a golden central couple, each partner with one face and two arms. The one in the upper right has a dark blue (he) and red (she) couple, fierce in aspect, each with one face and two arms. The lower right mandala centers on perhaps a Buddhakapala couple, he white and she golden, he with three faces and six arms and she with two faces and four arms. A pair of lamas occupies the central circle between the mandalas, the one on the left an

Indian pandit, perhaps Buddhashri (1339–1419), the one on the right a Tibetan monk, perhaps Ngorchen Kunga Zangpo (1382–1456), who commissioned such sets of thang kas containing four mandalas each. Smaller medallions between the mandalas, in directions and corners, contain the world-gods on their characteristic mounts. Clockwise from the bottom, they are Indra, Agni, Yama, Nairrtya, Varuna, Vayu, Kuvera, and Shiva (in the lower right-hand corner). There are sixteen deities in each of the top and bottom registers.

22
Four Mandalas from a Vajravali Series
❀

Tibet, Sakya order, 1430s–1440s

Ink and opaque watercolors on cloth

32 ½ x 29 inches (82.6 x 73.7 cm)

Private Collection

This is one of a set of fairly well-known mandalas in which four smaller compositions have been combined into one painting. An inscription at the top of the painting reads "Thirteenth of the Vajravali Paintings," while that at the bottom is translated "May the heart's intent of the glorious Lama Sazang Pakpa be completely fulfilled!" New research (Jackson 1996, p. 82, n. 182) shows that this set was commissioned by Ngorchen Kunga Sangpo (1382–1456) in honor of his late teacher Sazang Pakpa. It seems that each of the works in this set contains one or two mandalas from Abhayakara's *Diamond Garland* and other associated mandalas from the *Collection of Rites* (*Kriyasamuccaya*) by Darpanacharya. A red Amitayus occupies the central circle between the four main mandalas. He is attended by four smaller deities in little circles, with twenty-eight related deities in the other spaces outside the four main mandalas. There is a row of sixteen seated deities above, four each of white, yellow, red, and green; and a row of sixteen standing Vajrapani-type deities of five colors below. At the lower right, there is a Marichi mandala, conforming closely to the description found in the *Collection of Rites* (P, hu, 241a ff.), with twenty-four deities in her retinue. At the lower left is a mandala of a black standing Bhutadamara Vajrapani (similar to *Diamond Garland* no. 23), with a retinue of thirty-three deities; at the upper left, a mandala of a white, seated, eight-armed Vajradhatu (Vairochana) Buddha, with a retinue of forty-eight deities (similar to *Diamond Garland* no. 19); and at the upper right, a mandala of Shakyamuni in teaching gesture, with a retinue of thirty-six deities.

23
Chakrasamvara Mandala

❇

Tibet, 17th–18th century

Gilt bronze

Diameter 16 inches (40.6 cm)

The Virginia Museum of Fine Arts,
Richmond, Virginia
Gift of the E. Rhodes and Leona B.
Carpenter Foundation, from the
Zimmerman Family Collection,
91.478

This hammered metal Chakrasamvara mandala has an unusual
ring of thirty-two lama figures seated
within the lotus petals and ring of
flames, outside an inner mansion
with the Chakrasamvara archetype-
buddha (without consort) in the center surrounded by eight dakinis. This
unusual iconography, combining
exoteric and esoteric imagery within
one mandala realm, indicates it is a
regional variant, perhaps made for
ease of portability by an itinerant
yogi. The less-than-elegant casting
of this metal mandala and the somewhat sketchy treatment of the figures
indicate it was not made at any of the
major monastic centers, whose artists
had the resources—material, training, and time—to create more
polished works.

24

Mandala of Six Chakravartins

✳

Tibet, Sakya order, Ngor monastery,
15th century

Ink and opaque watercolors on cloth

42 x 31 inches (106.7 x 78.7 cm)

Philadelphia Museum of Art,
Purchased: The John T. Morris Fund,
1963-154-1

This mandala closely resembles the Six Chakravartin mandala listed by Abhayakara as no. 25 in his *Diamond Garland*, corresponding also with no. 76 in the Ngor monastery collection (Raghu Vira and Lokesh Chandra 1995, pp. 80, 214). The deity in the central inner mansion is Jnanadaka father-mother, with Buddhadaka, Ratnadaka, Padmadaka, Vajradaka, and Vishvadaka father-mothers occupying clockwise from the east (below) the five surrounding mansions. Each mansion has its complement of attending hero-heroine couples. In the doors and corners of the larger mansion that contains the six little ones stand the well-known eight Chakrasamvara fierce female protectors, Kakasya through Yamamathani. These deities are depicted again in the rows of sixteen deities at the top and bottom of the painting. There are twenty deities in medallions in the corners below and above the registers. The main ones, clockwise from the upper left, are the Naropa Vajrayogini, the Maitripa Vajrayogini, a white Vajranairatmya, and a red Chinnamasta. Each upper corner deity is attended by four guardian-couples, and each lower corner deity

by four single guardian deities. The concept of chakravartin (world-king or ruler), found in some of India's earliest traditions, is also important in Buddhism and refers both to the spiritual power of the buddhas and to the potential ability of a ruler to create a buddha-land in a temporal sphere. The precise composition and refined, painstaking detail exemplify fifteenth-century Tibetan painting. The central mandala palace is divided into four zones, symbolizing the four quadrants of the universe, and painted white, gold, red, and green. They are filled with lush flowering acanthus leaf arabesques arranged in horizontal and vertical grids, each with a slightly different pattern. The six smaller mandala palaces share this composition and color scheme. Their walls are identical to those of the larger palace and are also defined by patterns and colors. The multicolored circle surrounding the mandala palace is divided into three rings containing arabesques, vajras, and lotus leaves. The smaller circles in the four outer corners are equally detailed and are set against a background of swirling arabesques that echoes the designs in the mandala palace.

25

Paramasukha Chakrasamvara Mandala

Tibet, Sakya order, about 1500

Ink and opaque watercolors on cotton

20 ½ x 17 ¼ inches (52.1 x 43.8 cm)

Michael J. and Beata McCormick Collection

This brilliant Sakya order mandala, probably from Ngor monastery, depicts the three-faced, six-armed Chakrasamvara/Vajrayogini father-mother buddha, in a mandala surrounded by the four inner dakinis and the eight fierce female guardians, all the female deities having only two arms. There is an inscription below: "In order to secure the long life of the Holy Venerable Lama Konchokpel [*dkon mchog 'phel*], the Science Holder Hlachok Sengey [*lha mchog sen ge*] commissioned [this painting]." Hlachok Sengey (1468–1535) was a Sakya lama who studied at Ngor, obviously with the Venerable Abbot Konchokpel (1445–1514). As

he commissioned this mandala to ensure his teacher's long life, it is reasonable to assume the teacher was in the last decade or two of his life. The ring of charnel grounds is rendered exquisitely in Nepali-influenced style. There are top and bottom rows of eleven figures in niches: top, from left to right, blue Vajrasattva, flowery Mahasiddha, Mahasiddha Gandhapa, Mahasiddha Luyipa, dark-skinned Mahasiddha Kanhapa (see detail), dancing Mahasiddha in the middle, then five red-hatted monastic lamas. In the bottom row, left to right, are Amitayus; Amitabha; a standing red buddha holding a bowl; Vajradhara; six-armed

Prajnaparamita; two-armed Achala with sword; a six-armed, three-faced brown deity, hook in upper right; two-armed black Simhavaktra dakini; two-armed red Hayagriva; two-armed blue Hayagriva; and Vajrapani. All the figures are done in very animated, lifelike, individualized detail, especially the mahasiddhas. There are four sets of three lamas in medallions, all monks, in the corners between the mandala circle and the top and bottom rows; and a larger one in the central orb, flanked by two smaller ones. The typical Ngor-style acanthus leaf background is present everywhere.

26

Mandala of Jnanadakini

❈

Tibet, Sakya order, late 14th–early
15th century

Ink and opaque watercolors on cloth

33 ¼ x 28 ⅞ inches (84.5 x 73.3 cm)

The Metropolitan Museum of Art,
Purchase, Lita Annenberg Hazen
Charitable Trust Gift, 1987.16

Jnanadakini (Intuitive Wisdom
Angel) sits in the center on her two-
lion throne surrounded by the eight
goddesses of her inner circle, with
four female guardians seated in the
doorways. This painting corresponds
closely to the *Diamond Garland* no. 4
(Raghu Vira and Lokesh Chandra
1995, p. 28), as well as to no. 88 in
the Ngor monastery collection,
which attributes the origin of the
mandala to the *Diamond Four
Sacred Seat Tantra*. The eight death-
grounds are depicted in Nepali style
in great detail in a circle outside the
ring of flames. There are thirteen
lamas in a row above, with Sakya
Pandita in the center, the Kagyu lineage from Vajradhara through
Gampopa on the left, and a Kadam
lineage from the translator Ngog on
the right. On the bottom register, two
niches on the left have a donor—
with a Nepali-style red hat but a
Tibetan-style robe—making offerings. Then there are five niches
with wealth deities and protectors,
and six niches with fierce guardian
dakinis. Four large circles in the
corners contain four dakinis, each
with two attendants; each circle has
four smaller circles, with lamas
in the upper corners and dakinis in
the lower corners. The flat colors,
elegant figures, and beautifully
drawn details are characteristic
of most Sakya works from central

Tibet. The fluidity of details, for
example, and the relaxed poses of
the figures in the top and bottom
borders suggest a date in the late
fourteenth or early fifteenth century
for this painting.

27

Kalachakra Mind Mandala

❋

Tibet, Jonang or Zhalu order,
14th century

Ink and opaque watercolors on cloth

13 x 12 ½ inches (33 x 31.8 cm)

Dr. Wesley Halpert and Carolyn M.
Halpert Collection

This early painting of the Kalachakra
Mind-Palace mandala, that is, a mandala that depicts only the innermost
of the usual three palaces of the
Kalachakra, has some unusual features
indicating a southwestern Tibetan origin. Within the mandala, the crowns
of the main deity figures are unusually
wide, making them look almost like
brimmed hats, part of the naive
charm of the painting. Three of the
figures outside the mandala wear royal
robes and Central Asian turban-style
headdresses; they are apparently kings
of Shambhala, perhaps Suchandra in
the upper left with a blue complexion
as an emanation of Vajrapani (see
detail, left); Yashas in the upper right,
the emanation of Manjushri (see
detail, right); and Pundarika in the
lower left, the emanation of Lokesha.
The yellow-hatted lama figure in the
lower right may be Dolbupa
(1291–1361) or Buton (1300–1364),
depending on which order produced
the painting. A small blue Vajradhara
sits above. Around the central buddha-couple, Kalachakra (Time-
Wheel) and Vishvamata (All-Mother),
stand the eight shakti goddesses;
around them, the eight male and
female buddhas, each duplicated in
different unions; around them, the
twelve male and female bodhisattvas,
each also duplicated; and finally, stationed in the gateways, the four fierce
door-guarding couples (extra vases in
front of the east and west doors
apparently standing for zenith and
nadir guardians).

28
Kalachakra Mandala

❀

Tibet, 17th century

Ink and opaque watercolors on cloth

47 ⅜ x 30 ⅞ inches (120.4 x 78.4 cm)

Museum of Fine Arts, Boston,
Frederick L. Jack Fund 58.691

This masterpiece, from the time of the Great Fifth Dalai Lama, depicts the complete body, speech, and mind mandala palaces (one within the other) of the Kalachakra, with tiny representations of the 722 deities who reside within them. The Dalai Lama himself may appear in a blue robe with a bone apron, resembling a king of Shambhala, flanked by his regent, Desi Sangyey Gyatso, in a little scene opposite a Mongolian donor, probably Gushri Khan and his family. Surrounded by images of protectors, deities, and great adepts, Tsong Khapa sits above the mandala in the center, with a small one-faced, two-armed Kalachakra couple above his head, surrounded by the twenty-five kings of Shambhala and the lineage of gurus and lamas from the Kalachakra

beginning in the eleventh century and descending through Tsong Khapa to the Great Fifth Dalai Lama in the seventeenth. In the center below stands the Lone Hero form of Kalachakra, Vajravega (Diamond Force), surrounded by numerous deities. There are four mandalas in the corners around the main one: Manjuvajra Guhyasamaja in the upper left, thirteen-deity Yamantaka in the upper right, red Raktayamari in the lower left, and Vajrapani in the lower right, each with consort and eight attendants. This mandala seems to date from the period when the Kalachakra cult was being established as one of the central ritual activities of the Namgyal monastery, which moved into the new Potala Palace as the personal monastery of the Dalai Lama.

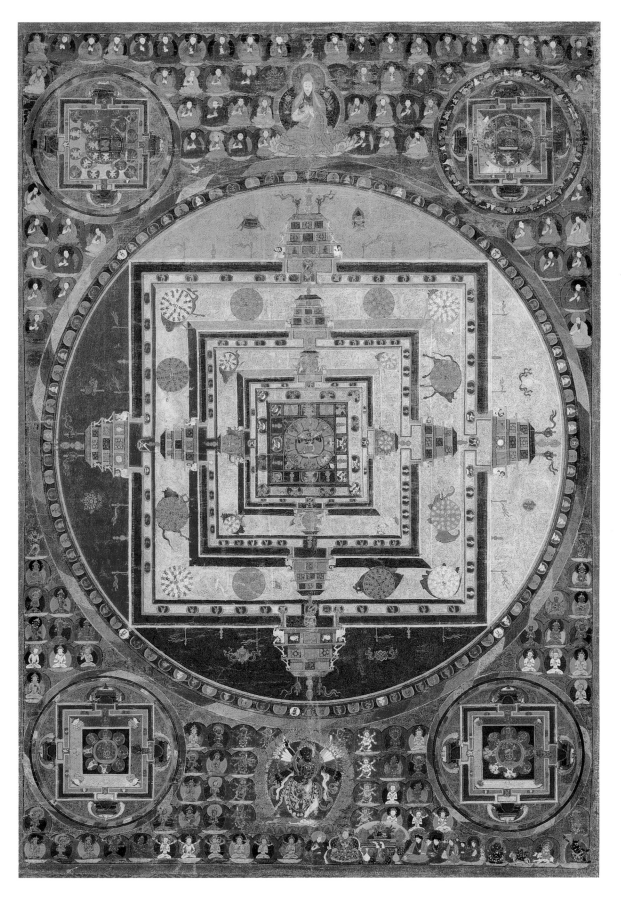

29

Kalachakra Father-Mother

Tibet, Sakya or Zhalu order,
15th century

Ink and opaque watercolors on cloth

21 x 20 ¼ inches (53.3 x 51.4 cm)

Museum of Fine Arts, Boston,
Gift of John Goelet, 67.821

In this delightful painting, the Buddha Kalachakra (Time-Wheel) stands in union with his consort Vishvamata (Universal Mother) upon divine personifications of lust and hate. Each buddha has four faces, he with twenty-four arms, she with eight. His torso is dark blue, right leg red, left leg white. Her whole body is golden. There is a hearty Yamantaka in the upper left corner of the central register, and a Hevajra father-mother in the upper right, with a Raktayamari father-mother standing near Kalachakra's right leg, and a Mahachakra Vajrapani father-mother near his left. Vajradhara and Jnanadakini begin the upper row from the left, which continues with eight pandits and lamas. Two more lamas are found beneath Vajradhara, and a donor lama sits in the left corner. The thirty-five registers down the sides and along the second from bottom row contain the whole panoply of Unexcelled Yoga tantra deities, with seven protectors and bodhisattvas, and a monk with offerings also on the bottom row.

30
Kalachakra Father-Mother

⊛

Tibet, 16th–17th century

Gilt bronze

15 ¾ x 11 ¼ inches (40 x 28.6 cm)

Collection of Mr. and Mrs. John Gilmore Ford

This breathtaking early sculpture allows a three-dimensional sense of the volume of the expansive male-female-union archetype-buddha. The figures have slender forms with full, square faces and powerful features. Their fanlike arms are filled with energy, while the weight and power of their bodies crush the demons beneath their feet. Every element of their intertwined bodies symbolizes an aspect of the cycle of time, the eternal omnipresence of the compassionate buddha-mind throughout the past, present, and future. Most of the hand implements are missing. He holds a flayed elephant skin in his two uppermost hands, which is an attribute of Shamvara rather than Kalachakra with consort. The mundane female deity beneath his left foot is also part of the Shamvara iconography. These details show the deep interconnection of the Shamvara and Kalachakra cults. In this Time-Wheel statue, wisdom and compassion in union are intently focused on each other, yet simultaneously seem to reach out and embrace all other beings and things in an eternal expression of poise and beauty.

31

Hevajra Mandala

❀

Tibet, Sakya order, late 16th–early
17th century

Ink and opaque watercolors on cloth

30 x 12 inches (76.2 x 30.5 cm)

Shelley Rubin and Donald Rubin
Collection

The powerful, boldly modeled figures of Hevajra, his consort, and all the other figures in this painting are hallmarks of seventeenth-century style, as are the elegant and precise details shown, for example, in the figures of the four monks seated around the central triangle (see detail, left). Such figures are common in Tibetan painting and often appear in works dating from the seventeenth to nineteenth centuries. The sense of volume in these figures, and the bulkiness of their robes, however, help to distinguish this painting from later renditions in which the figures have become more attenuated and the robes more stylized. This is an extraordinary mandala of Hevajra Buddha in union with Vajranairatmya, illustrating well their special connection with the blazing inner fury-fire, used to melt the rigid structures of ordinary awareness into the blissful omnivision of enlightenment. The large central triangle contains a Hevajra father-mother surrounded by eight inner dakini buddhas, with eight smaller buddha-couples in an outer ring. A red Hevajra couple occupies a smaller triangle below, surrounded by eight red buddha-couples. An identical set of Hevajra couples appears above in another tri-angle, all golden white. A blue Vajradhara sits above with a Naropa Vajrayogini in the upper left corner and a Lone Hero (without consort) Yamantaka in the upper right. The adept Virupa sits below Vajrayogini and the great master Sakya Pandita sits below Yamantaka. Below Virupa sits a lama identified by the inscription as Sangs-rygas phun-tshogs, perhaps the twenty-fifth abbot of Ngor monastery (1649–1705), with another unidentified lama across from him. A Brahamanarupa Mahakala occupies the lower left corner (see detail, right), and a Panjaranatha Mahakala the lower right. Because there are no mandala palaces outside the triangles, this is a Perfection Stage mandala, visualized within the subtle yogic nervous system, the large triangle probably at the heart center, and the lower and upper triangles at the navel and throat centers respectively. The idea is to kindle the inner fire at the navel, draw down white seed-energy from the brain, and intensify the process of melting into bliss at the heart center where the full form of Hevajra is visualized. This mandala doubtless corresponds to a special secret yogic teaching reserved for advanced initiates.

32

Indrabhuti Vajradakini Mandala

❊

Tibet, Kagyu order, late 17th–early 18th century

Ink and opaque watercolors on cloth

16 ⅛ x 13 ¼ inches (41 x 33.7 cm)

Collection of Mr. and Mrs. John Gilmore Ford

She is the form of the Vajradakini Buddha revealed to the adept king, Indrabhuti, of tantric legend. She is very similar to Vajravarahi, except there is no pig head emerging above or on the side of her human head. She dances on a sun disc, surrounded by the four inner Chakrasamvara goddesses, Dakini, Lama, Khandoarohi, and Rupini, and with four animal-headed female guardians, Kakasya and company, in the doors. The lion-headed Simhavaktra goddess is in the upper left corner and a red Vajradaka in the upper right. A lama donor sits in the lower left and the Chitipati skeleton couple, bizarre deities who guard the Chakrasamvara Mother tantras, appear in the lower right. The charnel grounds are rendered simply yet strikingly, divided by charming rainbow-colored rocks. The lush floral scrolls in the background of the mandala's interior illustrate the continuation of the central Tibetan style associated with the great Ngor monastery in later periods, as does the complex detailing of the mandala circles. The figures of Indrabhuti and her attendant retain the volume found in seventeenth-century paintings, but they are a bit static, indicating a date in the late seventeenth or early eighteenth centuries. The bright green landscape background and the elaborate treatment of the area around the seated teacher at the lower right reflect Chinese influence on later Tibetan art.

33
Vajravarahi Mandala
❋

Tibet, Kagyu or Geluk order,
late 18th century

Ink and opaque watercolors on cloth

26 x 17 ¼ inches (66 x 43.8 cm)

David Shapiro Collection

This eastern Tibetan painting presents a dancing Vajravarahi in her inner triangle within the double tetrahedonal mandala of the Vajradakini, surrounded by four Heruka couples and six fierce dakinis in the six corners. A pair of adepts floats from each of the four side points of the double triangle. Above the center is Vajradhara father-mother, flanked by Tilopa and Naropa (a standing Kalachakra father-mother and a dancing Hevajra father-mother), with a white Maitri dakini on the left, and a red Naro dakini on the right. Below stand three fierce dakini protectors, from the left a form of Kurukulla, a white Krodhini standing on a bull, and a fierce Nairatmya, with Vajrapani and Hayagriva on guard between them.

34

Fierce Deities of the Between (Bar do)

❀

Tibet, possibly Bri-gung type, late 18th–early 19th century

Ink and opaque watercolors on cloth

22 ⅝ x 14 ¾ inches (57.5 x 37.5 cm)

Museum of Fine Arts, Boston, Gift of George and Verena Rybicki in memory of William Stanley and Janet Morgan, 1992.233

This powerful painting depicts the fierce deities of the eighth through twelfth days after death, during the "reality between state" (Thurman 1994, pp. 149–66). It is thus a mandala of time, in that the deities appear sequentially to the deceased person's subtle body after death. It is also a spatial mandala, in that these fierce deities are thought to inhabit the brain center during life, in a micro-dimension. In the center are the five Heruka (Heroic) buddha-couples, with the Chemchok Heruka couple as the sixth. In the first ring around that are the eight Gauri goddesses, the eight Pishachi goddesses, and the four door guardian goddesses, all but the Gauris with animal heads. In the second ring are the twenty-eight animal-headed Ishvari goddesses. Around them are five Wisdom dakinis above and five Vidyadhara adept couples below. Although its green landscape background can be traced to the art of the sixteenth century, when Chinese-style landscape first became important in Tibetan art, the density of the composition, the lack of volume, and the exaggeration of static detail typify Tibetan works of the nineteenth century. This can be seen not only in the central part of the painting, where the iconographically mandated figures encircling the Heruka couple are placed against geometric backgrounds, but also in the static positions of all the figures in this dense composition. The physiques of the primary figures share the elongation common to late eighteenth- and early nineteenth-century works. Like the subsidiary figures in the mandala circles, they also lack volume and movement, and function primarily as icons or symbols rather than as representations of actual beings. The interest in surface patterning is also shown in the flaming mandorla around the principal deities—it suggests, but does not appear to generate, heat.

35
Yama and Chamunda Symbol Mandala

Tibet, Geluk order, 18th century

Ink and opaque watercolors on cloth

12 x 12 inches (30.5 x 30.5 cm)

Shelley and Donald Rubin
Foundation

This is a rare mandala used for secret initiation into the yoga of Yama Dharmaraja, the Indian god of death who was tamed by Manjushri in his Yamantaka form, to serve as the special protector of the teaching of the Geluk order. The deities are represented by their customary hand implements, he by skull club and noose, she by skull trident and skull bowl. The eight symbols in the holes of the circular blade are the special symbols of the eight Yama couples who are Yama's main minions and carry out his protector tasks.

36

Chamunda Fierce Fire Offering Symbol Mandala

❋

Tibet, Geluk order, 17th–18th century

Ink and opaque watercolors on cloth

24 x 18½ inches (61 x 47 cm)

The Zimmerman Family Collection

This is an extremely rare mandala, a model for the preparation of a hearth in which to perform a fierce fire offering (Sanskrit *homa*, Tibetan *sbyin bsregs*) to Chamunda, the consort of Yama. The flames of the background reflect the fact that the mansion of Chamunda, represented by the skull trident and skull bowl in the center of the innermost triangle (see detail), is visualized in the heart of the fire god, Agni, through whose fiery mouth the offerings are given to the goddess. The triangular hearth contains an ocean of blood, on which a continent made of a whole human skin supports a mandala mansion made of skeletons, adorned with intestinal garlands and impaled humans on the gates. Within the mansion is a circle of fire around a triangle of fire, which contains the further calm inner triangle where the goddess in symbol form stands on her sun disc. It is meant to be extremely macabre, eerie, and frightful, its ultimate goal being to eliminate the most deadly innermost enemy, insatiable egotism.

37

Offering Cosmos Mandala

Tibet, Geluk order, 18th century

Appliqué and embroidery on cloth

32 ¾ x 21 ½ inches (83.2 x 54.6 cm)

Collection of Mr. and Mrs. John Gilmore Ford

This is an unusual textile depiction of the cosmos. Mount Meru (the planetary axis) emerges from seven-fold rings of mountains, with cities of demigods and four guardian kings on its upper slopes, and Indra's capital, Sudarshana (the Indian gods' Olympus), rising on the top. The twelve mansions, three in each direction, represent the four main and eight minor continents extending out from Meru, the eastern three (below) held in trapezoids; the southern three (India, etc.) in circles; the western three, which should be in triangles, here look square; and the northern three in semicircles. Above, nets of pearls, jewels, bells, and yak tails hang from goblin mouths, as from the soffit of all peaceful mandala palaces. Below in the landscape are black vultures, horse, deer, yak, and mastiff, indicating that the visualization associated with this type of mandala also includes macabre offerings to the fierce protector deities.

38
Offering Cosmos Mandala

Tibet, 18th century

Gilt bronze and crystal

Diameter 12 ¼ inches (31.1 cm)

The Zimmerman Family Collection

This metal mandala represents the universe as pictured in ancient Indian cosmology. It is used in rituals to symbolize the offering of the entire universe to the enlightened beings, considered indivisible from the officiating lama. The eight auspicious signs are shown around the rim, interspersed with the Wheel of Dharma, amid a floral pattern. The outer part of the upper surface alternates between mountain and wave patterns, representing the cosmic oceans surrounding a sevenfold ring of mountains. The central axial mountain, Meru or Sumeru, is represented by the four-storied pyramid in the center. The four main continents, each with two subcontinents, are represented by the twelve geometric symbols ranged around the axial mountain. India, called Jambudvipa, is represented by the central circle in the southern direction from the mountain, the western continent complex by the three triangles, the northern Uttarakuru (probably the Americas!) by the three crescents (usually semicircles), and the eastern lands by the trapezoidal squares. In a ritual, the mandala is used as a base to visualize the entire cosmos, offered to all enlightened beings.

REGIONAL VARIATIONS:
MANDALAS FROM SOUTHEAST AND EAST ASIA

Paintings and sculptures from China, Japan, and Indonesia preserve some of the earliest variants of the mandala. Of these, the most well known and studied are the paired mandalas of the Womb and Diamond Worlds, used in the practices of the esoteric Shingon and Tendai sects of Japan. The Womb World is composed of an eight-petalled lotus center surrounded by square and rectangular courts, while the Diamond World is divided into nine courts arranged horizontally and vertically in rows of three. Mandalas of this type were brought to Japan from China in the eighth century and are based on texts brought to the Chinese court by Indian monks. The Womb World symbolizes the immanence of enlightenment in the phenomenal world, while the Diamond World serves as a guide to spiritual practices.

Little visual evidence remains for the development of mandalas of the Womb and Diamond Worlds in India, although sculptures in certain western caves such as Aurangabad have been interpreted in light of the better known Japanese tradition. The Diamond World mandala is also found in Indonesian art and is represented in this exhibition by ten small figures, remnants of larger three-dimensional images of this icon. Like their Japanese counterparts, these images illustrate the international nature of Buddhism from the seventh through tenth centuries, when traveling monks carried texts, icons, and practices from one part of Asia to the other.

Japanese Buddhism also preserves and uses mandalas that derive from indigenous practices based on pre-Buddhist traditions stressing an appreciation for natural beauty. These mandalas illustrate landscapes and buildings found at some of Japan's most revered sites, such as the Kasuga shrine near Nara or Mount Koya to the south of Osaka. Shintoism, which is the term coined for many of Japan's pre-Buddhist beliefs as formalized in later times, reveres beautiful—often remote—places, and imbues them and natural elements such as rocks and trees with spiritual potency that sometimes takes the form of deities known as *kami*. Such sites were frequently used by ascetics and other practitioners who chose a solitary path, some of whom were influenced by early forms of Esoteric Buddhism popular in Japan from the eighth through twelfth centuries.

Over the centuries, the sharing of ideas and practices among these varied seekers and the more settled monastic adherents led to the creation of a system known as *honji-suijaku*, or "true-nature manifestation," and its codification in Japanese Buddhism. According to this system, Shinto gods are native manifestations of imported Buddhist deities, and the two are interchangeable. Paintings illustrating these complicated ideas include representations of famous scenic sites with or without the Shinto shrines and Buddhist temples they house, representations of both Shinto and Buddhist manifestations of the deities associated with these sites, as well as those of the sacred animals or other emblems affiliated with the practices and beliefs of individual locations.

opposite: detail of catalogue no. 48

39

Four Deities from a Diamond World Mandala

❋

Indonesia, East Java, Nganjuk, Chandi Reja, late 10th–early 11th century

Bronze

Height each approximately 3 ¼ inches (8.3 cm)

The Asia Society Galleries, 1979.87.1-4

40

Four Deities from a Diamond World Mandala

❋

Indonesia, East Java, Nganjuk, late 10th–early 11th century

Bronze

Height each approximately 3 ½ inches (8.9 cm)

The Metropolitan Museum of Art, Samuel Eilenberg Collection, 1987.142.5, 7-9

Small sculptures such as these are now often identified as images from a larger set that were used to create a three-dimensional mandala. Two complete mandalas of this type have been discovered in Indonesia, one in the village of Chandi Reja in 1913 and another much more recently at Surucolo. Both groups have, at times, been identified as examples of a Diamond World or Vajradhatu mandala, thereby linking these images to the traditions of East Asia in which mandalas of this type were also very important.

Their small size indicates that these figures would once have been used to define the outer regions of a three-dimensional mandala. These Indonesian sculptures, bodhisattvas that function as attendant or retinue deities, have been linked to a commentary written in the reign of the Pala ruler Mahipala, some time during the last quarter of the tenth and the first half of the eleventh century, but the precise textual basis for the mandalas they depict has not yet been identified. The style of the sculptures is characteristic of the art of East Java in the late tenth and eleventh centuries. The figures have long thin bodies with strong faces, and each wears carefully cast beaded jewelry and a tall, mountain-shaped crown. The crowns and jewelry of each are different, as are the implements they hold in their hands; further research may identify them more specifically.

39. *Four Deities from a Diamond World Mandala*

40. *Four Deities from a Diamond World Mandala*

41

*Mandala of the Womb World
(Taizokai Mandara)*

Japan, Kamakura period,
13th–14th century

Hanging scroll, opaque watercolor,
ink, and gold on silk

46 $^{11}/_{16}$ x 38 $^{7}/_{8}$ inches (119 x 98.7 cm)

The Brooklyn Museum of Art,
Museum Collection Fund 21.240.2

The paired Japanese mandalas of the
Womb and Diamond Worlds are
among some of the earliest examples
of mandalas preserved in Buddhist
Asia. Images of this type are said to
have been brought to Japan from
China by the eminent master Kukai
(774–835) and to have been used in
the rituals of both the Shingon and
Tendai orders. Both mandalas center
on the image of Vairochana, the
Buddha of Infinite Light, who plays
an important role in the development of Esoteric Buddhism, particularly Yoga tantra, the precursor of the
Unexcelled Yoga tantra practiced in
Tibet today. The Womb World symbolizes the possibility of buddhahood in the phenomenal world as it
is perceived by a practitioner. The
Diamond World is a guide to the

42

Mandala of the Diamond World (Kongokai Mandara)

Japan, Kamakura period,
13th–14th century

Hanging scroll, opaque watercolor,
ink, and gold on silk

46 $^{11}/_{16}$ x 38 $^{7}/_{8}$ inches (118.9 x 98.7 cm)

The Brooklyn Museum of Art,
Museum Collection Fund 21.240.1

spiritual practice that leads to enlightenment. Mandalas of this type preserve some of the earliest compositions used in the creation of mandalas. The ninefold structure of the Diamond World parallels the composition of mandalas found in cave-temples such as Ellora in western India. The eightfold lotus at the center of the Womb World mandala, on the other hand, illustrates one of the earliest known pan-Asian mandala types—that of the mandala of the Eight Great Bodhisattvas, in which a central buddha figure is surrounded by eight attendant bodhisattvas. Recently restored in Japan, these paintings appear in this exhibit and catalogue for the first time since their conservation.

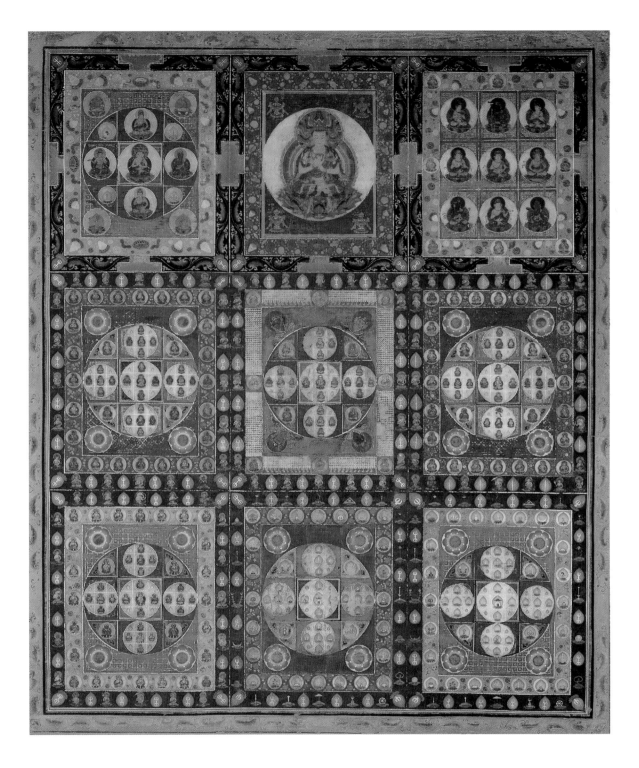

43

Mandala of the Womb World (Taizokai Mandara)

❈

Japan, Kamakura period, mid-13th century

Gold pigment, kirikane, and color on silk dyed indigo blue

35 ½ x 31 ⅛ inches (90.3 x 79 cm)

Private Collection, Cambridge, Mass.

This is one of the finest Japanese mandalas to reach the West. Lines of cut gold foil have been placed on silk dyed a dark purplish-blue to create horizontal courts, central lotus flowers, and figures. The foil delicately outlines the figures and delineates their hand gestures and ornaments. The use of purple silk links this mandala to the pair of Diamond and Womb mandalas (Takao Mandaras) preserved at Jingo-ji, which is located at the foot of Mount Takao. One of the earliest mandala pairs from Japan, the Takao Mandaras were executed in gold and silver pigments on a damask background that was also dyed purple. Despite its geometric structure, the mandala is filled with energy because of its animated representation of more than four hundred figures. Of the well-known Diamond World type, this mandala was once paired with an image of the Womb World mandala. Certain features, such as the image of the monk who commissioned it in the lower part of the painting, indicate that it was used in the rituals of the Tendai sect, one of two major branches of Esoteric Buddhism in Japan.

44

Kasuga Shrine Mandala

❀

Japan, Kamakura period,
around 1300

Colors on silk

31 x 11 inches (78.7 x 27.9 cm)

Private Collection, Cambridge, Mass.

Famous religious sites are often represented in Japanese mandalas of the true-nature manifestation (*honji-sui-jaku*) type. In these mandalas, native gods (*kami*) are explicated as manifestations of various Buddhist deities. Here, the gentle, rural landscape of the Nara plain is shown from the traditional bird's-eye perspective of indigenous Japanese painting traditions (as opposed to conventions imported from China). A subtle glow pervades this painting, and suggests the moonlight that is part of the iconography of Kasuga shrine mandalas. The five principal Buddhist deities of the shrine (Shakyamuni, Bhaishajyaguru, Kshitigarbha, Eleven-headed Avalokiteshvara, and Manjushri) are shown in a mirror carried by two angel-like beings at the top of the painting. Beneath them lie the conical Mount Mikasa and the heavily wooded Mount Kasuga, the principal landmarks of this site. The temple in the foreground is the Buddhist Kofuku-ji, the tutelary temple of the Fujiwara family. The Kasuga shrine that was the center of their Shinto practice is depicted in the background (see detail). Paintings detailing the two sites and emphasizing the ephemeral beauty of the Nara region were frequently produced during the thirteenth to sixteenth centuries as a result of changes in religious thought stressing both the need to escape from the imperfect phenomenal world to paradises and other perfected lands, and the growing belief that such pure lands were located in Japan. The cedars for which this region is famous and other trees are painted with delicacy and care, as are the small deer frolicking in the landscape shared by these two religious establishments.

45

Kasuga Deer Mandala

❀

Japan, Muromachi period,
15th century

Colors on silk

Hiroshi Sugimoto

The identification of actual places as
sacred to both imported Buddhist
and native Shinto traditions is one of
the distinctive features of Japanese
Buddhism. The Kasuga shrine near
Nara is one such site. By the twelfth
century the original gods (*kami*) of
this site had all been paired with
Buddhist deities affiliated with the
nearby Kofuku-ji temple. Deer, which
have long been associated with the
Kasuga shrine and remain protected
there, are believed to function as the
vehicles of these deities. In this painting, the deer carries a mirror (a longstanding religious and political symbol in Japan) set on a branch of the
sakaki tree, which is also sacred to
the site. The five principal Buddhist
deities for this region are shown at
the top of the painting above the
sacred mountains.

46
Mandala of the Four Deities of Mount Koya

Japan, Edo period, 17th century

Hanging scroll, ink, colors,
and gold on silk

40 ¾ x 20 inches (103.5 x 50.8 cm)

Property of Mary Griggs Burke

Mount Koya, south of Osaka, is the head-quarters of the Shingon order of Esoteric Buddhism. The staircase in the foreground suggests the entryway to the Shinto shrine that is represented in the center of the painting by the four deities seated on a platform beneath an elegant curtain in the center. The two gods at the top, Niu Myojin to the right and Kariba to the left, have long been associated with this shrine. The two at the bottom, Kehi and Itsukushima Myojin, are deities associated with other shrines some distance from Mount Koya. They were brought to Amano in the thirteenth century during a pilgrimage by the wife of the Kamakura shogun Minamoto Yoritomo. The god and three goddesses are seated on low seats before tripartite screens. The god seated in the upper right-hand corner wears the clothing of a Japanese courtier; the long-sleeved robes and tailored collars of the goddesses can be traced back to the costume of Song-period China. The figures are drawn with modulated outlines that give them volume and a hint of movement. The outlines are filled with opaque colors and covered by thin gold lines to create patterns, details, and an elegant surface. This is most evident in the delicate floral images decorating the screens or in the contrast between patterned and plainer garments that illustrate the many layers of clothing worn by the goddesses. The composition of this painting is consistent with Muromachi-period (1392–1673) paintings on the same theme, but the stylization of the figures and the architectural details suggest a date in the early part of the Edo period (1615–1868).

47

Star Mandala

❀

Japan, Edo period, 17th century

Gold and colors on wood

Diameter 21 ½ inches (54.6 cm)

Philadelphia Museum of Art, Gift of
the Friends of the Philadelphia
Museum of Art,
1978-45-2

Astrology played a large role in the Buddhist practices of Tang-period (617–906) China that spread to Korea and Japan. Amitabha, the Buddha of Infinite Light, seated on a lotus throne and holding a lotus with flaming jewels, is the center of this mandala. He is positioned in a sunlike circular disc surrounded with clouds and set against a dark blue background intended to represent the sky. Amitabha is surrounded by twenty-eight bodhisattvas, each paired with an image of a constellation. These are the twenty-eight lunar mansions (*xiu*) of early Chinese astrology. The thirty-six guardians, known as the auspicious stellar gods, are depicted in military costume at the outer edge. The buddha's physique and face, his clothing, and his lotus pedestal continue artistic traditions associated with Japanese Buddhist art of the Heian and Kamakura periods. The stiffness of the figures, the flattening of the forms, and particularly the mannered treatment of the buddha's scarves and the petals of his lotus pedestal, however, date the painting to the middle part of the Edo period. The round shape of this mandala and the use of wood can also be traced to longstanding traditions associated with Shintoism. The shape may derive from circular metal plaques (*kakebotoke*), that decorated Shinto shrines. They evolved from the mirrors important in Japan's first religious practices. The wood is reminiscent of the popular votive paintings (*ema-a*), usually of horses, that functioned as offerings in return for answered prayers.

48
Mandala of Marichi
❀

China, dated 1717

Ink and colors on silk

53 x 42 ½ inches (134.6 x 108 cm)

The Nelson-Atkins Museum of Art,
Kansas City, Missouri
(Purchase: Nelson Trust) 35-172

Marichi, the Buddhist goddess of the dawn, became prominent in China during the Tang dynasty as a result of both the prevalence of astrological speculations and the rise of Esoteric Buddhism. Also known in China as the Queen of Heaven and the Mother of the Big Dipper, Marichi was believed to offer protection from violence and peril, especially war. This representation of eight-armed, three-faced Marichi is most likely based on the *Marichi Bodhisattva Sutra* that was translated during the Song period (960–1279). Her left hands carry a rope, bow, flowering branch of the *ashoka* tree, and thread; her right hands hold a vajra, needle, hook, and arrow. Her left face is that of a pig and her right that of a young woman. She is attended by a host of deities representing constellations of other cosmological entities. The five seated buddhas at the top of the painting symbolize the five main buddhas familiar to later esoteric tradition. Many of the figures in the two large groups at the foreground of the painting are identified by inscription and appear to be semidivinities of various kinds. The long but partial inscription at the top of the painting gives a Chinese cyclical date in accordance with 1717.

MANDALA

THE ARCHITECTURE OF ENLIGHTENMENT

ROBERT A. F. THURMAN

Dedicated to the late Venerable Pema Losang Chogyen

PHILOSOPHICAL GROUND

In Buddhist usage, a mandala is a matrix or model of a perfected universe, the nurturing environment of the perfected self in ecstatic interconnection with perfected others. It is a blueprint for buddhahood conceived as attainment not only of an individual's ultimate liberation and supreme bliss, but also as the attainment of such release and bliss *by an individual fully integrated with his or her environment and field of associates.*

The traditional definition of *tantra* is process, continuum, or continuity (Tibetan, *rgyud,* thread). According to the striking insight of the late Venerable Tara Tulku, Abbot Emeritus of the Gyuto Tantric University, it is the process of demolishing the samsaric world by removing its foundation, ignorance, and then rebuilding that foundation on the basis of wisdom. Within the vision of tantra as a world-recreating process, mandalas are models used for creating buddha-worlds.

According to the Pali tradition, Shakyamuni Buddha's statement

opposite: detail of a gate from a three-dimensional Avalokiteshvara mandala, Library of Tibetan Works and Archives, Dharamsala, India

upon enlightenment emphasized the demolition process: "I have found you out, O house builder. I have torn down your rafters and walls. I have come out of your house. I am free at last."[1] This connects with his founding of the monastic life, the vocation defined as "escape from home to homelessness." In Monastic or Individual Vehicle Buddhism,[2] the mandala principle, the art of rebuilding a world attuned with nirvana, is difficult to discern, because the Buddha limited himself to negative definitions. He did not explicitly describe the monastic community as a model for a new world of liberated individuals that presaged—in its rules of interaction, its freedom from violence, its idyllic experiential matrix, its facility for new knowledge—the kind of buddha-world explicitly described in the Universal Vehicle literature. In the monastic literature, the ideal world is described indirectly in terms of the historical past, in *Jataka* stories of kingdoms the Buddha ruled in former lives and in the ideal communities of beings mentioned in the sutras as models for contemporary behavior.

In the Individual Vehicle, the mandala principle is thus mainly revealed in the often subliminal presentation of the Buddha's enlightenment as having a lasting impact on the world. This is symbolized by the stupa monument that memorializes the

Buddha's mental presence in his physical relics; by the idea of his verbal presence in the dharma body, the texts and teachings that provide access to the world of liberation; and by his physical presence in symbols and icons.

According to the Sanskrit tradition, Shakyamuni spoke more positively about buddhahood after his enlightenment: "Profound, peaceful, unproliferating, luminous, and uncreated—this reality I have found is like an elixir of immortality."[3] For the Universal or Messianic Vehicle, the mandala principle expresses the ideal of "the perfection of the buddhaverse." Such a cosmic transformation is possible because of the infinite nondual presence, in every atom and subatomic energy, of the truth- and beatific-bodies; it is actualized by the activities of countless emanation-bodies[4] of the Buddha, ceaselessly helping beings throughout the universes. The central theme of the *Vimalakirti Sutra*,[5] for example, is the perfection of this world, called *saha,* the (barely) tolerable, as Shakyamuni's buddhaverse. The world is revealed as a mandala for beings' optimal evolution toward their own enlightenments. The actual operations of the saha mandala, centering on Vimalakirti's magical house, resonate with ancient Indian visions of kingship, anointment, royal majesty and blessing, and the aesthetics of compassion. Vimalakirti's house functions in the same way as the central technology of the Apocalyptic Vehicle, architecturally enabling the person within it to reach out imaginatively and enfold his or her environment in the process of evolutionary transformation to which he or she is dedicated.

How does "mandala" come to have such a meaning? To judge from Tibetan translations, Sanskrit *manda* translated as Tibetan *dkyil*, which can mean essence (*snyingpo*), as well as seat (*khri*), mind (*sems*), and even center (*dkyil*). It goes with *bodhi*, enlightenment or awakening, to indicate the site under the Bodhi tree where full perfection of the sentient being occurs, where subjective awareness breaks free from addiction to frustrating compulsions and blossoms out in an understanding so vast and deep it knows the infinite by becoming it, bit by bit. Where could the essence or seat of such enlightenment be encapsulated? Where could it be held? *La* is said to be a circle, an enclosing perimeter that contains the essence, the jewel, the ornament.

In a conventional sense, then, every being *is* a mandala, rather than just a point of awareness. We *are* our environment as much as we are the entity in the environment. Thus my image of myself as living, conscious, human, male, white, fifty-five, American, English-speaking, and so on, goes along with a model of my parents, ances-tors, offspring, and posterity (and in some cultures, my own former and future lives), currently within the American social world centered on Washington, D.C. and its mandala of monuments and institutional structures. I exist within a physical model of being, a structure of atomic, molecular, cellular, and energy processes formed into a body held by gravity on the North American continent, between Atlantic and Pacific oceans, on the round planet Earth, third planet from the sun, with the moon encircling it, the sun a star in the Milky Way galaxy, in such and such a nebula, and so forth. If "I" refers to a point of awareness in the center of all this, then it presupposes the entire surround, the model which contains this "I," my imagined physical, social, and interpersonal environment.

When an ordinary being is described in Buddhism as a cluster of five heaps *(skandha)* or systems of matter (including sense objects as well as sense organs), of sensations, ideas, emotions, and consciousnesses, that being is described as a system of processes within an environment, not as a detached point of awareness. Correspondingly, when we become perfected buddhas, when we reach the culmination of our evolutionary potential, our environments also become transformed. Within our existing world-model are traces of the evolutionary culminations of other beings who became buddhas, such as Shakyamuni. The buddhas are not just superordinate points of awareness, they are different worlds, different mandalas or environments. The very fabric of our world is woven of the buddhaverses of infinite past and present buddhas.

The sacred space under the enlightenment tree in Bodhgaya is called the "essence of enlightenment" *(bodhi-manda)*, or the diamond seat *(vajrasana)*, and is considered completely impenetrable by any spiritual or physical entity. The souls of beings in the process of rebirth, the between state, cannot go through it, though they can traverse mountains and planets. This gives mythic impact to the inconceivable reality of an infinite being in a specific place, the infinite—beyond limits, yet having a center. The infinite cannot be excluded from any specific place; unbounded, it cannot be kept out of anything. Thus the infinite is ultimately indivisible from the finite. Infinite awareness enjoys absolute peace and unlimited bliss. It is utterly present everywhere, everything is its center. So a mandala is not an escape from anything: the infinite does not need protection from anything, as nothing can be other than it. A mandala is compassion, it is form, it is infinite wisdom expressing infinite love extended to those caught in the finite-infinite dichotomy to whom it opens a door of liberation, a gateway to freedom, a portal to the infinite.

Enlightenment is often expressed as twofold to suit our habit of binary thinking. It is the perfection of mind *and* the perfection of body, the transmutation of death *and* of life, the culmination of knowledge *and* merit, the enjoyment of perfected formlessness *and* perfected form. All these polarities are integrated through the evolutionary climax of wisdom and compassion, or bliss. When we focus on enlightenment primarily as union with absolute reality—the truth-body, the realization of voidness, the intuitive wisdom of selflessness—we see only one side of its inconceivability. We also must discover enlightenment as endarkenment, the creative engagement of infinite freedom with form. This is the continuing process of enlightened engagement with beings, the ceaseless structuring of emanations motivated by compassion and empowered by bliss. Thus the transparency of enlightenment is a clear light, not a white light, but a light that integrates black with white, a light that penetrates everything, including shadows.

These ideas are expressed in the *Diamond Pavilion Tantra*.

If voidness were the sole art for it,
One never would gain buddhahood.
An effect never differs in kind from its cause;
So voidness is not the whole art.
The Victors teach voidness to stop self-habits
Of both self-advocates and theory-less cynics.
But it is the mandala and environment
That incorporate the art of universal bliss.
It is the yoga of the Buddha-pride
That makes buddhahood accessible.
A Teacher has thirty-two excellent signs,
And is Lord of eighty auspicious marks.
Thus, the art is to assume the goal,
Which is the Teacher's actual Body of Form.[6]

The path to buddhahood has two aspects, absolute and relative. The mind attains the absolute, the body masters the relative. The mind's attainment of wisdom is the same for exoteric (*sutrayana*) and esoteric (*mantrayana*) Buddhist vehicles. It realizes ultimate reality through voidness yoga, evolves transcendent wisdom, and becomes the Buddha Body of Truth. The body's art is different in the two vehicles. On the exoteric vehicle it encompasses relative reality, travels on a causal or means vehicle, practices the yoga of the first three transcendences, evolves great compassion through the art of positive interaction, and through a progression of count-

less lives becomes the Buddha Body of Form. On the esoteric tantra vehicle, the body encompasses relative reality, travels on an effect or goal vehicle, practices deity yoga (develops buddha-vision and buddha-pride), evolves great compassion effectual as great bliss, packs eons of subtle reality evolution into one or a few lives on the gross body level, and becomes the Buddha Body of Form.

The path of tantra begins in the creative meditation that harnesses the imagination to "assume the buddha-form." It transforms the self and the universe into the experience and realm of enlightenment. It uses imagination to simulate buddhahood and buddhaverse in order to accelerate the actual transformations and fulfill the bodhisattva vow without waiting for the flow of history in ordinary time.

For this to be possible at all depends in Buddhist physics on the ultimate reality of voidness. This logically entails the relativity of all space and time, all things' ultimate voidness being exactly equivalent to their superficial relativity. Once ultimate reality is understood as empty of any intrinsic substantiality, reality, identifiability, or objectivity, its apparent nature at any level of experience is understood to be utterly conventional, merely constituted by collective designation (*prajnaptirupadaya*).

Ordinary beings dominated by misknowledge *(avidya)* structure their universe into a conventional world maintained by conditioned imaginations, coordinated by ordinary languages and conceptual systems. But buddhas structure universes according to the needs of the beings in them, which the buddhas' absolutely open, empathetic sensitivities unerringly reveal. Once the conventionality of realities is understood, even conceptually, the bodhisattva is liberated from the naive realism that traps him in misknowledge. He becomes free to reconstruct an extraordinary reality of enlightenment, if it helps to liberate self and others. The danger of becoming trapped in further illusions is avoided by the knowledge of selflessness. Naive realism about ordinary reality, already critically shattered, is not likely to arise in an imaginatively constructed extraordinary reality.

The initial realization of voidness, still mainly on the conceptual level, does not immediately eradicate instinctual self-habits, the deep structures of misknowledge that dominate habitual perceptions. In the ordinary Universal Vehicle, this deepening process, wherein the initial unmistaken conceptual understanding of voidness leads to the ultimate nonconceptual intuitive experience of voidness in the spacelike equipoised samadhi-wisdom, is called the path of the union of critical insight (*vipashyana*) and concentrative quiescence (*shamatha*). The process consists of an ever-narrowing oscillation between the spacelike samadhi, wherein all appearances vanish, like reflections of the moon in water, under the critical investigation of reified objective and subjective realities, and the illusionlike aftermath wisdom, wherein realities dawn once more.

The jewel-like practitioner, the genius fit for the Vajra, Diamond-Thunderbolt, or Apocalyptic Vehicle, can avoid this slower process of oscillation by perceiving apparent objects and their ultimate voidness simultaneously with equal intuitive force. She does not require a disappearance of objects in order to experience their voidness. Mere cognition of appearance *is* the effective critique of any reified substance outside of voidness, and such cognition of voidness precludes any sense of nothingness as a real voidness or absolute beneath the surface of appearances. In the eleventh Dalai Lama's famous metaphor, the practitioner is like the drunk whose blurred vision reveals two moons in the sky, yet who exuberantly calls out to his comrades, "There's the moon!"[7]

Therefore, the tantric yogin can play with appearances to cultivate purified perception of them as the buddhaverse in the form of the Akanishta mandala palace of the beatific-body buddha, and can play with voidness wisdoms to cultivate compassion as great bliss, as the actual embodiment of buddhahood. The yogin's bliss-void-indivisible wisdom itself becomes his buddha-body, and the clear light of voidness itself becomes his buddha-mind, the Dharmakaya Body of Truth. This nondual-from-the-beginning approach (feasible for the exceptional practitioner who already has the unmistaken, conceptual, critical understanding of selflessness or voidness) is far more rapid in bringing the subtle intuitive layers of consciousness into attunement with the philosophically enlightened layers of consciousness. It gets directly into the instincts by mobilizing the subtle and very subtle forms of consciousness, such as those experienced during orgasm and death, for the realization of voidness.

Thus, mandala is a matrix of embodiment. It is the architecture of enlightenment in its bliss- and compassion-generated emanations. It is a womb palace within which infinite wisdom and compassion can manifest as forms discernible to ordinary beings. It is also a structure perceived by misknowledge-dominated ordinary beings as symbolic of the qualities of enlightenment. Using its architecture of the sacred, they can imitate the buddha-form. It is natural that the model of the royal palace or the sacred precinct of the temple would suggest transcendence, security, and the glory of the exaltation of the divine.

We might call the mandala principle the idea that buddhahood is a perfected reality that does not exclude ordinary reality, thus transforming others as well as self, community as well as individual, environment as well as conscient being.

ORIGINS AND VARIETIES OF THE MANDALA

The mandala idea originated long before historical Buddhism. In the earliest level of Indian or even Indo-European religion, in the *Rg Veda* and its associated literature, *mandala* is the term for a chapter, a collection of mantras or verse hymns chanted in Vedic ceremonies, perhaps coming from the sense of *round*, as in a round of songs. The universe was believed to originate from the mantra hymns, whose sacred sounds contained the genetic patterns of beings and things, so there is already a clear sense of mandala as world-model.

A mandala is also any circle, such as the disc of the sun or moon, and, by extension, any environment or surround, the sphere of influence of a kingdom, the circle of acquaintances of a person, and so forth. The word *mandapa*, a tent or covered hall, also means temple or the central pavilion of the deity within a temple.

Thus very early on, *mandala* had the generative meaning of a circle as a universal symbol for womb, for breast, for the nurturing source of life. Divinities such as sun or moon are also round and emanate transformative rays. As with other central concepts of Buddhism, such as dharma and karma, Buddhism took a mainstream Indian concept and transformed or transvalued it for its own liberative use. The mandala concept functions on the sacred level in notions of cosmogony and their ritual and geometric resonance in religious performance. It also extends from the sacred into the secular in royal coronation rituals and in the mental model of social reality internalized within any society.

In a tantric account of the Buddha's enlightenment, as he sits in the ultimate ascetic samadhi of immovability on the bank of the Nairanjana River near Bodhgaya, having resolved never again to draw breath as an egocentric, unenlightened individual, he is interrupted by a goddess. She approaches, snaps her fingers, and arouses him in subtle body form, separating his dreamlike magic-body (*mayadeha*) from his entranced coarse body, and invites him to the Akanishta Heaven, to the presence of all the timeless communities of buddhas. There he is introduced to the Divine Palace of Enlightened Beings, initiated as an Unexcelled Buddha in the Secret Mandala of All Transcendent Lords and Ladies, and exalted by the feast of subtle energy of the tantric circle.[8]

After rejoicing in the perfection of the vajra-thunderbolt ultimate energy of the magic-body/clear light, bliss-void-indivisible intuition, Shakyamuni Buddha emanates effortlessly into innumerable worlds of beings to share his infinite happiness with them. He returns to his coarse body in samadhi to continue to teach beings in the saha world. His initiation, realization, and exaltation are the real reasons his body turns the color of shining gold, miraculously recovering from its emaciation and regaining its full form and luster (corresponding to the exoteric account of his partaking of the divine milk, rice, and honey presented by the cowherdess Sujata). While the Buddha spent forty-nine days in solitude in the grove around the Bodhi tree, he was actually teaching millions of gods and celestial bodhisattvas in innumerable pure lands and emanating teachers to countless other worlds of conscient beings.

In Tibetan Buddhist practice and performance today, we find a number of different kinds of mandalas in actual usage. There are natural mandalas. The five primary elements—earth, water, fire, air, and space, sometimes with the addition of consciousness—are each mandalas, in the sense of symbolic shapes representing their specific essences: a yellow square for earth, a white disc for water, a red triangle for fire, a gray semicircle for air, a drop shape for space, and a "drop-tail" or squiggle shape for consciousness. Important planetary bodies have mandalas that represent their essences: an orange disc for sun, a silver one for moon, a black one for Rahu (the eclipse planet), and a golden disc for Kalagni ("time-fire"— the supernova node).

There is an offering mandala, a sculptural cosmogram depicting Mount Meru (the planetary axis), the four continents and eight subcontinents, the solar pathways of the planets, the astronomical mansions, and the larger time cycles (see catalogue no. 37). This world-model can be represented by interlacing the fingers as compass points and center, by a stack of metal rings filled with grains and jewels, by a solid cast sculpture, or by a painting. The first two types of mandalas are models *of*, symbolic representations of elements or realms that, in a sense, allow the meditator to manipulate the originals through magical resonance.

Next we find "subliminal mandalas," including icons of Shakyamuni's Former Lives and his Buddha Life in narrative, drama, sculpture, and painting representing the stories that form the buddhaverse by adding the buddha-dimension to the ordinary universe. In this category also we can place Shakyamuni's miracle performances—represented in narrative, drama, sculpture, and painting—as well as the numerous buddhaverse visions originally given

in the Universal Vehicle sutras and richly presented throughout the Buddhist world, especially in painting. These mandalas are models *for*, in that they create an imaginative rift in the fabric of the ordinary world through which the extraordinary world of the buddhas can be glimpsed. Such mandalas are the implicit beginnings of the explicitly alternative-dimension mandalas of the tantric systems, the archetypal model *for* mandalas.

In the tantras themselves, where we first find the mandala principle explicated in detail, there are initiatory mandalas, which open the door for the practice of the Action, Performance, Yoga, and Unexcelled Yoga tantras. Because the Unexcelled Yoga tantras (corresponding to the Maha-, Anu-, and Ati-yoga tantras in the Nyingma categorization) are the most explicit about all the elements of the tantric enterprise, I will discuss these mandalas in Unexcelled Yoga tantra terms. Their practices are divided into the Creation Stage and the Perfection Stage: the primary practices of the former are contemplation and visualization; and of the latter, transcendence practices and performances in subtle dimensions opened up by the visualization processes. At the beginning of these multilayered practices, the mandala is essential to create the sphere within which these performances can be effective. The first encounter with the mandala of any Unexcelled Yoga tantra is during the initiation (consecration or empowerment).

The actual mandala itself, underlying all practices and performances, is a complete, three-dimensional environment, an alternative universe, a world centered on a divine mansion that contains buddha archetype-deities with specific types of bodies, surrounded by gardens and charnel grounds, replete with mountains, lakes, trees, and various divine, legendary, and historical beings. The borders of this world are sealed against all negative influences by rings of fire and diamond-thunderbolt energies, which, when desired, can be made permeable to absorb beings from ordinary worlds to bless and transform them. This real alternative mandala world exists in a realm of divine substance within the realities perceived by all buddhas, and can only be perceived in the trained holographic imaginations of tantric adepts, who see it as made of limitless quantities of jewel substances, exquisitely shaped by divine energies into inconceivably balanced and finely wrought exalting structures. During initiation ceremonies, however, these mandalas can be presented in a variety of materials through a variety of arts. They can also be imagined within the human body, or as fashioned from its dismantled parts.

For the moment, I will sort the types of mandalas according to the four main initiations, those of the vase, secret, wisdom-intuition, and word. There are sketched, painted, and two-dimensional mandalas drawn with colored particles, and architectural and visualized three-dimensional mandalas located in the coarse objective world, in the body, or in the micro-dimension. There are the relative spirit of enlightenment mandalas, another sort of drop or genetic mandala at the level of subtle mental and physical code; the female lotus mandala, divine realm for realization of ultimate reality; and the mandala of the ultimate spirit of enlightenment, mandala as the absolute itself, the infinite, eternal, immanent mind of all buddhas of past, present, and future.

In conferring the numerous subdivisions of the vase initiation, the initiate's imaginative experience of the real mandala can be triggered by mandalas created in two dimensions by lines painted on cotton, silk, or any smooth surface to produce a kind of blueprint. In a fully painted mandala, the buddha-deities can be depicted by seed-syllables *(bija),* hand symbols *(mudra),* or portraits. Conferring the initiation through a painting is considered an inferior procedure, though the use of a painted mandala or blueprint in subsequent meditation is considered quite helpful.

In textual descriptions from ancient India, it appears that initiatory mandalas were laid out in colored chalks carefully sprinkled on smoothed ground to create a sacred space as a foundation for the visualized three-dimensional holographic mandala in which the initiator and initiates actually interacted in the ritual. In Tibetan practice, a smaller but much more vividly detailed blueprint is made of colored sand in a separate space. It grounds the holographic divine mandala in such a vivid way that the imagination of the initiate is immediately catapulted into sensing the full mandala as present in enterable form. The particle mandala is considered essential for a valid initiation, and the ability to create one is an indispensable requisite of the tantric master.

Next there are architecturally constructed three-dimensional models of the real mandala. These can be made of any substance, though clearly no mundane substance can duplicate the divine architecture of the original, divine, holographic mandala universe, which uses huge slabs of solid diamond, ruby, topaz, emerald, and sapphire, seamlessly shaped into pillars, beams, rafters, flooring, and numerous structural and ornamental elements. Wood, clay, mundane gems, and precious metals, however, can be shaped into representations of the mandala to trigger the imagination. It is theoretically possible to construct an actual building in which someone could be initiated, though the immense expense has made this

rare in Buddhist history. The Manchu Chien Lung emperor made several buildings in Jehol, his ancestral capital, but these were containers for mandalas rather than direct representations.

The vase initiation enables the practitioner to enter the creative visualization stage, in which she learns to visualize the mandala palace and environment, and herself as the deity or community of deities resident therein. Therefore, it emphasizes the vision of the architectural space of the mandala which, with its divine realms and residents, can be imaginatively constructed in any size and at any location. By visualizing deities in their environments at specific vital points in the body, the yogin creates body mandalas, and in visualizing mandalas in micro-dimensions in awareness-drops *(jnana-bindu),* "drop" mandalas are created. These mandalas are important when the meditator nears the goal of the Creation Stage, which is to isolate his perceptions from any vestige of ordinariness, by vividly imagining all elements of the body and its environment as divine substances. Thus the tantric meditator enters the alternative dimension of the divine mandala and becomes safe and secure enough to practice the dissolution processes required to master the subtle, instinctual levels of the body-mind complex.

The secret initiation enables the initiate to practice speech- and mind-isolation, self-consecration Perfection Stages, wherein mantras and wind-energies are unified in the subtle body dimension. She attains the self-consecration vajra body, also called the superficial magic-body. At this point, the coarse architectural mandala is no longer emphasized, although the subtle body energies are stabilized and transformed within it. She receives the initiation within the "superficial enlightenment spirit mandala," the white and red drops of essences of semen and ovum from the father and mother guru-deities in union. Here the enlightenment spirit of love and compassion for all beings is associated with the genetic material of parents, seen as white and red drops; these drops themselves are called mandalas. Such drop mandalas are specific spiritual cells or genes, which code infinite enlightenment in subtle form: they communicate the genetics of supreme enlightenment to the initiate, as a means of helping him master his own unenlightened, instinctual genetic coding. The secret initiation uses this relative enlightenment spirit mandala to purify speech by isolating all verbal perception from any habitual ordinariness, arousing the vision of speech and breath as indivisible from divine mantra, poetic and creative sound. It is very subtle and recondite, and rather hard to understand and explain. But it definitely lies in the realm of the transmission of the genetic code from the divine parents to the practitioner, who is born as a magic-body buddha on the subtle level.

The third major initiation, the wisdom-intuition initiation, is said to enable one to practice the clear light translucency Perfection Stage, also called the Great Seal or Mahamudra. The initiation is received in the vulva of the "wisdom" or consort, as the practice of this Perfection Stage is beyond coarse personality constructs and directly involves moving the subtle energies (winds) and subtle senses (drops) through various sensitivity points in the central channel *(avadhuti)* of the subtle body, which runs from the tip of the sexual organ up to mid-brow, passing in front of the spine from its base to the crown of the head. This is different from the visualization of a micro-mandala in the lotus of the wisdom consort; the actual lotus itself becomes the mandala, a divine model of an enlightened universe, and the initiate therein discovers the infinite nonduality of bliss and void that is the ultimate translucent nature of reality. This mandala lies far beyond any trace of ordinary percept or concept in the delicate realm of nondual void and bliss, absolute and relative, mind and body, spirit and flesh, and so on, where the ultimate truth-body realization of the practitioner is attained.

The Great Fourth, or Supreme Word initiation enables the initiate to practice and attain the two-reality-indivisible Perfection Stage, the stage of the union of the perfected magic-body and the ultimate clear light. It is received in the mandala of the ultimate spirit of enlightenment. This attainment completes the total purification of the most subtle instincts and mastery of the most foundational energies. The initiation is received at the most subtle level of body and mind, in the ultimate clear light mind within the mandala of the indestructible drop, where body and mind themselves are indistinguishably nondual, infinite and infinitesimal are nondual, divine mandala and ordinary world are nondual, and all the attainments accessed by the previous three initiations are sealed and confirmed. The mandala of the ultimate spirit of enlightenment is thus also the ultimate mandala. It is the omnipresent, all-pervasive, indivisible mind of all buddhas which is absolutely immanent in all relative things through infinity and during all moments of past, present, and future eternity. It is thus, naturally, completely inconceivable.

THE MANDALA PRINCIPLE IN EXOTERIC BUDDHISM
Monastic Visions of the Buddha
Though the Individual Vehicle considers itself far from tantric ideas and attitudes, the Monastic Buddhist literature in Pali, Sanskrit, Tibetan, Chinese, and Mongolian is full of examples of the mandala principle, primarily in descriptions of the Buddha's presence. He is clearly portrayed as what we might call a "field being" as opposed to a point of subjectivity.

In what we have left of early Buddhist sculpture, he is never represented in anthropomorphic form, as if he were too chameleon a physical presence, too infinite and unencompassable in ordinary outlines, to depict in a static representation. His presence is symbolized as a wheel, a tree, or a jewel. When beings encounter him, they enter his field, and are thereby initiated into his mandala of exalted possibility and expanded awareness. They completely lose their ordinary self-identifications and are initiated by his presence into new possibilities of being. For example, the young playboy Yashas was drugged and robbed by prostitutes. Staggering nearly naked through the woods, angry and hung over, he bumped into the Buddha meditating under a tree.

"Have you seen some girls running away with some jewels and silks?"

"Do you really want to find those girls, jewels, and silks? Or do you want to find the reality of freedom?"

"Oh, freedom of course!"

And the boy sat down, listened to the Four Noble Truths, and within the day became an arhat, a liberated saint.[9] Did Yashas, in his demented state, simply encounter a man who spoke some words? Unlikely. He entered an intense field of energy, a buoyant space of exaltation that lifted his mind out of its swirling agitation and held him rapt in quickened receptivity. Whenever the Buddha goes to a new place, the gods come and transform the environment so that flowers bloom out of season and trees are festooned with jewels and other ornaments.[10]

There is a Tibetan story that King Bimbisara of Magadha commissioned a portrait of the Buddha to send to a distant king who had never had the blessing of seeing the Lord. No painter could capture the scintillating, coruscating energy field of the Buddha, with dazzling rays circling around his head. So the Buddha seated himself near a still pool so the painters could see his reflected form in the surface of the water, and thus paint his portrait.

The symbolism of the Buddha and his dharma is all royal symbolism, appropriate to a king as royal "we," the personage who represents the nation. The Wheel of Dharma is a new transvaluation of the royal wheel of sovereignty; the seat of enlightenment is a royal throne; the language of Fortunate Lord *(Bhagavan)* and Transcendent One *(Tathagata)* is transroyal and transdivine. The etiquette of dealing with a buddha is derived from royal practice: circumambulating thrice, kneeling on one knee, presenting offerings, making prostrations, folding the palms in supplication, taking refuge. The Buddha, however, renounces a royal throne to uplift the entire community. The whole symbolism of the Buddha is the same as of the Wheel-turning Raja *(Chakravartin)* and presents yet another depiction of enlightenment as a communal attainment. Then finally, there is the formation of the Sangha, a new monastic-centered community within the larger Indian society, which clearly expresses the institutionalization of the attainment, and indicates the possibility of membership in a new reality, a world in which buddhas live.

At the end of his life, the Buddha authorized construction of stupa[11] memorials, monuments to his physical presence in the world. Using them as markers, he designed a Buddha mandala or holy land in which pilgrims traverse the sacred space created by his deeds. This Buddhist holy land stretches from his birthplace at Lumbini to the site of his enlightenment at Bodhgaya, to the Sarnath of his teaching, to Kusinagara where he entered into parinirvana, and then back to Lumbini. Within this zone other stupas commemorate teachings: Shravasti, site of his most spectacular miracles; Vaishali, where he taught the laity; Rajagrha, site of his first monastery; Kapilavastu, where he taught his father, son, foster mother, ex-wife, and original subjects; and Shankhasya, site of his descent from Indra's Thirty-Three Heaven after teaching his mother the *Abhidharma.*

The pilgrims who enter this geographical mandala gain access to a new universe in which they can alter the course of their own evolution, by aspiring to total freedom from suffering, attaining a higher awareness of reality, and by following the footsteps of the Buddha.

The Mandala Principle in the Mahayana Sutras

In the Mahayana sutras, the Buddha's presence invariably manifests in miraculous displays that demonstrate the essence of his teaching in an initiatory way, even before he speaks a word. He enfolds his audience in a new dimension, a mandala that exalts them in an extraordinary setting that renders them receptive to his teaching of their own extraordinary possible destiny.

In the *Holy Teaching of Vimalakirti Sutra,* five hundred noble youths from the city of Vaishali visit him at a country estate where he is staying with his monks and bodhisattvas. They each greet the Lord by ceremoniously offering their ornate jeweled parasols. The Buddha then magically fuses all the parasols into a giant jeweled lattice dome, something like a modern planetarium. The interior surface appears to the audience as a dazzling vision of the entire multidimensional universe (or multiverse). Infinite stars, moons, suns, other planets and dimensions, and vast numbers of humans, animals, and gods are dwelling in it—all the varied phenomena of nature are visible in an extraordinary panorama of ecological interconnectedness. Later in the same meeting, presumably under the same dome, within the mandala of the interconnectedness of nature, Buddha places his big toe on the ground and demonstrates the underlying perfection of this world as his own chosen buddhaverse, a land wherein every element of matter, every energy, and every form ceaselessly functions to teach beings the dharma of the reality of their own freedom. Each member of the audience perceives the entire environment as jewels, feels his own body as ecstatically virtual in its reality, and experiences himself as sitting on an inconceivable jewel lotus in the best position for greatest evolutionary development toward the freedom, omniscience, and omnicompetence of buddhahood. Later in the sutra, the sage Vimalakirti uses his own residence as a magic mandala, receiving thousands of guests into its altered dimensions. Sometimes he transforms it into a zone of sheer voidness, and sometimes he seats his guests on giant thrones, hundreds of thousands of miles tall, and the guests themselves become giants in order to be enthroned on them. He bestows numerous visions of other universes upon his guests, and invites a group of extraterrestrial visitors from the Fine Incense buddhaverse to join them. He then serves a feast of elixir food from the Incense buddhaverse which alters everyone's awareness by changing their scents. Finally, he transports the entire assembly of thousands of persons in the palm of his hand to the country estate where the Buddha is residing and, after some notable conversations with the Buddha, at the Lord's request stretches out his magic arm and brings into everyone's clear vision the miniaturized solar system of his own planet of origin, the eastern Intense Delight (Abhirati) buddhaverse of Akshobhya.

In the *Transcendent Wisdom Sutras,* the Buddha begins by entering into the profound illumination samadhi mentioned in the *Heart Sutra (Prajnaparamitahrdaya Sutra)* or by extending his exquisite tongue to cover the entire universe, emitting rays of light that reveal to the audience a vision of multiple dimensions, universes, and worlds wherein the same Buddha is simultaneously teaching the profound reality of voidness to infinite assemblies of humans and gods.[12]

In the *Land of Bliss Sutra*, the Buddha describes in exquisite detail the heavenly fields of the universe of the Buddha of Measureless Light, Amitabha, occasionally bestowing a visionary glimpse of his celestial environment.[13]

In the *Holy White Lotus of Real Teaching Sutra (Saddharmapundarika Sutra)*, the Buddha announces that he will give the White Lotus teaching only after the White Lotus Virtual Reality mandala manifests from the power of the vow of the long-transcended Buddha Prabhutaratna. The ordinary terrestrial environment of the Vulture Heap Mountain is then suddenly transformed into a perfected realm: the rugged mountain setting becomes soft, flat, and radiant with sapphire and diamond surfaces divided by golden threads into chessboard segments, each with a jeweled lion throne under a magnificent jewel tree on which all the buddhas of infinite dimensions are enthroned. With an awesome rumbling noise, a gigantic jeweled stupa thousands of miles tall emerges from the jewel ground, and the entire assembly levitates high into space in a cloud-like formation around the domed chamber at the heart of the monument. Shakyamuni Buddha announces that the mummified body of Prabhutaratna Buddha is seated within: "Would the audience like to see him?" When everyone clamors for a view, the Buddha dramatically draws back a creaky bolt and the dead buddha sitting inside speaks up cheerfully, praising Shakyamuni Buddha for wanting to give the White Lotus teaching and inviting him to sit down beside him. The Buddha does so and proceeds to give the True Teaching within this powerful symbolic setting, where the cognitive dissonance of death in union with life must be held in awareness by the beholder.[14] (When we consider the dramatic vision at the heart of this most popular of Universal Vehicle scriptures, it is hard to comprehend why most East Asian Mahayana Buddhists persist in regarding the visionary spectacles of tantric mandalas as somewhat outlandish and even un-Buddhist!)

Finally, in the *Flower Garland (Avatamsaka) Sutras*,[15] the Buddha is surrounded by an enormous host of visitors, many from other universes, who sit in flower towers thousands of miles high, flown at more than warp speed across the reaches of space from worlds beyond as many worlds as there are grains of sand in sixty-two Ganges riverbeds (a typical distance). The towers are arranged in the cardinal directions, intermediate quarters, and at the zenith and nadir in a classical mandala formation. During the teaching, Shakyamuni Buddha now and then transforms himself into the sapphire-blue Buddha Vairochana, radiating magic light rays from his forehead that temporarily bestow on each member of the audience the intensely accelerated vision of all their past life experiences and all their future life attainments, up to and including attainment of perfect buddhahood in a future universe and performance of buddha deeds for the sake of all beings. At the end of the teaching, the Bodhisattva Maitreya introduces the hero of the tale, the pilgrim-seeker Sudhana, a banker's son, into the magical tower of Vairochana. There Sudhana beholds the entire evolutionary history of Maitreya from a self-centered, unenlightened being to a functioning buddha. At the same time, the panorama unfolds in infinite resonant variations in every atom of the universe, each containing infinite micro-universes, which contain infinite worlds where infinite living Sudhanas enter infinite Vairochana towers and behold infinite evolutionary panoramas of infinite living Maitreyas.

In sum, every single Mahayana scripture conveys the most extraordinary visions that engage the audience in creating a setting and developing a receptivity that makes it possible for them to receive the Universal Vehicle teaching of the profound freedom and magnificent destiny of all living beings. This is a graphic and lavish use of the mandala principle to create an ideal space, an exalting architecture, an initiatory model environment, wherein the practitioner is consecrated, imaginatively transformed and transported, and elevated to a new potential for understanding and sensitivity which is the goal of the teachings of transcendent wisdom and universal compassion.

It is unlikely that any concrete evidence will turn up to support the Tantric Buddhist claim that the Apocalyptic Vehicle was present, nested esoterically within the Universal Vehicle, itself nested within the Monastic Vehicle, right from the Buddha's time. Nevertheless, the mandala principle can undeniably be encountered at work within the texts of the Universal Vehicle, manifested by the Buddha's artistic creativity, which enfolds the audience in the optimal setting for understanding and incorporating his teaching.

THE MANDALA IN THE TANTRAS
The Initiation Ceremony

Tantric initiation is a consecration, like the anointment and coronation of a monarch, as indicated by the Sanskrit *abhisheka* (literally, anointment). It has often been translated from the Tibetan term *dbang bskur ba* (conferral of authority) as empowerment, which connotes that some sort of power is being transferred from guru to disciple. The power, however, the wisdom, lies in the innate genius of the disciple. Her anointment with the elixir of the wisdoms of all the buddhas blesses her with confidence to manifest her own innate genius and burdens her with the responsibility of doing so, giving up immature dependencies on anything external. So perhaps the older translation, "initiation," is less objectionable, as the four consecrations are truly initiatory. They initiate one not into any ordinary status in ordinary society, but rather into extraordinary status in the cosmic society of the buddhas.

The four main initiations provide a framework for the path of practice that follows.

CONSECRATION	BASIS	PRACTICE	RESULT
Vase (many parts)	Body Vajra (purge perception of ordinariness of body)	Creation Stage	Body of Emanation
Secret	Speech Vajra (purge perception of ordinary speech; dissolve neural energy–mantra duality)	Perfection Stage (to mind-isolation, superficial magic-body)	Body of Beatitude
Wisdom-Intuition	Mind Vajra (purge blocks to dawn of all appearances as bliss-void-indivisible)	Perfection Stage (to ultimate clear light)	Body of Truth
Word	Body-Speech-Mind Vajra	Perfection Stage (of two-reality-indivisible union)	Vajradhara Union Body

Initiation is conferred at the outset of tantric practice as its indispensable entrance, but the first consecration rarely "takes" fully in the beginning disciple. This is because it requires highly disciplined visual abilities actually to enter the mandala palace, perceive the building and ornaments in vivid detail, see the guru-deity there with his retinue of many deities, see oneself as a transformed deity with three faces and six arms, and so on. Indeed, the real mandala is in its own special universe, not in the ordinary world. It is an achievement even to find it with the inner vision, using the various objects, symbols, and persons in the room or temple in which the consecration

is conferred in ordinary reality. Further, the initiate must understand all the vows and pledges involved in the complex tantric ethic, and must have the ability to keep them, which itself requires a high degree of yogic mastery over mind, senses, and body.

The first consecration "takes" according to the ability of the devotee, and permits her to engage in the practice that eventually will enable her to attain full consecration. On both conscious and subliminal levels, the yogini is installed in the presence of her own enlightenment—physically, verbally, mentally, and intuitively. While she may still be far from full realization, her subsequent practice proceeds in the goal-vehicle orientation, the context that perfect enlightenment is immediate and practice removes blocks to its realization, rather than in the context that enlightenment is somewhere "beyond," as something to be reached by means of a path. Practice thus proceeds in the context of cognitive dissonance, being "there" immediately yet not there experientially.

The five systems (skandha) of matter, sensation, conception, emotion, and consciousness actually become, respectively, Vairochana and mirror-intuition, Ratnasambhava and equality-intuition, Amitabha and individuating-intuition, Amoghasiddhi and all-accomplishing-intuition, and Akshobhya and ultimate-reality-perfection-intuition. These transmutations are listed below according to a typical Unexcelled Yoga tantra, the *Esoteric Communion*.[16]

SYSTEM	EMOTION	BUDDHA	ELEMENT	WISDOM
matter	delusion	Vairochana	diamond	Mirror Wisdom
sensation	pride/avarice	Ratnasambhava	gold	Equality Wisdom
conception	lust	Amitabha	ruby	Individuating Wisdom
emotion	jealousy	Amoghasiddhi	emerald	Wonder-working Wisdom
consciousness	hate	Akshobhya	sapphire	Absolute Perfection Wisdom

It is important to understand that every element of any mandala environment is created symbolically from the visionary substance of enlightened attainments, so it becomes a kind of enlightenment "memory-palace," an architecture that encodes states of awareness and positive energies. To quote a typical explanation, the mandala is

> square because Buddhas and non-Buddhas are not unequal in ultimate reality. The four foci of mindfulness make the eastern door. The four authentic exertions make the southern door; the four magic feet make the western door; the five spiritual faculties such as faith make the northern door. The inner Vajra garland (on the circular beam) stands for the perpetual turning of the wheel of Dharma of the Apocalyptic Vehicle. The purity of the consciousness aggregate and the Ultimate Realm Wisdom are Great Glorious Vajrabhairava. The sequence of the ritual actions of the Master are the commitments of defense, eating, rites of food sacrifice, protection, reversal, visualization of the mandala, and introducing disciples.

The Creation Stage

Within the aesthetic context of the protective womb of the mandala, one practices the Unexcelled Yoga, with its Creation and Perfection Stages. Elaborate and difficult as it is, the Creation Stage is just preparatory for the Perfection Stage, which goes beyond imagination and actually accomplishes the transition from the coarse world of ordinary reality to the subtle realm of extraordinary reality. The Creation Stage is systematic creative visualization that forms the stuff of vision into a universe of fulfillment. It can be learned through the scheme known as the "three conversions": conversion of death into the Body of Truth, the between (bar do) into the Body of Beatitude, and life into the Body of Emanation. These conversions emerge from two main foundations: the critique of the habitual perception of the outer environment as the ordinary life cycle, and the critique of the ordinary sense of being an imperfect and dissatisfied self. In their place, pure perceptions and conceptions are systematically cultivated. A cultivated "pure perception" and a "buddha-self-image" open the door to the outer world of great bliss, wherein nature itself is spontaneously fulfilling, and to the inner "jewel self of selflessness," able to help all beings. I will sketch the process of meditation in a typical *Esoteric Communion (Guhyasamaja) Tantra* Creation Stage session.

Prepare a quiet place, sit comfortably cross-legged, with vajra,

bell, drum, and offering vessels of various kinds, especially a skull bowl *(kapala)* filled with ambrosia (representing your ordinary skull as a vessel containing the rest of your ordinary body chopped up and cooked into the nectar of immortality which delights and nourishes all beings). Invoke the lineage gurus, from Vajradhara Buddha through Nagarjuna and the other great adepts and yogis down to one's personal vajra guru. They appear one by one, merge into the guru and thence into oneself. Then dissolve the universe and yourself through the vision of death as the Body of Truth, visualizing a kind of black hole that swallows everything into absolute voidness, with the mantra OM SVABHAVA SHUDDHA SARVA DHARMAH SVABHAVA SHUDDHO 'HAM! All becomes a perfect void, before this universe began. Offering sequences emerge and dissolve in this void. In this realm of void, wind stirs, fire explodes, water shimmers, earth crystallizes, and the four elements thus emerged fuse into a vajra-cross of the five wisdom colors, blue (center), white (east), yellow (south), red (west), and green (north). It radiates tiny vajra-thunderbolts like laser bullets, which form an impenetrable enclosure hanging in this void. A lotus-moon seat emerges in the center upon which oneself as a terrific Akshobhya emerges embracing a consort of similar appearance, both with three faces, blue, red, and white; and six arms, holding vajra, bell, and wheel in the right hands, and lotus, jewel, and sword in the left hands. Then the ten fierce deities are evoked from HUM syllables and stationed around the enclosure, emerging from your heart one by one. Each of them is seen in vivid detail. Then, oneself as central couple dissolves, experiencing death/Body of Truth as fearless oneness with the void, experiencing the between/Body of Beatitude as jewel seed-syllables radiant on moon-disc, and then entering the womb of life/Body of Emanation in the immeasurable mandala palace.

The mandala palace itself is made of diamond, gold, ruby, emerald, and sapphire. It is systematically built up as a square with four gates with intricately decorated arches and doors, with jewel pendants hanging from the eaves, dharma-wheels and deer over the arches, and a second-story pagoda in the center of the roof, surmounted by a lighthouselike giant jewel and an upright five-pronged vajra. Offering goddesses, deities, and yogis dance on the balcony and hover in the sky around the building. Within the building, whose floor and ceiling have the same directional colors as the original vajra-cross, are thirty-one seats. The whole building is made of five wisdoms, appearing like a jewel holograph.

It is precise in its details. One must practice combining one-pointed concentration with artistic vividness until the building can be seen in every detail, and one experiences being within it, opening the doors, walking around, looking up at the ceiling and molding ornaments. Like Vimalakirti's house, it is experienced as a real structure, yet it can be seen through like a holograph, from inside and outside without any obstruction. The palace has the radiance and glory of the jeweled lotuses, jeweled rays, and jeweled trees in the *Land of Bliss Sutra*, as it is a manifestation of the same beatific-body.

Now, life/emanation-body is completed as one arises on the central dais within the palace as Akshobhya Buddha father-mother, oneself as both father Akshobhya and mother Sparshavajra, surrounded by an inner circle of eight deities, Vairochana and so forth; an outer circle of eight bodhisattvas and four goddesses, Samantabhadra and the others with Rupavajra and her companions; and with the ten terrifics in the doors, corners, above, and below. When this splendor is fully manifest, all the innumerable living beings stream into the palace from all directions drawn by jewel-laser beams from the sapphire HUM syllable in one's heart, are themselves transformed into *Esoteric Communion* Akshobhya father-mothers, and then stream forth into pure land mandala universes of their own.

This outlines the main Creation Stage, and must be contemplated until clarity of detail and stability of vividness are achieved. At that point, one can experience the full aesthetic range of the Three Bodies, the fruition of enlightenment in the alternate reality one has imaginatively constructed. The next section of the Creation Stage involves moving from this still coarse level of imagination to subtler levels, progressing inwardly to the realm of the Perfection Stage. One focuses on oneself as the central Akshobhya, then brings all the thirty-two deities in miniature to points in one's own body, stabilizing them there vividly. One then dissolves them and oneself into clear light in a specific progression, designed to rehearse the dissolution of the elements of the body at death.

One becomes a clear void again with the mantra OM SHUNYATA JNANA VAJRA SVABHAVATMAKO 'HAM! Then on a sun, moon, and lotus seat, glowing diamond, ruby, and sapphire OM AH HUM letters emerge as oneself. They merge together and absorb the entire universe, changing into a giant moon, with the mantra OM DHARMADHATU SVABHAVATMAKO 'HAM! Then again the white OM, red AH, and blue HUM pop out of the moon like bubbles and send light rays outward, drawing back all buddhas and bodhisattvas and goddesses and terrifics who dissolve into the moon. Then, with the mantra OM VAJRATMAKO 'HAM! the moon turns into a diamond vajra with OM AH HUM in its center.

The whole sequence is slowly and vividly visualized from within and without simultaneously, oneself actually being the moon, syllables, and vajra, rehearsing imaginatively the experience of the five enlightenments in the after-death between. One then takes rebirth as a white *Esoteric Communion* Vajradhara, and emanates replicas of oneself all over the universe, permeating the fields of all living beings with the blissful spirit of enlightenment. Then, one visualizes one's own body as the mandala palace, identifying parts of the body, even intestines and bones, as parts of the building, and then again populating it with the thirty-two deities.

The front, back, right, and left sides of my body become the mandala palace's four corners. My mouth, nose, anus, and urethra become the four doors. My five-colored pure energies that carry thoughts become the fivefold wall. My tongue-cognition becomes the precious molding. My intestines become the jeweled nets, and the sinews become the half nets. Parts of my white spirit of enlightenment become the half-moons, my eye cognition becomes the mirrors, and my nose cognition becomes the garland of flowers. My tongue sense becomes the bells, and the body sense becomes the yak-tail fans adorning the nets and half-nets. My ear and body cognitions become the banners and victory-standards flying on the parapet. My eight limbs, calves, thighs, forearms, and biceps become the eight pillars. My belly becomes the mandala's interior vases. My ear senses become the half-moon-vajras in the corners. My pure five systems become the five colors of the mandala palace. My four vital points: secret spot, navel, heart, and nose-tip, become the four triumphal arches, and my eye senses become the dharma-wheels above them, with my mind cognition the deer, and my nose sense the triumphal arches' banners. My mind sense becomes the central lotus. Thus all parts of my body become parts of the mandala palace.

From my crown to hair line, the reality of the material system, white OM transforms into white Vairochana, Akshobhya-crowned, with three faces, white, black, red, and six arms holding wheel, vajra, and white lotus in the right hands and bell, jewel, and sword in the left hands. From my hairline to throat, the reality of the notion system, red AH transforms into red Amitabha, Akshobhya-crowned, with three faces, red, black, white; six arms, upper left hand holding the bell with the stem of a red lotus, upper right hand holding the lotus open at the heart, other right hands holding vajra and wheel, and left hands holding jewel and sword. From throat to heart between my two breasts, the reality of the consciousness system, blue HUM transforms into blue Akshobhya, Akshobhya-crowned, with three faces, blue, white, and red; six arms holding vajra, wheel, and lotus in the right hands and bell, jewel, and sword in the left hands. From heart to navel, the reality of the sensation system, yellow SVA transforms into yellow Ratnasambhava, Akshobhya-crowned, with three faces, yellow, black, and white; six arms holding jewel, vajra, and wheel in the right hands, and bell, yellow lotus, and sword in the left hands. From navel to groin, the reality of the emotion system, green HA transforms into green Amoghasiddhi, Akshobhya-crowned, with three faces, green, black, and white; six arms holding sword, crossed vajra, and wheel in the right hands, and bell, green lotus, and jewel in the left hands.

This kind of imaginative meditation on the jewel-like plasma of buddha-forms continues in precise detail, becoming ever more subtle, until one can visualize the entire palace and thirty-two occupants as contained within a drop of seed on the tip of the genital, and hold that precise holograph stable for several hours. The three kinds of drop mandalas—syllable, symbolic implement, and deity—are described in the same text:

All the gods of the body mandala are satisfied, the melted drop falls into the consort's lotus and that very drop becomes the source of all deities, the Transcendent Lords and the Five Clans and so on. One part of the drop becomes a BHRUM which transforms into the square four-doored mandala palace, replete with all its characteristics, including seats. The other part of the drop becomes the thirty-two parts, each upon a lotus seat. They instantly transform into HUM, KHAM, OM, SVA, AH, HA, LAM, MAM, BAM, TAM, JAH, HUM, BAM, HOH, MAIM, THLIM, OM, OM, OM, HUM, OM, SAM, HUM, HUM, HUM, HUM, HUM, HUM, HUM, HUM, HUM, HUM. These thirty-two seed-syllables respectively transform again into vajra and vajra, wheel, jewel, lotus, vajra-cross, wheel, vajra, blue lotus, vajra-cross, red mirror, blue lute, perfume-conch, food vessel, wheel-marked naga tree flower, wheel, jewel, jewel, lotus, lotus, sword, sword, staff, vajra, lotus, vajra-cross, sword, vajra, blue vajra-marked staff, black vajra-marked staff, vajra and vajra. These implements one after another again transform into the thirty-two deities. On the central seat I myself, peaceful blue-black Akshobhya.

At that point, one is ready for the Perfection Stage yogas. The Creation Stage meditation sessions always end with the dissolution of whatever visionary realms have been created into the clear light of universal voidness. They also rehearse—at a certain point in the process of offerings—the experience of the four joys, which are offered to all the assembled buddha-deities. These joys are central to the practice of the Perfection Stage.

The Perfection Stage

Mandalas as recognizable architectural realms of divine inhabitants are not the focus of the Perfection Stages, though their vivid and stable imaginative creation is presupposed. Rather, the Perfection Stages focus on the subtle realms of physical experience and mental awareness. Containing the energies of these stages requires special relative enlightenment spirit drop mandalas, relative/ultimate-boundary body mandalas, and ultimate enlightenment spirit, inconceivable, and formless mandalas. In order to explain these most subtle forms of mandala, it is necessary to sketch the Perfection Stage, which is surrounded by deep mystery and perhaps even deeper confusion.[17]

The Creation Stage ends in a form of body-isolation. The yogin's body is perceived as perfectly divine, utterly isolated from any ordinariness. The practitioner of, for example, the *Esoteric Communion Tantra* actually experiences herself as the three-faced, six-armed *Esoteric Communion* Akshobhya, feeling as hers the faces, eyes, and arms, and the consort's body as well, just as we have sensations of our ordinary body now. Though purified, beautiful, and blissful, body-perception is still on the coarse level.

The gateway for entering the Perfection Stage realm is the subtle visualization of the Creation Stage. By using body mandalas to visualize tiny deities in every pore, the yogin loses the discrete sense of the coarse body and feels every atom of every part of his body and senses as a buddha-deity. The visualization explodes beyond the organizing capacities of the ordinary imagination and the practitioner perceives himself as a jewel-like subtle body, a vajra body, composed of nerve-channels, neural wind-energies, and endocrine drops (*rtsa rlung thig-le*). The subtle mind is the instinctual consciousness of the three luminances. Finally, he attains an extremely subtle body and mind which are called, respectively, the indestructible drop body (a kind of gene-stream of subtle wind-energies), and the mind of translucency—these being ultimately a nondual body-mind. It is useful to schematize the gross, subtle, and extremely subtle bodies and minds:

	BODIES	MINDS
gross	elemental body	fivefold sense consciousness
subtle	nerve-channels, neural wind-energies, endocrine drops	three luminances (luminance, radiance, imminence) involved with eighty natural instincts
extremely subtle	wind-energy carrying clear light and staying in indestructible drop	mind of translucency and indestructible drop (nondual body-mind)

As we can see, the mandala emerging from the relative enlightenment spirit drops of the secret initiation is a kind of subtle energy–cracking complex, with five nerve wheels ranged along a triple tube, with an enormous number of small tubes emerging to anchor the structure to the usual five-limbed coarse body.

There are 72,000 nerve-channels radiating outward from the heart wheel. There are two main right and left channels, *rasana* and *lalana*, running from nostrils to genital tip, as does the all-important central channel, the *avadhuti*. In ordinary beings it is squeezed shut by the lalana and rasana channels, which entwine it tightly. Blossoming from the stem of the avadhuti are five main wheels (*chakra*): at the brain, a 32-petalled lotus; at the throat, a 16-petalled lotus; at the heart, an eight-petalled lotus; at the navel, a 64-petalled lotus; and at the genitals, a 32-petalled lotus. Although the nerve-channels are not physiological in a coarse materialistic sense, still the Creation Stage yogini with her powerful imagination is able to open them as real structures through holographic visualization.

The mandala-palace and deity-body visualizations function as coarse imagination patternings that subliminally open the subtle neural patternings of the subtle wheel system. By the time the yogin reaches the Perfection Stage, this internal opening process is consciously pursued. There are ten neural wind-energies: five main energies—vital, respiratory, digestive, muscular-motor, and evacuative—and five branch energies, which power the senses.

These energies are now perceived as deities. The endocrine drops are the male hormonal essence as in semen and the female hormonal essence as in ovum, called white and red spirits of enlightenment.

The extremely subtle indestructible drop is positioned in the center of the heart wheel on the avadhuti channel. Its mind of clear light is the Buddhist soul, which is not only relative and impermanent in its changing, genetic process, but also indestructible in that it takes rebirth after dying. Finally, it attains the infinite life of buddhahood after beginningless wanderings through samsara in various life-forms, but it does not exist as an absolute. It is the ultimately subtle self of selflessness, the ultimate subjectivity which realizes the objective clear light of universal voidness. Its body is extremely subtle wind-energy, a kind of virtual energy, like the energy of a dream image in the mind. At this extremely subtle level there is no body-mind duality.

I know of no source that explicitly discusses the following speculation. It seems likely that the architecture of the various mandalas is based on dimensions and proportions that resonate with the structure of the internal subtle structure of nerve-channels, perceived from the perspective of the extremely subtle body-mind inhabited by stabilized contemplative awareness. Thus, when the practitioner is able to visualize himself as a mustard seed–sized Vajrasattva or Manjushri, seated on a lotus-sun-moon cushion in the center of the heart complex, with a great shining blue-red jewel tube above, flowering in the 16- and 32-petal lotus complexes at throat and brain, the tube continuing below to the 64-petal lotus at navel and 32-petal lotus at the genitals—he becomes, as it were, a resident of a giant jewel space-station, with tunnels and catwalks and round towers. The experience of the jewel mansions of the mandalas of the various Unexcelled Yoga tantras will have prepared him aesthetically for this type of experience. Once the yogin is capable of being secure in such a space, he is ready for the yogic processes of melting and dissolving through developing the inner fury-fire (*gtum mo*), cultivating the ecstatic joys in the various centers of the subtle nervous system, and keeping those joys in balanced concentration on the ultimate void nature of reality.

The Perfection Stages are numbered variously, usually as five: body-isolation, speech-isolation, mind-isolation (also called self-consecration or magic-body), translucency or clear light, and union.

The body-isolation Perfection Stage yogini reaches a point of stable concentration, where she experiences the process normally undergone only at the time of physical death. Coarse inhalation and exhalation stop entirely. She traverses four dissolvings: earth into water, water into fire, fire into air, air into gross consciousness (identified with ether or space in some systems), accompanied by subjective signs called mirage, smoke, fireflies, candle flame. Then the coarse consciousness dissolves into the subtle levels of consciousness, the three intuitions—luminance (*aloka*), radiance (*alokabhasa*), and imminence (*alokopalabdhi*). The state of the extremely subtle mind is called translucency or clear light (*prabhasvara*), and is the same as enlightened awareness—infinite, eternal, beyond subject and object, nondual, blissful, peaceful, all-pervading, and so on—the level of living diamond. The subjective signs of the progressive dissolving of one state to another are called moonlit clear sky, sunlit clear sky, radiant black clear sky, and pre-dawn clear sky.

	DISSOLUTION	SIGN
1	earth to water	mirage
2	water to fire	smoke
3	fire to air	fireflies in sky
4	air to consciousness	candle flame
5	to luminance	moonlit clear sky
6	to radiance	sunlit clear sky
7	to imminence	radiant black clear sky
8	to clear light	pre-dawn clear sky

The melting down of coarse consciousness through luminance intuitions into clear light is accomplished by bringing all the neural wind-energies into the central channel. All the white and red life-drops, withdrawn from the outer nerve-channels, come along with them, usually entering the central channel through the mid-brow aperture, or through the tip of the genital. An unprepared being would actually die at this point: once the tightly closed central channel is broken open, the vital energies would leave the gross body. Because the knots around the central channel have been carefully loosened, the yogin avoids this danger and the subjective death experience becomes the threshold of the clear light realm of the bliss and vision of enlightenment.

Heat from all the captured vital energies blazes from the navel up the central channel: when the energies and drops melt down from the brain wheel and permeate the throat wheel, the yogin feels intense joy locked in luminous void. When they descend to the heart wheel, he feels supreme joy in extreme void. When they reach the navel wheel, he feels intense joy in great void. When they reach the genital wheel, his total being becomes orgasmic joy in universal void, immersed in clear light awareness, the virtual clear light. The yogin then feels the four joys and four voids in the reverse order, as the energies and drops gradually move back up through navel, heart, throat, and brain wheels, where reverse-order joy merges with universal void a second time.

The whole process is called the Waking State Truth Body Merger of the Nine Mergers (*bsre ba dgu*) precept, from an oral tradition brought to Tibet by the translator Marpa.

After enjoying the orgasmic joy universal void clear light, the yogini resurrects herself by traversing the eight levels, the eight signs (pre-dawn sky and so forth), in the reverse order, from subtle to coarse. This process is called the Waking Beatific Body Merger. The energies then emerge from the central channel and circulate in the gross body, which the yogini experiences as if being reincarnated in the former body. She perceives a couple in sexual union, falls in love with the partner of the opposite gender, enters into the union as if being conceived, and then reanimates the old body. This is the Waking Emanation Body Merger.

The next stage is speech-isolation (*vagviveka*) or vajra repetition (*vajrajapa*). It has the precise aim of unraveling the knots constricting the central channel. The wind-energies are united with mantras, especially OM AH HUM, the vajras of body, speech, and mind of all buddhas. This union is cultivated with refined meditative technique until the yogini feels she has become a vibrant, divine OM AH HUM, alone on a moon-disc in the center of an empty universe. When such concentration reaches the stability of trance, breathing stops effortlessly and the dissolution process begins again. It is much more powerful now that the channel knots are looser—the orgasmic joy in universal void can occur even in the central chamber of the heart complex.

The opening of the heart wheel is dangerous if forced, and so the vajra repetition takes years for even the most able practitioners. Here we can see what Milarepa was doing for so long in Himalayan caves, implementing this highly sophisticated spiritual technology in the context of the vivid mandala of the Hevajra Buddha archetype-deity. At this level of attainment, the subtlest mind of great bliss is mobilized as the ultimate subjectivity for the realization of the still merely virtual clear light of universal void.

Beyond this mind-isolation, the yogin has the power to postpone an immediate return to coarse body reality by mobilizing the subtle wind-energies to arise in the subtle magic-body, shaped by stabilized visualization into the archetype-buddha-body cultivated in the coarse reality mandala palace, replete with the signs and marks of buddhahood. This is the Waking Beatific Body Merger. With that magic-body, the yogin can explore universes in virtual reality, accumulating lifetimes of merit from virtuous deeds and wisdom from deep insights, all in an accelerated evolutionary timeline. It is this special dimension, made possible by the Perfection Stage, that makes tantra the superquick path to buddhahood.

When the yogini does reactivate her previous coarse body, it is called the Waking Emanation Body Merger. Subsequently, when she falls asleep, she enters the clear light automatically in the Sleep Truth Body Merger. When she dreams, she arises in the Sleep Beatific Body Merger. When her dream body returns and she wakes, it is the Sleep Emanation Body Merger. If she decides to leave her former ordinary body due to some circumstance, she will employ the three Death Mergers, death being the final Body of Truth, the between the Body of Beatitude, and reincarnation the Body of Emanation.

WAKING YOGA PRACTICE

Waking Truth Body Merger	meditational attainment of clear light
Waking Beatific Body Merger	arisal in neural energy body back from clear light via imminence to earth
Waking Emanation Body Merger	reentry of gross body by subtle body as if through crown of head; respiration restarts

SLEEP YOGA PRACTICE

Sleep Truth Body Merger	dissolution yoga at sleep moment into clear light
Dream Beatific Body Merger	arisal from clear light into dream body, neural energies formed as rainbow body of *Esoteric Communion*
Waking Emanation Body Merger	dream body reenters gross body, awakens, respiration begins again

DEATH YOGA PRACTICE

Death Truth Body Merger	entrance into clear light after gross body death
Between Beatific Body Merger	arisal in neural energy deity body in between state
Birth Emanation Body Merger	incarnation into seeds of father and mother, choosing an embodiment suitable for Unexcelled Yoga tantra practice, *vis à vis* planet, country, class, accessibility of teachings, etc. (human form preferable to pure land incarnation)

The mind-isolation/self-consecration stage that makes the magic-body practices possible requires the yogin to meditate with a sexual consort. Sexual union between coarse bodies is the only situation, other than death, in which all the neural wind-energies dissolve into the central channel. Thus the consort is essential to reach such depth in this life. For the process to work, both partners must be at the same stage, neither using the other as a mere instrument. Both must have the same visualization, the same understanding, the same motivation, and the same concentration. Therefore, the genuine performance of this level is rather rare. The magic-body is still called impure at this stage, and is described by five similes: dream body, Vajrasattva's mirror image, moon in water, phantom, and bubble.

Beyond the third-stage magic-body, the yogin has no need of coarse forms of mandalas or even the subtle body of channels, winds, and drops. The stabilization of wind-energies and thoughts is so complete, imagination itself can engineer any structures or feelings that it wishes. Therefore, the last two-and-a-half stages are sometimes called the Great Seal Stage, the Great Perfection Stages, or even just the Great Perfection, and are sometimes thought of as a separate stage of formless and inconceivable tantra. As this is the very culmination of the path, there is also a natural, though quite dangerous, tendency to jump impatiently straight to this level, comparable to someone thrilled at seeing astronauts in action who just can't wait to experience spacewalking personally. The sensible procedure is to join a space program, train in many disciplines and knowledges, get on a shuttle mission, learn how to wear a space suit, and finally go out into space. In the meantime, the aspiring astronaut might safely dream of spacewalking without a suit, and not come to any harm. In the tantric disciplines, the astronauts are "psychonauts" and the mandala palace is their flight simulator. The archetype buddha-deity body, with its symbolic multiple heads, arms, and legs, its many eyes, and so on, is like a practice space suit. The subtle body of channels is the actual space shuttle. The stabilized imagination, holding subtle energies in the fixed pattern of the archetype-deity, generates the magic-body that is the actual space suit. And the space in which one walks is the sky of the clear light, virtual and actual, the miraculous infinite realm which nondually enfolds all space and time. Its vacuum contains all energy, all knowledge, all bliss, and unites one with the awareness of all enlightened beings throughout time and space. Like the astronaut in 2001 and 2010, it may ultimately be possible to walk there without any suit or ship. But it is clearly impractical for someone to stow away on a space shuttle, sneak to a hatch, and jump into the void without a suit!

The fourth stage of clear light or enlightenment begins after six to eighteen months of the performance of magic-body deeds. The yogin constantly plunges into clear light, returns to the coarse body, teaches beings, and develops the field of beings in the old society. Eventually, he reaches the actual or objective clear light, no longer the virtual clear light. In this objective clear light, the magic-body attains the irresistible path that transforms the deepest unconscious instincts. There is the usual series of joys and voids. At the moment of arising from objective clear light into the imminence-intuition of the reverse order, he becomes a saint *(arhat),* gains the pure magic-body, gains the liberation path, abandons all emotional obscurations, and achieves the experimental union.

The fifth stage of perfect union is accomplished after further immersion practice conquers the cognitive obscurations, the blocks to omniscience that prevent even the highest bodhisattva from sharing the buddhas' total understanding of all the levels of absolute and relative realities and the causality of the relative worlds of beings. The "union" is the union of the pure magic-body, perfection of compassion as infinite orgasmic joy, with the objective clear light, perfection of wisdom as universal voidness intuition.

It is not absolutely essential to know the general nature of the advanced levels of the paths of tantric contemplation in order to appreciate the beauty and refinement of the various mandalas of two and three dimensions we encounter as artifacts of various Asian civilizations. But it does enhance our appreciation to gain an overview of the entire scientific and artistic enterprise that provides the context for the production of mandalas. It heightens our respect for those civilizations when we recognize how their advanced enterprises provided a general knowledge of the aesthetics of visual art, literature, architecture, dance, and music. It is amazing to see how tantric arts employ all aspects of material culture to reach into the depths of the human nervous system, into the most intimate feelings and sensitivities of people, in order to

share with them the evolutionary opportunity to unfold their own inner potential to the maximum degree allowed by their own predispositions, the tolerance of the economy, and the level of culture of their era.

THE MANDALA PRINCIPLE IN THE ARTS AND SCIENCES OF ASIA

To return to what we might call the ordinary world (perhaps much less ordinary when we consider the extraordinary opportunities some suggest it affords), we now can look back around the landscapes of Asia to see the resonance of tantra's deep aesthetic principles—the mandala principle—in the daily lives of people from all walks of life in many civilizations.

The cosmogony and cosmogram of any people provides them with a world-picture or world-model within which their feelings, perceptions, and thoughts take place. Our insight into the mandala principle allows us to see that this is not only a matter of vague cultural imagery contributing to a vague personal sense of things, but is rather a matter of imaginal world-patterning directly affecting inner structuring of physical and mental senses through actual brain organization. Thus, a world-picture of a flat earth with its fixed ups and downs relates directly to the inner ear's sense of balance. When some heretic suggests the world might be round, is careening through a solar system, is spinning swiftly on its axis, and so forth, it can threaten inherited brain organization and cause visceral intolerance reactions, as we have seen again and again throughout human cultural history. Similarly, the structures and rituals of a people tend to conform to the cosmic pictures they share.

What emerges from the tantric sciences and arts of India that spread through Asia is a self-conscious employment of the mandala—or cosmogrammatic—principle to reinforce new values within various preexisting cosmic realities and value systems. Cultures based on sacrificial cosmogonies developed religions, rituals, city plans, architectures, and other arts and crafts that reinforced the sacrificial sense of life, wherein the individual life-purpose was subsumed into the collective survival purpose. With cultural developments that made life more secure for collectivities and allowed individuals leisure and liberty to seek an inner evolutionary purpose of their own, tantras—evolutionary technologies—became possible.

These tantric technologies then naturally moved into the artistic media, redesigning the life worlds of the peoples. They relativized all cosmogonies and cosmograms, adding new heavens and new earths to the world-model. They loosened the social structures, beginning with the families, by adding more individualistic life roles, such as the monastic and the ascetic. They expanded the aesthetic possibilities open to individuals, developing sciences and arts that provided new models: pleasure-science *(kamashastra)* to allow a greater range of sensual and sexual experience; wealth-science *(arthashastra)* to allow a greater range of social experience, with more fluid economic and political arrangements; theater-science *(natyashastra)* to allow a greater range of emotional experience; experiential science *(yogashastra)* to allow a greater range of interior experience through contemplative discipline; artistic science *(shilpashastra)* to allow a greater range of development of material culture; literary science *(alamkarashastra)* to allow a greater range of perceptual and conceptual sensibility; moral science *(dharmashastra)* to allow a greater range of religious and ethical development; philosophical science *(siddhantashastra)* to allow a greater range of intellectual development; and finally, evolutionary science *(tantrashastra),* to allow a greater range of evolutionary development within a given human life.

Thus when we look at a reliquary stupa from a Greco-Indian civilization of the Indus valley, a sculptural tableau from Bengal a thousand years later, a temple model from Bihar, a pagoda model from China, new visions of heavens from Tibet or Japan, cosmograms and city plans from various civilizations, everywhere we can see the workings of the mandala principle. We can see an evolving cosmogrammar that brings the inner achievements of each culture's deepest and most daring self-transformers, yogis and yoginis, monks and nuns, each culture's psychonauts, into resonance with the broader material culture that forms and transforms the general sensibility of the civilization.

This of course opens up the discussion of our contemporary cosmogrammar, the structures that shape our culture, the great mall at Washington, D.C. with its monuments and memorials, the plan and buildings of our fair island city, our internet-interwoven world. But this we must leave for further explorations of the mandalas operating in our daily lives.

NOTES

1. Paraphrased from the *Dhammapada*.
2. I translate the Sanskrit term *Hinayana* as Individual Vehicle or Monastic Buddhism, in that it facilitates the individual's focus on his own liberation. *Mahayana* is rendered as Universal Vehicle or Messianic Buddhism, as it encourages the individual to undertake the universal liberation of all beings. *Vajrayana* translates as Diamond Vehicle or Apocalyptic Buddhism because it aims to liberate all beings immediately, putting an end to the ordinary time of the world of suffering in the apocalyptic revelation of the enlightened universe.
3. From the *Lalitavistara Sutra*.
4. Dharmakaya = Body of Truth, Sambhogakaya = Body of Beatitude, Nirmanakaya = Body of Emanation.
5. See Robert A. F. Thurman, trans., *The Holy Teaching of Vimalakirti: A Mahayana Scripture* (University Park: Pennsylvania State University Press, 1976).
6. *Vajrapanjara Tantra*. This particular verse is often quoted by Tibetan scholars. See Tsong Khapa and Dalai Lama, *Tantra in Tibet* (London: Allen and Unwin, 1988).
7. Mentioned by Jangkya Rolway Dorjey in the auto-commentary to his ecstatic poem, "Recognizing the Mother Void," translated by this author and published in *Vajra Bodhi Sea* (1976).
8. See Ferdinand D. Lessing and Alex Wayman, trans., *Khedrupje's Fundamentals of the Buddhist Tantras*, 2d ed. (The Hague: Reidel, 1975).
9. The story of Yashas, the first lay disciple of the Buddha, occurs in all *Vinaya* sources.
10. Especially in the later accounts, such as the *Lalitavistara Sutra*.
11. As recorded in the Pali *Parinibbana Sutta*.
12. For the *Heart Sutra*, see Geshé Rabten, *Echoes of Voidness*, translated and edited by Stephen Batchelor (London: Wisdom, 1989). For the *25,000 Line Transcendent Wisdom Sutra*, see Edward Conze, *Large Sutra on the Perfection of Wisdom* (Berkeley and Los Angeles: University of California Press, 1982).
13. See Edward Cowell, *Buddhist Mahayana Texts* (New York: Dover, 1968).
14. For the *Lotus Sutra*, see Bunno Kato et al., *The Threefold White Lotus Sutra* (New York: Weatherhill, 1983).
15. See Thomas Cleary, *The Flower Ornament Sutra* (Boston: Shambhala, 1995).
16. *Guhyasamaja Tantra*. All *Esoteric Communion* excerpts are from my translation of the visualization manual by Jey Tsong Khapa (1357–1419), partially published in Robert A. F. Thurman, *Essential Tibetan Buddhism* (San Francisco: Harper, 1995).
17. My presentation of the Perfection Stage in the *Guhyasamaja Tantra* here parallels the Perfection Stage in the *Guhyagarbha Tantra*, published in the introduction to my translation of the *Tibetan Book of the Dead* (New York: Bantam, 1994).

APPENDIXES

GLOSSARY

SELECTED BIBLIOGRAPHY

INDEX

APPENDIX A

The central focus of our exhibition and study is how the mandala's diagrammatic shape in two dimensions translates into three-dimensional space and structure—how a pattern of balance turns into a world of harmony. The Kalachakra mandala in painting is perhaps the most widely known of Tibetan mandalas, while the three-dimensional palatial environment for which it is the blueprint is only dawning in public awareness. In this section we present an essay from Barry Bryant on the process of the creation of the sand mandala by the highly trained monk artists of Namgyal monastery, as well as photographs of the mandala palace commissioned by H. H. the Thirteenth Dalai Lama in Tibet. —R.A.F.T.

CHART OF THE FIGURES REPRESENTED IN A KALACHAKRA MANDALA

MUSEUM OF FINE ARTS, BOSTON (CATALOGUE NO. 28)

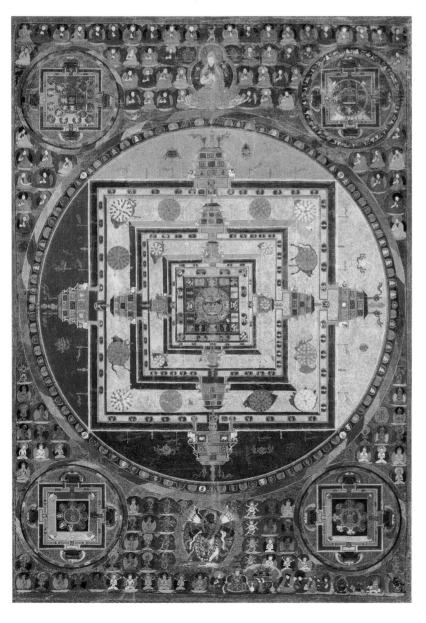

1. Kings of Shambala

2. Lamas who have upheld the Kalachakra lineage

2a. Tsong Khapa

3. Thirty-two deity Manjuvajra Guhyasamaja Mandala

4. Thirteen deity Yamantaka Mandala

5. Kalachakra father-mother

6. Eight shaktis

    ] = Great Bliss Mandala

7. Male and female buddhas

8. Male and female bodhisattvas

9. Guardian protectors

10. Eighty Speech Mandala deities
    (Seventy-two female deities and eight father-mother deities)

11. Twelve animals carrying thirty deities each symbolizing the three hundred deities of the days of the year, according to the Kalachakra system

12. Offering goddesses

13. Eighty-eight charnel ground deities

14. Vajravega

15. Red Raktayamari Mandala

16. Vajrapani Mandala

17. Various deities associated with Kalachakra

18. Standard Geluk order protectors

19. Desi Sangyey Gyatso and Mongolian patrons

20–21. Father-mother figure associated with Kalachakra teachings

22. Mind Mandala Palace

23. Speech Mandala Palace

24. Body Mandala Palace

25. Kalachakra father-mother

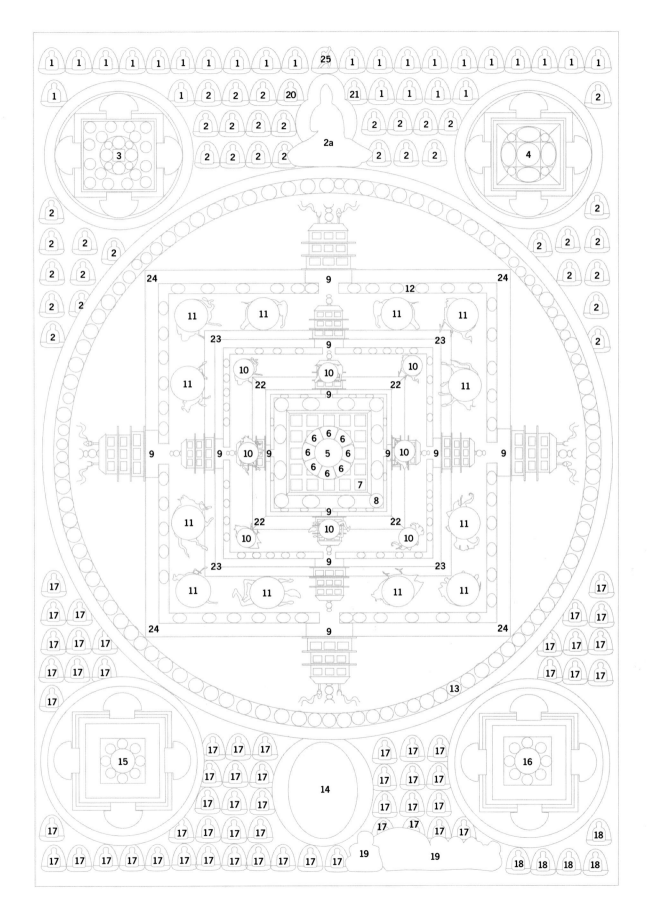

Views of a three-dimensional Kalachakra mandala in the Potala Palace, Lhasa, Tibet

Monks creating a Kalachakra sand mandala in Dharamsala, India

CHART OF THE ELEMENTS IN A KALACHAKRA SAND MANDALA

1. Mandala of Great Bliss with a lotus flower center housing six deities including Kalachakra and Vishvamata, Akshobhya and Prajnaparamita, Vajrasattva and Vajradhatvishvari surrounded by eight shaktis

2. Mandala of Enlightened Wisdom

3. Mandala of Enlightened Mind

4. Mandala of Enlightened Speech

5. Mandala of Enlightened Body

6. Animals representing the months of the year

7. Half vajras with half-moons, each adorned with a red jewel

8. Geometric shapes symbolizing the six elements, which are the five physical elements (fire, water, earth, air, and space) plus the wisdom element

9. Thirty-six offering goddesses represented by Sanskrit seed-syllables

10. Double vajras which correspond to each of the four directions

11. Hanging garlands and half-garlands of white pearls surrounding the eight auspicious signs

12. Downspouts, which release rainwater from the palace roof

13. Half-lotus petal design symbolizing protection from afflictive emotion

14. Seven animals pulling a chariot that holds two protective deities; seven elephants are here in the western quadrant

15. Western gate of the Mandala of Enlightened Body

16. Offering garden

17. Earth element circle filled with interlocking crosses representing earth's stability

18. Water element circle containing wavelike ripples

19. Senge Kangpa Gyepa, an eight-legged lion pulling a chariot containing two wrathful protective deities

20–21. This whole area is known as the cemetery grounds and is composed of the fire element circle (20) and the wind element circle (21)

22. Wheel of Dharma with a pair of protective deities in the center

23. Sanskrit seed-syllables

24. Space element circle containing an interlocking fence of golden vajras

25. Wisdom element circle, also known as the Great Protective Circle

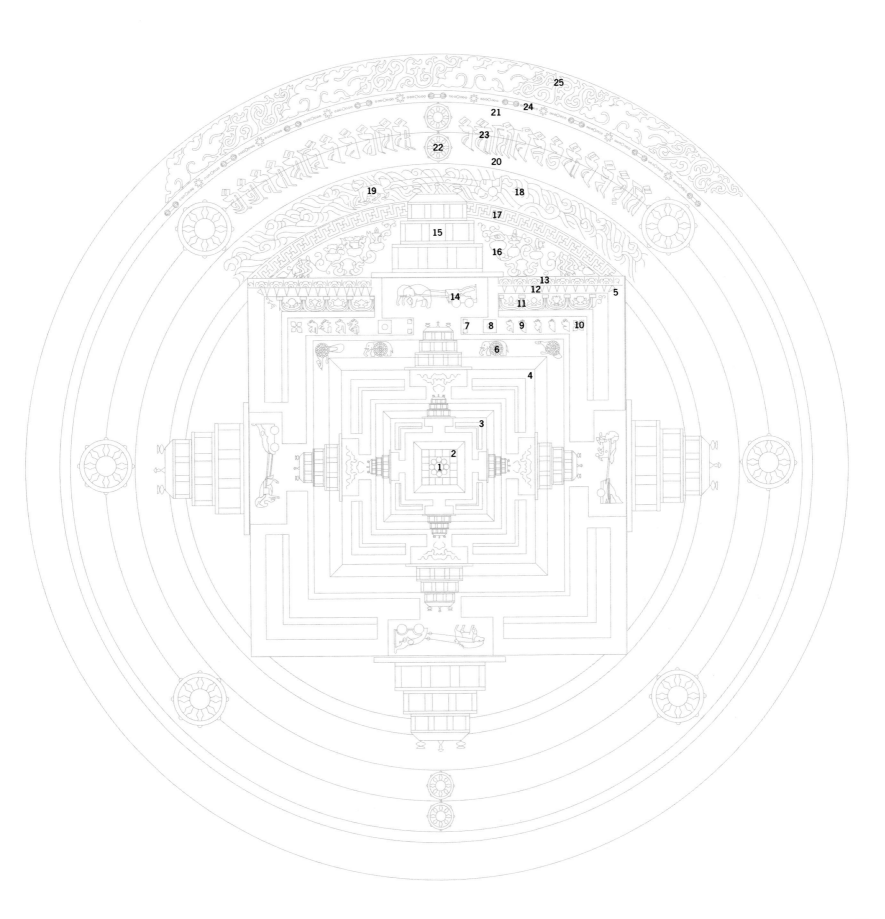

THE KALACHAKRA SAND MANDALA
(EXCERPT FROM *THE WHEEL OF TIME SAND MANDALA*)

BARRY BRYANT

(Throughout this text, references to the sand mandala chart on pp. 152–153 have been added in brackets.)

The Kalachakra Sand Mandala is a two-dimensional representation of the five-story palace of the deity Kalachakra. It is one of the colored-particle mandalas, a generic term used to describe any mandala made of crushed materials such as jewels, flower petals, rice, or, most commonly, sandlike stone ranging in density from soapstone to marble.

The Kalachakra Sand Mandala consists of five square mandalas, one within the other, surrounded by six concentric circles. Each square mandala represents one of the five levels of Kalachakra's palace. The largest is known as the Mandala of Enlightened Body.

Painting the Mandala

During the initiation, four monks begin applying the sand to the Kalachakra mandala. They are joined by four more monks as the mandala grows larger. The drawing of the mandala is completed on the second day [of the Kalachakra Initiation] and from the third to the eighth day the monks apply the sand for a total of seven days' work.

The Kalachakra sand mandalas depicted in this book measure 6^1/$_2$ feet in diameter. No matter what the mandala size, the work of applying sand is always started at the very center and progresses outward. In the early stages of painting, while the sand mandala is smaller than three feet in diameter, the monks sit on the outer part of the unpainted mandala base, always facing the center.

In the tantric teachings, it is said that if one steps over or on or sits on a ritual instrument, image of the deity, scripture, or mandala, it is not only a sign of disrespect but is also equivalent to the breaking of one's vow. To avoid such an incident, the monks recite prayers each day, visualizing the lines of the drawing of the mandala as being lifted above the mandala base and remaining suspended above it until the workday is completed. When the mandala is about halfway completed, the monks then stand on the floor, bending forward over the base in order to apply sand.

Traditionally, one monk is assigned to each of the four quadrants. At the point where the monks stand to apply the sand, an assistant joins each of the four. Working cooperatively, the assistants help by filling in areas of color while the primary four monks outline the other details with sand.

The monks memorize each detail of the mandala as part of Namgyal monastery's training program. It is important to note that the mandala is explicitly based on the scriptural text, and that there is no creative invention along the way. Any creative inspiration is manifested within the perfecting of skill.

At the end of each work session, the monks dedicate any artistic or spiritual merit accumulated from this activity to the benefit of others. This practice prevails in the execution of all ritual arts.

There is a good reason for the extreme degree of care and attention that the monks put into their work: they are actually imparting the Buddha's teachings. Since the mandala contains instructions by the Buddha for attaining enlightenment, the purity of their motivation and the perfection of their work allows viewers the maximum benefit.

Each detail in all four quadrants of the mandala faces the center, so that it is facing Kalachakra. Thus, from the perspective of both the monks and the viewers standing around the mandala, the details in the quadrant closest to the viewer appear upside down, while those in the most distant quadrant appear right side up.

Generally, each monk keeps to his quadrant while painting the square palace. When they are painting the outer six concentric circles, they work in tandem, moving all around the mandala. They wait until an entire cyclic phase or layer is completed before moving outward together. ... This insures that balance is maintained, and that no quadrant of the mandala grows faster than another.

In the tradition of Namgyal monastery, sand is applied through the end of a long, narrow metal funnel,

or *chakpu* in Tibetan. Each chakpu is part of a pair; one is used to rasp a corrugated metal strip attached to the other, which is filled with sand. This rasping vibrates the chakpu, causing the sand to be released through the smaller opening.

There are different sizes of chakpus. Those with larger openings, through which sand flows liberally, are used for filling in background space and making thick walls and borders. Other chakpus, with smaller openings for the elaboration of fine details, release sand grains in more delicate streams. The flow of sand is also controlled by the speed and pressure used in rasping. Slow, soft rasping causes the sand to trickle out, even just a few grains at a time, while harder, faster rasping causes it to pour out in a steady stream. Mastery of this technique takes great patience and diligent practice.

The chakpu is not grasped; rather, it lies flat in the open palm of the left hand (assuming one is right-handed), with the thumb placed on top to balance it. The rasping side is facing up. The hand itself is supported by the mandala base, which allows for ease of lateral movement from the wrist. The right hand holds the second chakpu, which does the actual rasping. The monks interpret the sound of the hollow metal chakpus being rubbed together as an expression of the Buddhist concept of emptiness, or the interdependence of phenomena.

The two chakpus symbolize wisdom and compassion; their action symbolizes the Buddhist practice. The result of their action, the completed mandala, symbolizes the enlightened state.

Traditionally, in ancient times, the Indian Buddhist sand painters used their fingers to apply sand, as monks in some Tibetan monasteries do today. The chakpus used by the Namgyal monks were invented in the eighteenth century by the Tibetans.

Special wooden scrapers, known in Tibetan as *shinga*, usually measuring one to four inches wide, are used to adjust and straighten lines of sand into narrow, raised walls and other demarcations. The shinga are also used to remove excess sand.

Within Namgyal monastery, before a monk is permitted to work on constructing a sand mandala he must undergo at least three years of technical artistic training and memorization, learning how to draw all the various symbols and studying related philosophical concepts.

Because of the monks' level of concentration and the high degree of cooperation among them as they work, mistakes or accidents are rare. But occasional errors made within the mandalas may be discovered too late for correction by the wooden scrapers. In such a case, a piece of cloth is placed over the large end of a chakpu, and a monk will gently suck up the sand of the mistake into the chakpu.

Viewers of the sand mandala often ask, "What keeps the sand in place?" The answer is that the layers of sand simply rest one upon the other. Gravity is the only adhesive used.

Entering the Mandala

During the Kalachakra Initiation, the ritual master introduces the students to the deities. His description of the mandala begins at the outermost concentric circle, moving inward toward the center of the innermost mandala, wherein he describes the principal deity Kalachakra and his consort Vishvamata.

We begin our description of the mandala in the center and move gradually outward, the way it is painted. Every motif depicted in the mandala has symbolic meaning and can be interpreted on various levels.

The Mandala of Enlightened Great Bliss

The Mandala of Enlightened Great Bliss [see chart, no. 1] represents the transcendent experience of enlightened awareness. To the practitioner, this is understood as the consummate union of Kalachakra and Vishvamata; that is, the union of wisdom and compassion.

1. The mandala represents the fifth and uppermost level of the five-story, three-dimensional palace of Kalachakra.

2. A solitary monk sitting in the eastern quadrant of the mandala begins by painting the outline of a small circle at the center, which is the center of the lotus flower. ...

3. In the center of the lotus flower, five layers of colored sand are painted, one on top of the other. ... These layers serve as cushions for the central deities, Kalachakra and Vishvamata ... The eight petals surrounding the center of the lotus flower are filled with green sand. The petals serve as seats for the eight shaktis. ...

The Mandala of Enlightened Wisdom

The Mandala of Enlightened Wisdom [see chart, no. 2] represents the subtle mind.

1. The mandala represents the fourth level (second to the top) of the five-story palace of Kalachakra.

2. It contains sixteen black pillars, four in each direction. ... The spaces between these pillars form sixteen chambers.

3. Four of the sixteen chambers are located in the four cardinal directions and four in the four corners. Each houses an eight-petaled lotus flower, which acts as a cushion for a pair of male and female peaceful deities represented by dots of colored sand. ...

4. The remaining eight chambers located between the chambers of the eight pairs of deities house eight white vases, each between two white lotus flowers.

The Mandala of Enlightened Mind

The Mandala of Enlightened Mind [see chart, no. 3] represents the coarse mind, which perceives relative truth and absolute as one. It houses 70 deities.

1. The Mandala of Enlightened Mind represents the third level of the five-story palace of Kalachakra.

2. The area surrounding the light blue border of the Mandala of Enlightened Wisdom, which appears as four trapezoids, is called the "color space," because the colors of this area correspond to the colors of their respective directions.

3. The white square surrounding the color space is called the lhanam, which, in Tibetan, means the actual place where the deity resides. This lhanam is home to twelve pairs of deities, represented by colored dots. ...

4. The area immediately beyond the border surrounding the white lhanam is a very narrow passageway in the colors of the four directions.

5. Surrounding the passageway are the foundation walls, composed of three parallel lines. ... These three foundation walls represent the three vehicles or paths: the Theravada, the Mahayana, and the Vajrayana. ...

6. At each of the four entrances, a pair of wrathful deities resides on a red or white lotus flower. ...

7. The white areas just beyond the foundation walls are known in Tibetan as the dhoenam. ...

8. At each of the four corners of the dhoenam there is a multicolored double vajra, which symbolizes the four means of a bodhisattva to gather students. ...

9. The red area outside the dhoenam is decorated with a golden rosary of precious jewels. This area symbolizes wisdom, and the jewels represent method.

10. The next three areas beyond this red area contain architectural decorations and offerings. ... There are four gates in the Mandala of Enlightened Mind. Each is made up of eleven levels which appear as three stories. ... These eleven levels represent the levels leading toward the realization of Buddhahood. ...

The Mandala of Enlightened Speech

The Mandala of Enlightened Speech [see chart, no. 4] represents the pure qualities of the Buddha's speech. ... This mandala houses 116 deities.

1. The Mandala of Enlightened Speech is the second level of the five-story palace of Kalachakra.

2. The color space, the white lhanam, and the narrow passageway of the Mandala of Enlightened Speech are the same as those of the Mandala of Enlightened Mind.

3. This lhanam contains 80 deities. ...

4. Five parallel colored lines beyond the narrow passageway serve as foundation walls of this mandala, giving structure to the four entrances. ...

5. In each of the four entrances of the Mandala of Enlightened Speech are colorful offering goddesses. ...

6. The four white, L-shaped dhoenams ... found just beyond the five colored walls are home to 36 dhoema, or offering goddesses, represented here by Sanskrit seed syllables. ...
The four gates of the Mandala of Enlightened Speech are the same as the gates of the Mandala of Enlightened Mind, except the pillars are decorated with multicolored sand. ...

The Mandala of Enlightened Body

1. The outermost mandala, the Mandala of Enlightened Body [see chart, no. 5], is the bottom level of the five-story palace of Kalachakra. Here are housed 536 deities, including the 108 deities depicted in the cemetery grounds.

The three areas surrounding the parapet of the Mandala of Enlightened Speech are, moving outward, color space, lhanam, and the narrow passageway of the Mandala of Enlightened Body.

2. 360 deities reside in this lhanam. Here we see 12 animals, each carrying one of the 12 months of the year.

Each animal [see chart, no. 6] bears a lotus with 28 petals. Each of the 28 petals supports a deity representing one day of the 28-day lunar cycle, and a pair of deities in union, symbolizing the full moon and the new moon, resides at the lotus center. Thus, every figure bears a lotus flower which serves as a cushion to 30 deities representing the 30 days of the lunar month, totaling the 360 days of the lunar year.

3. The five colored lines surrounding the narrow passageway of the Mandala of Enlightened Body ... represent the walls. Here the five walls symbolize the five powers: faith, effort, memory, concentration, and wisdom.

4. The four white, L-shaped dhoenam found just beyond the five colored walls are home to 36 offering goddesses, represented by Sanskrit seed-syllables [see chart, no. 9]. The colors of the syllables correspond to the colors of their respective directions, with the exception of one syllable in each direction. East and north each have a single blue syllable, and the south and west a single green syllable. All of these goddesses are known as Chir-Doema in Tibetan.

5. Just as in the Mandalas of Enlightened Mind and Enlightened Speech, in each corner of the dhoenam of the Mandala of Enlightened Body double vajras are painted in four colors which correspond to each of the four directions [see chart, no. 10]. Half-vajras with half-moons, each adorned with a red jewel, appear on either side of the entrances [see chart, no. 7].

6. In the dhoenam and in the space between the Sanskrit seed-syllables and the half-vajras are geometric shapes symbolizing the six constituencies, which are the five elements (water, earth, fire, air, and space) plus the wisdom element [*see chart, no. 8*]. On either side of the eastern entrance, two gray crescent shapes symbolize the element of wind, and to the left of the entrance a green circle symbolizes space. On either side of the southern entrance, two red triangles symbolize fire. On either side of the western entrance, two yellow squares decorated with the green swastika (a symbol of stability) symbolize earth, and on the right side of the entrance a blue circle symbolizes the wisdom element. Two white circles on either side of the northern entrance are symbolic of the element of water.

These four geometric shapes represent the types of tasks performed by the Buddha and the protective deities:
- pacifying (circle)
- increasing (square)
- empowering (bow)
- enforcing (triangle) ...

7. Just as in the Mandala of Enlightened Speech, the red area beyond the dhoenam is decorated with a golden rosary of precious jewels. The red area symbolizes wisdom, and the jewels represent method. The different shapes of the jewels represent the four tasks performed by the Buddha, described above.

8. The next three areas beyond this red area contain offerings to Kalachakra [*see chart, no. 11*]. ... In the first, a black background is filled with hanging garlands and half-garlands of white pearls, symbolizing the qualities particular to the Buddha which are not shared by others. These pearls spill out of the mouths of decorative designs meant to evoke sea monsters. At the ends of the garlands are offerings symbolized by dots representing mirrors, yak-tail fans, bells, half-moons, and flowers. Inside the garland of white pearls are offerings to the deity.

The choice of what kind of offerings to depict here is left to the artists, as an expression of their devotion to Kalachakra. They can draw symbols representing the five sensual objects, eight auspicious signs [*as seen here*], eight auspicious substances, seven precious royal emblems, or the five Buddha families.

The next area, painted blue and representing the sky, contains triangular shapes representing downspouts, which release rainwater from the palace roof [*see chart, no. 12*].

The last and outermost detail of the Mandala of Enlightened Body is a white parapet with a half-lotus petal design outlined in black [*see chart, no. 13*]. The parapet symbolizes protection from afflictive emotions as well as fortification against obstructions on the path. ... At the entrance of each of the four quadrants of the Mandala of Enlightened Body, seven animals pull wheeled chariots, each carrying a pair of wrathful protective deities on a green lotus flower cushion [*see chart, no. 14*]. These chariots are symbolic of attaining the realization of emptiness mind through the conceptual mind. ... The four gates ... are essentially the same as those in the Mandala of Enlightened Mind and the Mandala of Enlightened Speech [*see chart, no. 15*]. ... On each side of the square palace are four crescent-shaped gardens formed by the innermost circle surrounding the palace [*see chart, no. 16*]. ... Each crescent contains various offerings to the deities.

The Six Outer Circles

The six concentric circles that surround Kalachakra's square palace represent the six constituencies. From the innermost to the outermost circle are the elements of earth, water, fire, wind, space, and wisdom.

1. The first, innermost circle of earth is characterized by the earth color, yellow [*see chart, no. 17*]. An unbroken chain of green swastikas, or interlocking crosses, represents the earth's stability. ...

2. The water circle is white [*see chart, no. 18*], containing continuous, wavelike ripples and two mythical animals, each pulling a chariot. In the east we see Khading Anila, king of the bird kingdom; in the west is Senge Kangpa Gyepa, otherwise known as the "eight-legged lion" [*see chart, no. 19*]. Each chariot bears a lotus flower upon which sits a pair of wrathful, protective deities in the form of dots. ...

3 and 4. Beyond the water circle, the pink and gray circles represent the elements of fire and wind respectively [*see chart, no. 20–21*]. This whole area is known as the cemetery grounds. The ten wheels include one red wheel in each of the four cardinal directions, one white wheel at each corner, and an additional two red wheels, one each in the east and west [*see chart, no. 22*]. Seated on a lotus flower at the center of each wheel is a fierce female deity embraced by a male naga deity, each represented by a dot of sand. In each great cemetery are eleven Sanskrit seed-syllables [*see chart, no. 23*]. These 88 seed-syllables represent the main elemental spirits among millions.

5. Surrounding the dark gray wind circle is the green circle representing the element of space, which has an interlinking fence of golden vajras [*see chart, no. 24*]. The vajras depicted here have five points and are joined by a golden decorative design. This protective circle of vajras prevents evil spirits from harming the practitioner.

6. The outermost circle is also known as the "great protective circle," as well as the mountain of flames, circle of wisdom, or blazing light [*see chart, no. 25*]. Symbolic of the wisdom element, it has a design of 32 alternating sections of shaded colors. The red and yellow are drawn as fire, whereas the blue and green are drawn as leaves. These four colors, plus white used in shading, represent the rays of the Buddha's five wisdoms in the form of a rainbow.

There is no border surrounding the great protective circle, illustrating that there are no limitations for the deeds of the Buddha and that his great compassion for all beings is extended with complete equanimity.

Dismantling Ceremony

At the conclusion of the Kalachakra Initiation on the twelfth day, the sand mandala is dismantled. During its presentation as a cultural offering, the mandala is usually dismantled on the final day of the exhibition as follows:

1. Prayers request that the deities return to their sacred abodes. Once the monk presiding over the prayers is satisfied that the deities have left, the dismantling process is begun.

2. All 722 deities symbolized by the colored sands are skillfully picked up one by one by the head monk as he recites the Kalachakra mantra, and the sand is placed in an urn.

Deities that are singular or in a yab-yum grouping are picked up individually. For larger groupings of deities, the monk simply passes his fingers through them, picking up a portion of each. The dismantling is done in the reverse order of the making of the sand mandala. The head monk begins at the perimeter, picks up the protective deities in the cemetery grounds, and works clockwise toward the center until he removes Kalachakra and Vishvamata.

3. Next, starting at the outer edge of the eastern quadrant, the head monk cuts through the mandala along the Brahman lines with a vajra, thus cutting the energy of the mandala. This is repeated, in turn, in the southern, western, and northern quadrants, and along the diagonal lines in the southeast, southwest, northwest, and northeast corners.

4. Standing in each of the four directions, the monks sweep the remaining sand into the center of the mandala. It is then placed in a specially prepared urn.

The monks carry the sand to the river or ocean, in a procession. At the water, the monks sit on a carpet with the vase containing the sand in front of them. In their prayers, they request that the protective spirits of the water accept the consecrated sand for the benefit of all beings. They visualize the aquatic life blessed by the essence of the sand. When the purified water rises from the ocean to the clouds and falls from the clouds as rain on the land, it purifies the environment and all its inhabitants. The monks then pour the sand into the water, saving some to give to those assembled in celebration of the event. Each person receives a small amount of blessed sand, which he is instructed to take home and place in a body of water or around the foundation of a house for protection.

The dismantling of the sand mandala may be interpreted as a lesson in nonattachment, a letting go of the "self-mind." The ceremony reflects the Buddhists' recognition of the impermanence and transitory nature of all aspects of life. The monks believe that the dismantling of the mandala is the most effective means of preserving it.

APPENDIX B

It seems as if there is no end to the richness of the mandala. Our essays for this volume are presented from the art-historical and Buddhological perspectives, respectively. We would like to present as well a few of the many perspectives of other practitioners, scholars, and analysts—those that have touched us most profoundly in our own explorations of the mandala. We begin with a pithy essay by Matthieu Ricard, a Tibetan Buddhist monk and scholar of the Nyingma tradition. We include a comparison with the sacred sand painting tradition of the Navajo by Peter Gold. And we conclude with a brief excerpt from the writings of Carl Jung, in which he describes his spiritual and therapeutic work with mandalas, reconceived by him as a space within which the unconscious can reveal itself. —R.A.F.T.

INTRODUCTION TO THE PURPOSE AND SYMBOLISM OF THE MANDALA IN TIBETAN BUDDHISM

MATTHIEU RICARD

This introductory explanation of the meaning and purpose of mandala meditation is based on oral teachings received from H.H. Dilgo Khyentse Rinpoche (1910–1991), on words of Guru Padmasambhava as recorded in various spiritual treasures (termas), *and on other Tibetan commentaries, especially those written by Shechen Gyaltsab Pema Namgyal (1871–1926).*

In the Buddhist tradition, mandalas are objects of meditation with a specific purpose: to transform our ordinary perception of the world into a pure perception of the buddha nature which permeates all phenomena. But how does such meditation come about within the whole range of Buddhist practices?

As H.H. the Dalai Lama often stresses, the Tibetan tradition seems to be the main surviving culture in which all the various aspects of Buddhism—Hinayana, Mahayana, and Vajrayana—have not only been preserved, but can be practiced in an integrated, harmonious, and effective way. These three *yanas*, or "vehicles," correspond to the three fundamental aspects of the Buddhist teachings: renunciation, compassion, and pure perception.

Renunciation, the foundation of the Hinayana and therefore the root of all subsequent vehicles, implies the strong wish to free oneself not only from the current sorrows of life but from the seemingly unending sufferings of samsara, the vicious cycle of conditioned existence. Renunciation accompanies a profound weariness, a dissatisfaction with the conditions of samsara, and a heartfelt disillusionment with worldly concerns.

Compassion, the driving force of the Mahayana, is born from the realization that both the individual "self" and the appearances of the phenomenal world are devoid of any intrinsic reality. To misconstrue the infinite display of illusory appearances as permanent entities is ignorance, which results in suffering.

An enlightened being, that is, one who has understood the ultimate nature of all things, naturally feels boundless compassion for those who, under the spell of ignorance, are wandering and suffering in samsara. From similar compassion, the Mahayana student on the spiritual path does not aim for his own liberation alone, but vows to attain buddhahood in order to gain the capacity to free all sentient beings from the suffering inherent in samsara.

Pure perception, or *pure vision*, the extraordinary outlook of the Vajrayana or Adamantine Vehicle, is to recognize buddha nature in all sentient beings and to see primordial purity and perfection in all phenomena. Every sentient being is endowed with the essence of buddhahood, just as oil pervades every sesame seed. Ignorance is nothing more than lack of awareness of this very buddha nature, as when a pauper does not see the golden pot buried beneath his own hut. The spiritual path is thus a rediscovery of this forgotten nature, just as one sees again the immutable brilliance of the sun once the clouds that were masking it have been blown away.

The remarkable feature of the tradition of the three vehicles is how each step of the gradual path is enhanced with the practice of the next. Just as an alchemist might transform a piece of iron, first into copper and finally into gold, so the renunciation of the Lesser Vehicle is ennobled and widened by the universal compassion of the Great Vehicle, which itself becomes infinitely vast and profound when suffused by the view of the Adamantine Vehicle.

It is within the context of Vajrayana that one makes use of mandalas to train into pure perception.

What, then, is meant by pure perception? The way we usually experience the outer world, our bodies, and our feelings is impure, in the sense that we perceive them as ordinary, substantially existing entities. From this erroneous perception comes the negative emotions that perpetuate suffering. However, take a closer look at all these appearances; you will find that they have no true existence. From a relative point of view they appear as a result of various causes and conditions, like a mirage or a dream, but in reality nothing that arises from causes and conditions has any true existence at all. In fact, there is not even anything to appear. As it is said, "He who realizes voidness is the true sage."

If you continue investigating, you will find that there is nothing anywhere, not even a single atom, which has a verifiable existence. Now, to see things otherwise, as truly existing, is the deluded perception underlying samsara—but even that deluded perception itself has never left the realm of voidness. Ignorance, therefore, is no more than a transient veil without intrinsic existence. When you recognize this, there is no impure perception, there is only the limitless display of the buddha's body, speech, mind, and wisdom; and there is no longer any need to try to get rid of the three worlds of samsara or to suppress suffering, because neither samsara nor suffering actually even exist. Once you realize that samsara is as void as a mirage, all the karmic patterns and negative emotions that lie at its root are severed.

Voidness, however, is not just nothingness or empty space, for, as the *Prajnaparamita* says, "Form is voidness, voidness is form; voidness is no other than form and form is no other than voidness." So voidness is inseparable from the display of phenomena. When you realize that true voidness of phenomena, you will spontaneously feel an all-embracing, nonconceptual compassion for all beings who are immersed in samsara's ocean of suffering because they cling to the notion of an ego.

The function of the sense consciousness is simply to perceive its corresponding objects—forms, sounds, smells, and the rest—without adding anything. But the mind then elaborates on these perceptions, thinking, "This is beautiful ... that is ugly ... this might harm me ... that will bring me pleasure." It is neither the form of the external object, nor the eye, nor the visual consciousness that produces these subjective elaborations which in the end lead to the accumulation of karma; it is the mind. A beautiful object has no intrinsic quality that is good for the mind, nor an ugly object any intrinsic power to harm it. Beautiful and ugly are just projections of the mind. The ability to cause happiness or suffering is not a property of the outer object itself—for example, the sight of the same man to two people can cause happiness to one and suffering to the other. It is the mind which attributes such qualities to the perceived object.

When in this way an object encountered by one of the sense organs is perceived by the mind as either pleasurable or offensive, this distorted perception is brought about by grasping. Here is the very basis of samsara. But if there is no grasping, the perception is liberated into wisdom. This is the experience of the purity of nirvana, where it is no longer necessary to reject pleasurable sensations. It is to be free of grasping that one trains in recognizing all appearances as a mandala, a buddha-field with all beings considered as deities. To see things in this way transforms one's perception of the world into primordial purity and allows one to realize all the qualities of buddhahood.

As you examine carefully the nature of all the infinite and varied phenomena in the universe and all the beings it contains, you find that nothing has ever left the continuity of voidness. It is said, "The truth of voidness is the truth of everything." Voidness, in fact, is what makes it possible for infinite phenomena to appear. The phenomenal world we perceive, being the spontaneous display of voidness, is a buddha-field, and all beings are male and female deities. This is the very basis of the Vajrayana.

When one perceives all phenomena as pure, all sense perceptions can be used as the path. When one sees that everything arises out of voidness and thus recognizes the expanse of infinite purity, one no longer discriminates between good and bad, pure and impure; it is all the display of the deity. Friends are the deity, enemies are the deity, all are one as the deity.

First of all, there are several meanings to the word *mandala*. The "mandala of the universe" refers to the whole cosmos, as explained in the *Abhidharma*, with Mount Meru at its center surrounded by the various continents, planets, etc., that constitute the universe. In the course of one's spiritual practice, to accumulate merit, one makes the offering of this "mandala of the universe" to one's spiritual teacher and to all the buddhas and bodhisattvas, as if one were the universal monarch owner of the world.

One also speaks of the "mandalas of the elements," referring to the symbolic shapes of the five elements (space, wind, water, earth, and fire) upon which the universe is said to be built. As for the "mandalas of the sun and of the moon," these expressions simply allude to their circular shape.

In our present context, that of the Mahayoga section of the Vajrayana, *mandala* refers to a divine abode, a perfect buddha-field, and to the enlightened deities, or buddhas, abiding in it. There is a main deity at the center of the mandala, surrounded or not by a retinue of

other deities. As we will see below, each aspect of the divine residence and of the resident deities is highly symbolic and is meant to develop in us enlightened qualities related to the path of enlightenment.

The meditation upon a mandala focuses on the process of visualization. One sees oneself as the main deity, which is considered not as a "god" or as a separate entity, but as the manifestation of one's own wisdom nature. The outer world is seen as a buddha-field and the other beings therein as male and female deities. The purpose of such meditation is to help one to recognize the primordial, unchanging purity of phenomena.

Sentient beings are tormented by countless forms of suffering in the six realms of samsara simply because they fail to recognize the true nature of things. Their usual impure perceptions are totally false delusions without the slightest grain of truth—like mistaking a piece of rope for a snake, or thinking a mirage is really the shimmer of water in the distance.

In any visualization practice one should think that everything has been perfect from the very beginning, that what one visualizes is not an intellectual product but primordially true. Through meditating on the mandala, one comes to perceive the whole universe as a buddha-field, all the sounds in the universe—the sounds of water, fire, wind, the cries of animals, human voices—as the reverberation of mantras, and one experiences all thoughts as the play of awareness.

If one sees the place around one as ordinary, it will not help one. But, if one visualizes it as a pure buddha-field, it will become so, or to be more exact, one will come to realize its natural purity. If one holds in one's mind the visualized mandala, one's manner of perceiving things will gradually change. If, for instance, we see frescoes depicting the life of Lord Buddha on the walls of a temple, our devotion increases. If the walls were simply left plain white, they would inspire nothing. To keep visualizing a place as a mandala or buddha-field works in a similar way.

The purpose of such meditation is thus to uncloud our mistaken perception of things and to realize, instead, their innate purity.

Symbolism of the Deities

To explain the symbolism that is intimately associated with any visualization, let us take the example of Guru Padmasambhava, the Lotus-born. Padmasambhava is considered to be both the union and essence of all the buddhas of the past, present, and future. His body has the indestructible nature of a vajra, or diamond. To indicate his attainment of immortality, he has the countenance of an eight-year-old child resplendent with youth.

He is dressed in the nine gowns/robes that signify his mastery of the nine *yanas*, or vehicles, of the Buddhist teachings. These include a garment of white beneath a blue gown, and the three monastic robes. Over these he wears a brocade cape. The three monastic robes indicate his mastery of the teachings of the Hinayana; the blue

garment indicates his mastery of the teachings of the Mahayana, the path of the bodhisattvas; and the brocade cape indicates his mastery of the secret teachings of the Vajrayana, the Secret Mantra Vehicle.

He has one face, indicating the oneness of absolute truth; two arms, indicating the union of wisdom and means, that is, emptiness and compassion; and two legs, indicating the ultimate sameness of samsara and nirvana. His eyes are wide open, gazing straight into the sky, indicating that he is always of the absolute nature. He is seated in the posture called "royal ease," his right leg slightly extended and his left leg drawn up into a sitting posture. Just as no one would disobey the command of a king, there is no one in the three worlds of samsara who would disobey the command of Padmasambhava, the King of Absolute Wisdom. In his right hand, he holds a five-pronged golden vajra, symbolizing the transmutation of the five poisons (desire, hatred, ignorance, jealousy, and pride) into the five wisdoms.

His left hand, which rests in the mudra of equanimity, holds a nectar-filled skull surmounted by the Vase of Immortality, indicating that Padmasambhava's wisdom is beyond birth and death.

Padmasambhava wears a lotus crown, the five petals of which symbolize the five buddha families (buddha, vajra, ratna, padma, and karma). The lotus crown also indicates that, like a lotus rising unstained from the mud below, Padmasambhava manifested miraculously, unstained by the obscuring process of an ordinary birth. At the top of the hat are a sun and a moon symbolizing means and wisdom, surmounted by a white vulture feather symbolizing the realization of the ultimate view, the Great Perfection. In the crook of his left arm rests the *khatvanga*, or trident, the three prongs of which symbolize the void nature of all appearances, its expression as pure luminosity, and compassion that is all-encompassing.

Boundless and infinite rays of light stream from his body in all the ten directions. From this streaming light Padmasambhava can emanate all the buddha-fields of the ten directions, as well as all the buddhas and bodhisattvas, and all the deities of the Three Roots. All of these are emanations of his wisdom heart. He can in the same way gather them back into his body, thereby demonstrating that they are all one with him.

To correct our ordinary impure perception of phenomena, we should not visualize these deities with gross material bodies of flesh, bone, and blood, but rather, as bodies of light, clear and transparent, with a vivid rainbowlike appearance. They appear clearly, yet are empty of substance, like the reflection of the moon in water. At the same time, we should not feel that they are inert, lifeless displays of rainbow light, but instead that they are completely filled with wisdom, loving kindness, and ability to benefit beings.

Although we visualize Padmasambhava as a main figure surrounded by an infinite retinue, there is in actuality no distinction or separation between them: all deities and beings in the visualization are emanations of Guru Rinpoche himself. Since they are the display of his mind and are thus by nature identical with him, their wisdom and compassion are equal to his own. As Guru Padmasambhava himself said:

The limitless number of peaceful and wrathful deities and their host of retinues correspond to the multiplicity of the methods necessary to transform beings. Since in the sphere of the absolute they all have but one taste, it is enough to meditate on one deity of your choice. Though the deities manifest various aspects of their Body, Speech, and Mind, in reality, doing the practice of one deity or of many deities is the same.

If you attain spiritual accomplishment by realizing one deity you have realized them all. If you realize yourself and the deity to be one, and the deity to be nothing other than the unborn absolute Body, you are then becoming very close to the deity.

However, if you build the deity out of your dualistic clinging to subject and object, feelings of like and dislike will alternate. This is a serious mistake.

Moreover, when deities have many heads and limbs, three heads represent the three *kayas*, six arms the six transcendent perfections, and four legs the four boundless ideas. The diversity of the symbolic objects they hold indicates the manifold aspects of the Dharma. These are some of the many symbols by which all sorts of qualities are represented: there is no ordinary tangible body. When they have one face and two arms, these respectively represent the immutable Dharmakaya, and the union of wisdom and method performing the benefit of beings; two legs represent absolute space and awareness, inseparable. Whichever aspect you are meditating upon, in the absolute Body there is no good or bad, great or small.

Symbolism of the Mandala as a Divine Abode

The palace in which Padmasambhava and his retinue reside is made of various jewels that symbolize the wisdom, compassion, and activity of the buddhas arising as forms and colors to fulfill the hopes and needs of beings. Its perfect square shape indicates that the absolute space of wisdom is without aberration. The four doors symbolize bringing the four boundless thoughts—loving kindness, compassion, sympathetic joy, and equanimity—into the palace of great bliss. They also symbolize the four enlightened activities of pacifying, increasing, mastering, and subjugating. The eight steps at the doors, four on either side of the threshold, indicate that the eight first vehicles, or *yanas*, of Buddhism lead to the effortless Great Perfection, Ati-yoga.

The four levels of the porticoes above the doors symbolize the four attracting qualities of a bodhisattva (to please beings with presents, to please them by saying gentle things suited to their minds, to teach them in accordance with their needs and capacities, to behave and practice in accordance with what one teaches). The golden wheel surmounting the portico symbolizes the ceaseless turning of the Wheel of Dharma. The four pillars of the portico symbolize the four bases of mastering evil and developing goodness: nonvirtue that is not yet born should not be born; nonvirtue already born should be controlled; virtue not yet born should be generated; and virtue already born should be increased. The four rooms on the upper part of the portico symbolize the four types of absorption: interest, diligence, thoughtfulness, and reason.

The walls of the palace, made of five transparent layers of five colors, symbolize the five wisdoms (wisdom of the absolute nature, wisdom of perfect equality, mirrorlike wisdom, all-distinguishing wisdom, and all-accomplishing wisdom), which are purified aspects of the five poisons (ignorance, hatred, jealousy, desire, and pride). They also symbolize the five purifying factors: faith, endeavor, mindfulness, concentration, and insight.

The five-level structure between the walls and the roof symbolizes the five strengths that prevent these five purifying factors from declining. The ornaments of jeweled laticework and filigrees, flowers, silken pendants, mirrors, moon crescents, and yak-tail whisks symbolize seven limbs of awakening.

The eight pillars inside symbolize the eightfold noble path. The eight ornamental structures between the pillars and the beams symbolize the eight aspects of liberation. The four master beams symbolize the four fearlessnesses about abandoning concern for oneself and replacing it with concern for the benefit of others. The twenty-eight secondary beams symbolize the eighteen kinds of voidness and the ten transcendent perfections (generosity, ethical discipline, patience, effort, concentration, insight, means, aspiration-prayer, strength, and primordial wisdom). The roof symbolizes the inconceivable qualities of enlightenment and the pinnacle that crowns it indicates that all the mandalas of the buddhas are included within the expanse of one's own awakened mind.

At the four corners of the roof are canopies, parasols, standards, and banners symbolizing, respectively, the purity of the absolute nature; the sense of responsibility that protects all beings; great compassion; and total victory over ignorance. Tinkling bells ring the sound of emptiness. Dazzling rays of light emanating from the whole palace bear witness to the inexhaustible display of the buddha's enlightened body, speech, and mind.

Fully transparent, made of light, without any shadow, the palace has neither outside nor inside, symbolizing that all phenomena are nothing other than the display of primordial wisdom.

The palace rests upon a cross of vajras symbolizing the indestructible pristine wisdom, which has emptiness as its nature. The twelve prongs of these crossed vajras symbolize the purification of the twelve links of interdependence (ignorance, impulse, consciousness, name and form, sense bases, contact, feeling, craving, drive toward existence, birth, old age, and death). The disc of the sun below the double vajra symbolizes the luminosity of the absolute nature, and the lotus upon which the sun rests symbolizes that this nature is immaculate.

The eight cemeteries that surround the palace symbolize the purification of the eight aspects of consciousness (the basic consciousness, the consciousnesses of the five senses, the consciousness associated with obscuring emotions, and the intellect) and also the eight similes describing the nature of phenomena (like a dream, a bubble about to burst, a reflection, a mirage, an image of the moon on the water, a visual aberration, an echo, and a magical emanation).

The fence of vajras that comes next represents the indestructibility of primordial wisdom, which transcends intellectual concepts.

Finally, the fire of wisdom that surrounds the whole mandala indicates that ignorance and all the other obscurations of the mind have been burnt forever.

A similar symbolism can be described in the case of mandalas of wrathful deities.

The length of this description shows that there is not a single element of the mandala that is fortuitous: everything has a symbolic meaning that the meditator must bear in mind. In this way, meditating upon the mandala is not a mere daydream musing through an enchanting paradise disconnected from reality, but the rediscovery of the very framework of our being and of the phenomenal world. Its purpose is not to escape reality but to see it as it is. It is not to build up additional concepts and fabricate unneeded entities, but to realize the unity of appearances and emptiness. It is not to cut oneself off from others, but to generate boundless compassion for beings who have lost awareness of the buddha nature within themselves.

Shechen Monastery, Baudhanath, 1995

EXCERPT FROM *NAVAJO & TIBETAN SACRED WISDOM: THE CIRCLE OF THE SPIRIT*

PETER GOLD

The Navajos of the high American Southwest and the Tibetans at the roof of the world in the heart of Asia have continued to live what we call a mystical or spiritual way of life, based on how the cosmos properly operates without and within. Tibetan and Navajo life is a process of constant rebalancing and perfecting of one's actions, expressions, and thoughts into an ideal state as befits each culture's ultimate role models: tutelary deities and spiritual heroes and heroines of the past who are remembered and celebrated in myth and ritual. Both groups see the process of living as a spiritual journey, an individual and communal effort to develop each person into the best version of him or herself, in the company of like-minded people dedicated to the integration of matter and spirit.

This journey into ideal understanding and being is so inextricably woven into the practicalities of daily living that in neither culture is there a word for religion as we know it. Our word derives from the Latin *religare*, "to bind back." For Navajos and Tibetans there is no such concept of linking back. They are already fully on the path toward the desired goal of the unity of matter and spirit. Accordingly, both are often heard to say that theirs is not a religion, but a way of life.

By establishing a synthetic dialogue between two exemplary spiritual cultures on opposite sides of the earth, I have attempted to uncover the bare essentials of living a life of the spirit. I have called the principles that underlie the Tibetan and Navajo systems of natural philosophy the Circle of the Spirit. Both systems envision a special kind of circle. It consists of a small, inner circle connected to an outer, larger one by means of four lines, creating four quadrants. It is a spiritual draftsman's diagram, a sacred shorthand for the four universal principles of the spiritual path.

The third principle is called Centering in the Mandala of Self and Cosmos. ... Knowing that real and ideal, ordinary and extraordinary are one, this third principle explores the way in which the two-in-one

unity differentiates into four phases or aspects—just as the cycle of the day and night has four periods, the year has four seasons, and a lifetime has four phases. Tibetans and Navajos artistically render these fourfold states of being, expressing, and knowing in the form of sand-painted circles of the spirit, which herein are called by their universally recognized Sanskrit name, *mandala*.

The third principle has to do with finding one's center in an ideal but terrifyingly real world of ever shifting and changing actions, energies, and thoughts. Although one stands as if at the summit of a sacred mountain— balancing and unifying earth and sky—one must find equipoise and dynamic equilibrium in the immediate reality. Accomplishing this deft balancing act requires becoming fully present at the center of one's sacred reality, the mandalas of self and cosmos. To assist in the process of centering, Navajos and Tibetans employ mandalas that map out—encode—the model of how to abide at the center of one's world-reality. A mandala shows the four naturally occurring vectors of insight and energy operating in the cosmos-at-large and within one's own bodymind, particularly as they manifest in the course of sacred rites and in daily spiritual practices. Despite the almost limitless variation in the sand-painted mandalas of the Tibetan and Navajo spiritual traditions, the directional meanings, colors, and symbols are uncannily similar, encoded as they are according to the same system of logic, the dialectical language of nature.

The two traditions' mandalas serve identical purposes. They are interfaces between a yet-to-be-perfected "real world" outside the mandala and a sacred "ideal world" whose qualities and divine beings temporarily abide in the mandala's inner sanctum. Navajos know these mandalas to be arenas in which the deities, or Holy People, "come and go," interacting with the beneficiary of a particular rite in order to restore his or her body-mind into Beauty, in the manner by which the rite's first spiritual hero or heroine had been trans-

formed. Tibetans focus on a single sand mandala during the course of Tantric Buddhist initiation rites; the mandala serves as a focal point for identifying with ideal characteristics of the initiating deity and transforming the participants into spiritual hero(in)es, or bodhisattvas.

People and Place

Tibetans and Navajos dwell atop two of the world's highest inhabited plateaus. The Tibetan Plateau lies at the heart of Central Asia, and the Colorado Plateau lies at the core of central North America. They rise at the identical latitude and nearly the same longitude but on opposite sides of the earth.

Clearly, in every respect, Tibetans and Navajos see themselves as crystallizations of the substance and energy of their places on earth. They are the inhabitory, indigenous peoples of their respective high lands. With such deep physical roots comes an even deeper conceptual connection with place; their views of reality, their material and spiritual works all reflect this connection. But to attribute their continued presence and cultures solely to the power of place would be a half truth. It is likely that informed choices have been made over the centuries regarding coming to and remaining in these special places above the rest of the world. Why did the ancient Navajos and Tibetans finally make these plateaus their homes? I believe it is because they are places of deep inspiration and insight, in addition to being sites of pure water, readily available food, and abundant materials for shelter. The Tibetan and Colorado plateaus provide endless food for thought in their deep blue skies, powerful weather, vivid rainbows, fresh air, snowcapped mountains, vast plains, deep red rock canyons, massive rivers, varied wildlife, forests, lakes, and springs. In both places, one vividly perceives a balanced partnership of the four primal essences: the elements of earth, water, (sun's) fire, and air. What better physical models can be found for the alchemical distillation of the four primal essences into the fifth essential element, the "quintessence" of ethereal energy and mind, whose attainment is a goal of every spiritual path?

———

The Navajo and Tibetan mandala view of self and cosmos prepares them for the journey into the ideal reality, or primordial ground. The journey and goal are recreated in the teachings and mandalas of all the major Navajo and Tibetan spiritual lineages. Their mandalas are spiritual draftsmen's schematic diagrams of an ideal place populated by deities—ideal beings. By being imbued with holiness, through various ritual procedures in partnership with the powers of the imagination, the sand mandalas transcend their designs to become sacred realities, versions of the ideal state abiding at the primordial ground of Beauty and the Void.

Navajo Sand Mandala Realities

In the Navajo tradition the sand paintings depict Holy People acting in the sacred world. Interacting with them in the myth, but never shown in sand, are certain of the earth-surface walkers. Such a man or woman, youth or maiden, is the chantway's hero(ine) and a model for the Navajo to emulate. The spiritual hero(ine) is a Holy-Person-to-be who will successfully end his or her quest for sacred knowledge by becoming empowered with *diyin* [spiritual power making one immune to fault and harm] and taking the form of one of the generalized, blue-faced yei tutelaries [deities] known as *hashch'baad* (female) and *hashch'baka* (male). By deeply identifying with the sand mandala's Holy People and with the spiritual hero(in)es, the one(s)-sung-over (a person or persons for whose direct benefit the sand mandala rite is being held) begins to take on the ideal thoughts and energies that are, in turn, aspects of the mind and energy of the cosmos-at-large.

Navajos create their compelling schematics of spiritual reality by sprinkling fine grains of naturally colored sand upon a smooth palette of clean, locally acquired sand that is usually salmon or beige in color. The (generally four or more) sand painters—under the direction of the chanter—let flow a thin stream of sand grains from between their thumb and their index and middle fingers. In some cases, flower petals, corn pollen, and even powdered jewels are used.

This is *iikááh*, "where they come and go." It is the sacred arena into which the empowered Holy People arrive and in which they interact with the participants in the rite, just as the spiritual hero(ine) met the divinities during the chantway's formative times. After the powers of the Holy People are invoked—brought into the sand painting—the one-sung-over, whose body-mind they will transform into Beauty, is brought psychologically and physically into the center of the mandala. In this sense, the Navajo sand painting is a ritual osmotic membrane in whose ideal reality the Holy People mingle with those yet-to-be-empowered people for whom the rite is being done.

Depending on the number of sand painters that are available, and the fee paid by the family of the one-sung-over, the sand painting can take either linear (single-line) form or radial (mandala) form. The latter is preferred, although it is not necessary for invoking the powers and blessings of the Holy People. When the sand painting is done in mandala form, the painters sit at the periphery and work from the center out to the four directions. In this way, pulverized colored rock slowly becomes transformed into an altar of the cosmos without and the universe within.

The Whirling Logs Sand Mandala stretches several yards in diameter (almost to the walls of the ceremonial hoghan) on a bed of fine sand. It spreads out, too, on a plane intermediate between earth and sky, a microcosm—painted in Beauty—of the universe. The sand mandala also perches halfway between the two realities of the ordinary (by its sandy form) and the ideal (by what it symbolizes and contains after being consecrated). It is the place of what Gladys Reichard called "spiritual osmosis" between the powers of the Holy People and the "feet, hands, body, mind, and voice" of humanity. The sand painting becomes the arena for the absorption of one into the other. The powers of the yeis (who are designed in sand and invited in by song and prayer) enter the one-sung-over as he or she sits on the western arm of the log cross made of sand ... And through the powers of the imagination the one-sung-over begins to transcend the state of body-mind that is in disharmony with the cosmos. The one-sung-over thus enters, by way of the sand mandala, the ideal reality of the Dreamer [invincible spiritual teacher] and the Holy People.

The crossed logs of sand, surrounded and protected by a rainbow goddess, symbolize the process of balancing and entering within an ideal cosmos. The logs emanate from the project toward the four quarters of a sacred world of Beauty. Little wonder then that the cross within a circle is as widespread a symbol among Native Americans as the mandala is among Asians.

In the actual sand painting, the sand logs intersect at a small bowl of water—placed there to signify the Lake of Whirling Waters. Between the logs, at the semicardinal points, "grow" sandy figures of the four sacred plants. They are colored according to the basic directional scheme (sunwise, beginning in the southeast, white, blue, yellow, black). Their white roots extend into the lake. The lake is the hub, the font of the directional elements and powers that are embodied in the four pairs of male and female yeis riding the cross of logs. The eight tutelaries are the unity of male and female energies and body-mind qualities that compose the Navajos' directional teachings. Visually, the logs and deities create a swastika figure, a symbol of ultimate union.

The Whirling Logs Sand Mandala signifies a cosmos in motion that exists, simultaneously, within one's own body-mind. The cross and its holy riders are the attributes and elements of this ideal universe at the primordial ground. And it is set into motion on the sacred lake through a vision by a spiritual hero who becomes one with the one-sung-over (and with the chanter himself).

This deep identification is supported through various physical actions by the chanter and his assistants toward the one-sung-over, who sits upon the mandala's western quarter facing eastward. At various points in the rite a masked yei figure abruptly enters the hoghan and wets his hands in the liquid from the medicine bowl placed in the outstretched hands of the encircling rainbow goddess. He touches, with his wet and outspread hands, a part of the body of a divinity in the painting—such as its head—then touches the crown of the head of the one-sung-over (and similarly, the other main energy points of the body). The powers of the yeis are transferred to the patient just as they had been given the Dreamer during his journey to the Lake of the Whirling Waters.

The sand mandala is the symbolic medium for restoring the patient to a state of Beauty. For all intents and purposes, the one-sung-over has become the Dreamer through the partnership of his or her imagination, the sand painting, and the powerful ambience created by the songs, prayers, and masked figures, as well as preknowledge of the meaning of the rite. Like the Dreamer, the one-sung-over has endured a long and difficult transition from a flawed, ordinary state of body-mind into the ideal state in which the Holy People abide. The one-sung-over has become restocked with diyin, the spiritual power of universal mind, and thus "re-stored" to Beauty.

This process is sealed by ritually destroying the sand painting after others in attendance have had a chance to bless themselves by placing particles of sand from the bodies of the deities onto the appropriate parts of their own bodies. The Navajo will tell you that the sand mandala is destroyed so that its power cannot be misused and so that the disturbed state of the sand painting does not displease the deities. Since the sand is imbued with power of the Holy People, it must be deposited by the chanter's assistants in the direction of power and protection (north of the hoghan), once the painting is obliterated.

Seen on a more primal level, the painting will continue to serve an important purpose by its very destruction. By this point in the rite, the transformation of the patient's body-mind is already well under way. If, however, the patient were to rely too heavily on a permanent rendering of the ideal realm, rather than his or her own memory and imagination, then the transformation might be minimized. Perhaps that is why the Holy People refused to give the Dreamer the "permanent" mandalas that were painted on clouds.

EXCERPT FROM *MANDALA SYMBOLISM*

C. G. JUNG

The Sanskrit word *mandala* means "circle" in the ordinary sense of the word. In the sphere of religious practices and in psychology it denotes circular images, which are drawn, painted, modeled, or danced. Plastic structures of this kind are to be found, for instance, in Tibetan Buddhism, and as dance figures these circular patterns occur also in Dervish monasteries. As psychological phenomena they appear spontaneously in dreams, in certain states of conflict, and in cases of schizophrenia. Very frequently they contain a quaternity or a multiple of four, in the form of a cross, a star, a square, an octagon, etc. In alchemy we encounter this motif in the form of *quadratura circuli*.

In Tibetan Buddhism the figure has the significance of a ritual instrument (*yantra*), whose purpose is to assist meditation and concentration. Its meaning in alchemy is somewhat similar, inasmuch as it represents the synthesis of the four elements which are forever tending to fall apart. Its spontaneous occurrence in modern individuals enables psychological research to make a closer investigation into its functional meaning. As a rule a mandala occurs in conditions of psychic dissociation or disorientation, for instance in the case of children between the ages of eight and eleven whose parents are about to be divorced, or in adults who, as the result of a neurosis and its treatment, are confronted with the problem of opposites in human nature and are consequently disoriented; or again in schizophrenics whose view of the world has become confused, owing to the invasion of incomprehensible contents from the unconscious. In such cases it is easy to see how the severe pattern imposed by a circular image of this kind compensates the disorder and confusion of the psychic state—namely, through the construction of a central point to which everything is related, or by a concentric arrangement of the disordered multiplicity and of contradictory and irreconcilable elements. This is evidently an *attempt at self-healing* on the part of Nature, which does not spring from conscious reflection but from an instinctive impulse. Here, as comparative research has shown, a fundamental schema is made use of, an archetype which, so to speak, occurs everywhere and by no means owes its individual existence to tradition, any more than the instinct would need to be transmitted in that way. Instincts are given in the case of every newborn individual and belong to the inalienable stock of those qualities which characterize a species. What psychology designates as archetype is really a particular, frequently occurring, formal aspect of instinct, and is just as much an *a priori* factor as the latter. Therefore, despite external differences, we find a fundamental conformity in mandalas regardless of their origin in time and space.

The "squaring of the circle" is one of the many archetypal motifs which form the basic patterns of our dreams and fantasies. But it is distinguished by the fact that it is one of the most important of them from the functional point of view. Indeed, it could even be called the *archetype of wholeness*.

Whereas ritual mandalas always display a definite style and a limited number of typical motifs as their content, individual mandalas make use of a well-nigh unlimited wealth of motifs and symbolic allusions, from which it can easily be seen that they are endeavoring to express either the totality of the individual in his inner or outer experience of the world, or its essential point of reference. Their object is the *self* in contradistinction to the *ego*, which is only the point of reference for consciousness, whereas the self comprises the totality of the psyche altogether, i.e., conscious *and* unconscious. It is therefore not unusual for individual mandalas to display a division into a light and a dark half, together with their typical symbols.

The fact that images of this kind have under certain circumstances a considerable therapeutic effect on their authors is empirically proved and also readily understandable, in that they often represent very bold attempts to see and put together apparently irreconcilable opposites and bridge over apparently hopeless splits. Even the mere attempt in this direction usually has a healing effect, but only when it is done spontaneously. Nothing can be expected from an artificial repetition or a deliberate imitation of such images.

———

We shall now pass on to individual mandalas spontaneously produced by patients in the course of an analysis of the unconscious. ... [T]hese are not based on any tradition or model, seeming to be free creations of fantasy, but determined by certain archetypal ideas unknown to their creators. For this reason the fundamental motifs are repeated so often that marked similarities occur in drawings done by the most diverse patients. The pictures come as a rule from educated persons who were unacquainted with the ethnic parallels. The pictures differ widely, according to the stage of the therapeutic process; but certain important stages correspond to definite motifs. Without going into therapeutic details, I would only like to say that a rearranging of the personality is involved, a kind of new centering. That is why mandalas mostly appear in connection with chaotic psychic states of disorientation or panic. They then have the purpose of reducing the confusion to order, though this is never the conscious intention of the patient. At all events they express order, balance, and wholeness. Patients themselves often emphasize the beneficial or soothing effect of such pictures. Usually the mandalas express religious, i.e., numinous, thoughts and ideas, or, in their stead, philosophical ones. Most mandalas have an intuitive, irrational character and, through their symbolical content, exert a retroactive influence on the unconscious. They therefore possess a "magical" significance, like icons, whose possible efficacy was never consciously felt by the patient. In fact, it is from the effect of their own pictures that patients discover what icons can mean. Their pictures work not because they spring from the patients' own fantasy but because they are impressed by the fact that their subjective imagination produces motifs and symbols of the most unexpected kind that conform to law and express an idea or situation which their conscious mind can grasp only with difficulty. Confronted with these pictures, many patients suddenly realize for the first time the reality of the collective unconscious as an autonomous entity.

———

I need say only a few words about the functional significance of the mandala, as I have discussed this theme several times before. Moreover, if we have a little feeling in our fingertips we can guess from these pictures, painted with the greatest devotion but with unskillful hands, what is the deeper meaning that the patients tried to put into them and express through them. They are *yantras* in the Indian sense, instruments of meditation, concentration, and self-immersion, for the purpose of realizing inner experience ... At the same time they serve to produce an inner order—which is why, when they appear in a series, they often follow chaotic, disordered states marked by conflict and anxiety. They express the idea of a safe refuge, of inner reconciliation and wholeness.

I could produce more pictures from all parts of the world, and one would be astonished to see how these symbols are governed by the same fundamental laws that can be observed in individual mandalas. In view of the fact that all the mandalas shown here were new and uninfluenced products, we are driven to the conclusion that there must be a transconscious disposition in every individual which is able to produce the same or very similar symbols at all times and in all places. Since this disposition is usually not a conscious possession of the individual I have called it the *collective unconscious*, and, as the bases of its symbolical products, I postulate the existence of primordial images, the *archetypes*. I need hardly add that the identity of unconscious individual contents with their ethnic parallels is expressed not merely in their form but in their meaning.

Knowledge of the common origin of these unconsciously preformed symbols has been totally lost to us. In order to recover it, we have to read old texts and investigate old cultures, so as to gain an understanding of the things our patients bring us today in explanation of their psychic development. And when we penetrate a little more deeply below the surface of the psyche, we come upon historical layers which are not just dead dust, but alive and continuously active in everyone—maybe to a degree that we cannot imagine in the present state of our knowledge.

GLOSSARY

Abhirati—Ecstatic Land. The abode of Akshobhya, described in the *Vimalakirti Sutra*. *See also* Akshobhya.

absolute reality—*See* reality.

adept—*See* mahasiddha.

Akanishta (S. Akaniṣṭha)—The highest heaven of the form realm, which lies between the desire realm and the formless realm in the Buddhist cosmos. Akanishta is on the boundary between form and formlessness, the horizon where mass becomes infinite. The Indian monotheistic deity Brahma dwells there; it is also the location of perfected buddhaverses such as Amitabha's Blissful Land (Sukhavati) and Akshobhya's Ecstatic Land (Abhirati). *See also* buddhaverse.

Akshobhya (S. Akṣobhya)—Literally, unshakeable. One of the five transcendent (*tathāgata*) buddhas, the primary lords of the five buddha-clans. Akshobhya is lord of the vajra clan. He presides over the Abhirati buddhaverse in the east and the eastern direction in many popular tantras. He or Vairochana holds the center in the advanced Unexcelled Yoga tantras. Akshobhya represents the transmutation of delusion or hate into mirrorlike wisdom (or reality wisdom), and the purity of the form or consciousness system. His color is white or blue. *See also* archetype-deity, clan.

Amitabha (S. Amitābha)—Literally, infinite light. Transcendent buddha of the west, lord of the lotus clan. He represents the transmutation of lust into discriminating wisdom, the color of ruby, the purity of the conceptual system. Associated with the Buddha Amitayus (Infinite Life) and the Bodhisattva Avalokiteshvara, he is widely known outside of Tantric Buddhism as the buddha of the Blissful Land buddhaverse of the west (Sukhavati), and is worshiped by numerous Pure Land believers throughout Asia. *See also* archetype-deity, clan, Sukhavati.

Amoghasiddhi—Literally, unerring accomplishment. The transcendent buddha of the north, lord of the action clan, he represents the transmutation of envy into all-accomplishing wisdom and the purity of the performance system. His color is emerald. *See also* archetype-deity, clan.

Apocalyptic Buddhism—Tantric or Vajrayana Buddhism, from its usual emphasis on the relatively immediate (within this life or a few lives) possibility of complete enlightenment. *See also* Buddhism, Esoteric Buddhism.

archetype-deity (S. *iṣṭadevatā*, T. *yi dam*)—A deity-form of enlightenment chosen by a tantric practitioner as a model of or template for his or her ideal goal of embodied enlightenment. Such a divine buddha-form is approached as an independent being in some ritual, contemplative, and narrative contexts; it is also adopted as a contemplative role model when the yogin identifies with the deity, seeking to become the deity itself. Thus the deity's form becomes an ideal or archetypal structure of the enlightenment desired by the practitioner. There are five main mild archetype buddha-deities who represent the five wisdoms: Vairochana—reality wisdom; Akshobhya—mirrorlike wisdom; Ratnasambhava—equalizing wisdom; Amitabha—individuating wisdom; and Amoghasiddhi—all-accomplishing wisdom. They also represent the transmutation of the five systems—consciousness, form, sensation, conceptions, and volitions—and of the five poisons—delusion, hate, pride, lust, and envy. *See also* clan, five wisdoms.

arhat (S. *arhat*)—A Buddhist saint who has fully realized selfless reality and is thereby assured of attaining nirvana at death. The ideal type of the Individual Vehicle, which does not focus on the distinction between arhat and perfect buddha.

art (S. *upāya*)—In the broadest sense, an ingenious method, system, or technology. Often translated as means, method, or technique, in the Buddhist context it refers to activity that frees and develops beings for enlightenment. It is the expression of compassion in dynamic action.

Avalokiteshvara (S. Avalokiteśvara)—"Lord who looks with compassion on suffering beings," Avalokiteshvara is a celestial bodhisattva, the archetype of universal compassion throughout the Buddhist world. He became a buddha millions of eons ago, but vowed that he would emanate himself as bodhisattvas *after* his perfect enlightenment of buddhahood, in order to stay close to suffering beings and help them find freedom and happiness. In his celestial forms, he is associated with the Buddha Amitabha and the lotus clan. In his male forms, he is associated with benevolent kingship throughout Buddhist Asia—His Holiness the Dalai Lama is believed to be an emanation of Avalokiteshvara. In his female forms, he is associated with nurturing mother figures such as White Tara and Kwanyin.

beatific-body (S. *sambhogakāya*)—The beatific-body of buddhahood. The evolutionary perfection of buddhahood is said to be experienced in three bodies. The beatific-body represents the ultimate but subtle subjective enjoyment of being a buddha who has realized perfect union with the infinite freedom of ultimate reality. *See also* buddha-body.

bell (S. *ghanta*, T. *dril bu*)—The vajra bell has a half-vajra as its handle and symbolizes the ultimate wisdom that is the source of, and always complements, universal compassion. Wisdom is the understanding of reality, especially the emptiness or voidness of all things. Realizing one's own selflessness results in liberation from egocentric suffering. Ringing the bell prefigures the joyful teaching of the nature of reality that flows spontaneously from perfect wisdom.

between (T. *bar do*)—In colloquial usage, between indicates the whole period between death and rebirth. Technically, it represents the six betweens—life, dream, meditation, death-point, reality, and existence. It also refers to the phase in which the experience of a particular period in one of the six betweens is itself called a between.

bhagavān—*See* buddha, lord.

Bhaishajyaguru (S. Bhaiṣajyaguru, J. Futsunushi no

Mikoto)—The medicine buddha, usually a deep blue color, worshiped in many Buddhist countries as the patron of medicine and healing and the archetype-deity of physicians.

bodhi (S. *bodhi*)—A complete and precise knowledge of the nature of reality and a total sensitivity to the condition of others. *See also* enlightenment.

Bodhi tree—The pipal tree in Bodhgaya under which Siddhartha Gautama took his last seat as an ordinary self-centered person and attained unexcelled perfect enlightenment.

bodhicitta (S. *bodhicitta*)—The spirit of, or will to, enlightenment. When a person develops the universal, messianic motivation to become someone who can perfectly satisfy the needs of all beings, he or she conceives this spirit, thereby becoming a bodhisattva.

bodhisattva (S. *bodhisattva*)—*Bodhi,* enlightenment or wisdom of selflessness, and *sattva,* hero or heroine. A person who lives by the spirit of enlightenment life after life, dedicated to becoming a buddha for the sake of all beings. Sometimes even after reaching that goal, a buddha will emanate incarnations into the world as bodhisattvas, in order to be near sentient beings to help them more effectively. Celestial bodhisattvas—Avalokiteshvara, Manjushri, Tara, Vajrapani, Samantabhadra, and others—may be considered buddhas acting as bodhisattvas. One becomes a bodhisattva by conceiving the spirit of enlightenment, through (1) imagining the possibility of enlightened consciousness, (2) seeing that it alone conveys the ability to help others find happiness, (3) seeing that dedicating all one's lives of efforts toward that goal is the only sensible way to live, and (4) resolving to undertake that universal responsibility oneself. This transformation from ordinary being to "enlightenment hero/heroine" is formally sealed by the bodhisattva vow.

body, speech, and mind—A basic triad in Buddhist thought, constituting the three levels of evolutionary existence. Buddhist ethics divides its ten basic laws into three of body—not to kill, steal, or commit sexual misconduct; four of speech—not to lie, slander, chatter, or revile; and three of mind—not to covet, hate, or hold misguided views. Each person must therefore be responsible on all three levels. At buddhahood, ordinary body becomes the emanation-body, speech becomes the beatific-body, and mind becomes the truth-body.

body-mandala—*See* mandala.

body-mind complex—In the tantric context, the body-mind is seen as gross, subtle, and extremely subtle, a scheme that is important in analysis of the death, between, and rebirth processes. The gross body-mind is the ordinary elemental body as nexus of the five sense organs and the six sense consciousnesses. The subtle body-mind is the "diamond body" of neural channels, winds, and drops coordinated with the three subtle intuitions—luminance, radiance, and imminence. And the extremely subtle body-mind is the indestructible drop of the subtlest wind-energies coordinated with the

clear light transparency intuition, the subtlest mind, and the seed of enlightenment. *See also* five systems.

buddha—An awakened or enlightened being, one who has reached the peak of evolution by developing his or her wisdom and compassion over countless lifetimes until both have become perfect. Wisdom is perfect when it knows all things and compassion is perfect when it frees all beings. A buddha is thus said to have completely fulfilled both his or her own self-interest as well as all altruistic concerns for others. Shakyamuni, who lived in India about 2,500 years ago, is the Historical Buddha of our era on this planet. In the absolute sense, there is only one buddha, as the truth-bodies of different buddhas cannot be distinguished from each other. But in the relative sense, there are countless buddhas, as each being who consummates all evolutionary possibilities enjoys his or her own beatitude and extends emanations for the sake of other beings. A buddha can manifest as male, female, or both in union.

buddha-body—A buddha is no longer an ordinary being, a self-habit-ridden individual caught inside his skin: his extraordinary qualities are expressed as three bodies of the experience of enlightenment. At the evolutionary culmination of full enlightenment, the ordinary mind expands in an experience of oneness with the infinity of beings and things—this becomes a permanent awareness, called the Body of Truth or Body of Reality. This is the highest fruit of wisdom, a state of virtual omniscience, nirvana—a perfect, ultimate freedom, and the utmost fulfillment of all selfish concerns. At the same time, the ordinary speech and body do not lose their continuity with ordinary life. Speech expands as a celebration of the mind's attainment of infinite oneness, becoming a consummate and infinite joy experienced as the Body of Beatitude, a subtle or ethereal body made of the sheer joy of being free of suffering. It is as infinite as reality, a subtle radiant omnipresence of a buddha's joy throughout all things. The ordinary body expands with enlightenment into an emanation-body, a limitless number of individuated manifestations arising from the background energy of the beatific-body when a buddha wishes to interact with ordinary beings.

buddha-deity—*See* archetype-deity.

buddha-land—*See* buddhaverse.

buddhaverse (S. *buddhakṣetra*)— The environment of a buddha. The evolutionary transmutation of the finite individual into an infinite body of awareness also transforms the environment. Beings are relational nexi of relative self and environment, so the enlightenment of one implies the transformation of the other. In popular Buddhism, this is expressed in descriptions of the heavenly lands of the archetype-buddhas such as Amitabha's Sukhavati, an environment which is as otherworldly and unearthly as it is radiant and exquisite. The Buddhists accepted all the culturally commonplace heavens, such as the Olympus-like Thirty-Three Heaven atop the cosmic mountain, Meru, presided over by Indra, king of the gods; the Tushita Heaven where

future buddhas dwell; and the sixteen Brahma heavens of the realm of pure form. In addition, they envisioned buddhaverses, universes transformed by individual buddhas into environments perfectly suited to the spiritual evolution of all the beings in them. The buddhaverses include the heavens of the ordinary deities in the highest of the Brahma heavens, the Akanishta. Universe indicates a world turning around the single, self-centered individual, whereas the buddhaverse turns around enlightened wisdom which sees no ultimate distinction between self and other. *See also* Abhirati, Akanishta, Sukhavati.

Buddhism—The religion, education system, or way of life founded on the enlightenment attained—and proclaimed possible and necessary for others to attain—by Shakyamuni Buddha beginning around 530 BCE. The Three Jewels—the Buddha (teacher), the Dharma (teaching) and the reality of freedom it presents, and the Sangha (community of practitioners)—are the three most precious things for a Buddhist. He takes refuge in them to find a haven from the extreme dangers of the suffering life cycle, and assurance of the positive evolutionary direction of his life. Among the many types of Buddhism are three overarching categories, all developed in India from ca. 500 BCE to 1100 CE, and known as the Three Vehicles by those who accept them. The first, Monastic Buddhism (early, original, or primitive Buddhism), is centered on the Four Noble Truths and aims for the individual's freedom and enlightenment. We call it the Individual Vehicle, without negative connotation. The second, Messianic or Mahayana Buddhism of the post-Ashokan period, is centered on emptiness and great compassion and all beings' freedom and enlightenment. We call it the Universal Vehicle. The third, variously known as the Diamond Vehicle or Mantrayana, Tantrayana, or Vajrayana Buddhism, is the esoteric vehicle of post-Gupta Tantric Buddhism, centered on the implementation of compassion as great bliss, the use of artistic imagination to reconstruct the self and the universe, and all beings' accelerated freedom and enlightenment. We call it the Apocalyptic Vehicle from the lightning-swift and revelatory connotation of vajra as diamond and thunderbolt. There are also national forms such as Indian, Sri Lankan, Burmese, Japanese, Tibetan, or Chinese Buddhism. Finally, there are separate orders or sects within various cultures, such as Zen Buddhism, Theravada Buddhism, Shingon Buddhism, or Pure Land Buddhism.

chakravartin (S. *cakravartin*)—Literally, wheel-turner. In Indian myth, a world-conquering king whose virtue—earned by good deeds in former lives—gives him effortless power to subjugate all lesser kings around him and rule the world.

chorten—*See* stupa.

clan, five buddha-clans (S. *kula*)—Often translated as family, which has the modern connotation of nuclear family (parents and children), clan rather conveys the ancient extended family which includes cousins, uncles, aunts, and so forth. The five clans—vajra, buddha, jewel (ratna), lotus (padma), and action (karma)—are headed by the archetype-deities Akshobhya, Vairochana, Ratnasambhava, Amitabha, and Amoghasiddhi respectively. *See also* archetype-deity, five wisdoms.

clear light (S. *prabhāsvara*)—The subtlest light, transparent rather than bright, that illuminates the most profound reality of the universe. It is a light like glass or diamond, like the pre-dawn twilight, different from the lights of sun, moon, and Rahu, the planet of the darkness. It is an inconceivable light, beyond the duality of bright and dark, the self-luminosity of all things.

compassion (S. *karuṇā*)—The will to free others from suffering, based on empathetic sensitivity. Its opposite is hatred, which wills others to suffer. Its counterpart is love (S. *maitri*), which wills others to have happiness, in addition to freedom from suffering. Universal compassion is the automatic reflex of perfect wisdom, as the realization of essential selflessness is an experience of the ultimate unity of self and other. This causes the sufferings of others to become one's own, making the will to eliminate suffering spontaneous and immediate.

consort—The partner, usually female, in a buddha-couple. Sometimes each figure is considered a different divine being, sometimes they are the double manifestation of a single being. The Buddhist belief is that all beings, whatever their superficial sexual identity, are potentially both male and female, each having both male and female aspects and energies. The empathetic ability to transcend sexual identity–habits is cultivated by tantric archetype meditation wherein a male sees himself as a female archetype-buddha, a female sees herself as a male archetype-buddha, or either meditates as a buddha-couple in union. The various consorts are: *karmamudrā,* action consort, the physical partner with whom one practices tantric sexual yogas; *dharmamudrā,* a visualized consort; *jñānamudrā,* an angelic consort who unites with one emerging from the subtle dimensions of reality; and finally *mahāmudrā,* ultimate reality itself experienced as a consort in the enlightenment experience of orgasmic union with infinite reality. *See also* couple, Great Seal, mudra.

couple, buddha-couple (T. *sangs rgyas yab yum*)—Literally, buddha father-mother. A single enlightened individual seen as two beings, a male and female in union. In the process of enlightenment, a bounded, singular, self-centered individual—usually with one sexual identity or another—is transformed into an infinite, multibodied, omnipresent, universalized individual, capable of manifesting whatever embodiment interacts most beneficially with beings. The representation as a pair in sexual union demonstrates the union of wisdom (mother) and compassion (father) and the resulting capacity to adopt all beings, help them out of the life cycle of suffering, and give them a new life of happiness in the buddhaverse.

Creation Stage—The first stage of the Unexcelled Yoga tantras in which the yogin visualizes the mandala palace with its environment and ornaments, and the blissful body, speech, and mind of the archetype-deity as the pure embodiment of enlightenment. The practitioner develops the ability to totally transform his perception and conception, so that he stably perceives his environment as the pure mandala, his body as a deity body, his speech as buddha-mantra, and his mind as buddha-wisdom, all four isolated from ordinariness, imperfection, and impurity. *See also* Perfection Stage.

dakini (S. *ḍākinī*)—Dakas (male) and dakinis (female) were originally fierce angels or deities of popular Indian religion, associated with the Hindu goddess Kali and with the tantric adepts of Buddhism. In Indo-Tibetan Buddhism, the dakinis became more prominent and were associated with both mundane and transcendent female deities called yogini. They are slightly fierce but also erotic female deities who appear to tantric practitioners to teach, inspire, assist, and admonish. The Vajradakini (Diamond Angel) is a female form of perfect buddhahood, equivalent to a Heruka, a male buddha-deity manifestation. *See also* fierce deity, Heruka.

Dalai Lama—Dalai is Mongolian for oceanic, lama is Tibetan for spiritual master. Sonam Gyatso, a reincarnate lama of Drepung monastery, was given this name as an honorific title by Altan Khan of the Mongols, and it was applied retroactively to his two immediately previous incarnations. In 1642 the Great Fifth Dalai Lama was invested with secular and spiritual authority over Tibet, and subsequent Dalai Lamas exercised it until 1959 when the fourteenth Dalai Lama fled into exile from the Chinese occupation. He still heads the Tibetan Government-in-Exile, in Dharamsala, India.

Dharma—One of the Three Jewels, the Jewel of the Buddha's teaching, though it can also mean the ultimate reality itself that is taught in the teachings, the path that leads to its realization, the qualities that derive from it, and so forth. In Indian usage prior to the Buddha's time, it tended to mean religion, law, duty, custom, and so forth, patterns that hold human behavior and thought under control. These "pattern-maintaining" meanings still coexist in Sanskrit and other Buddhist languages with the Buddha's more liberating or "pattern-transcending" meanings, causing considerable confusion for translators in some contexts. *See also* Three Jewels.

diamond—*See* vajra.

Drepung monastery—The largest monastery in Tibet, founded in 1416 by Chamchen Choje. The name comes from the Dhanyakataka stupa in southern India, where Buddha is believed to have first taught the Kalachakra system.

drop (S. *bindū*)—Physical or chemical essences (something like modern neurotransmitters) that focus awareness within the subtle nervous system. In the subtle body, the channels form the structure, the winds serve as the energies that move things and cause transformations of experience, and the drops serve as the nodes of subjectivity that focus awareness within this realm, which opens up when consciousness has been withdrawn from its ordinary functions of receiving and coordinating sense-data. These drops are also associated with the genetic material that is the essence of the male and female sexual fluids; the yogic mastery of their subtle potentials represents the sublimation of the creative energies that ordinarily build up the suffering life cycle into the reconstruction of the divine realm of the enlightened mandala. Thus, red drops represent the female genetic essence carried in blood, and white drops represent the male genetic essence carried in semen. *See also* energy, spiritual gene, soul.

drop mandala—*See* mandala.

emanation (S. *nirmāṇa*)—A creation of enlightened mind, made for the sake of communicating freedom and joy to other beings. *See* buddha-body.

energy, neural energy—Subtle inner winds that contribute activity to the subtle body by moving drops through the channels. The five main winds are the life, evacuative, articulative, digestive, and pervasive energies, each associated with a particular channel-wheel, a particular archetype-buddha, a particular wisdom, and so forth. The branch energies are associated with the buddha consorts, the five elements, and so forth. These energies are also important in Buddhist medicine; they underlie the technology of acupuncture and the understanding of most mental and many physical disorders. *See also* drop.

enlightenment (S. *bodhi, buddhatvam*)—The perfection of wisdom, the direct understanding of the true nature of reality and its result, compassion, the open connection with others. Wisdom creates the enlightened mind, considered an infinite, blissful, omniscience technically inconceivable to human or even divine mentalities. Compassion creates the enlightened body (or bodies) to communicate blissful reality to other beings so they can be inspired to seek their own liberation.

Esoteric Buddhism—The Buddha often criticized teachers who held back their best teachings out of stinginess or lack of compassion for their disciples. Buddhism, however, does consider some teachings better kept secret, or esoteric, until students are advanced enough to understand them properly. Such was (and still is, in some respects) the tradition surrounding the tantras. On the surface, the erotic and terrific imagery needed to explore the unconscious provide good reason for a modicum of secrecy, as such imagery can lead to misunderstanding. More importantly, though, secrecy is required to keep ambitious practitioners from getting ahead of their appropriate stage and hurting themselves by premature attempts to plumb the depths of the psyche. Before exploring passions and transmuting them into the path, they need a secure capacity for detachment and restraint. Before encountering the ferocious and terrific forces of the psyche, they need a determined commitment to universal love and compassion that can withstand confrontation with the demonic. And most importantly, before cultivating buddha-pride and divine confidence by rehearsing an enlightened identity, they must have rigorous insight into identitylessness in order to avoid delusional enlightenment megalomania.

Esoteric Communion (S. *Guhyasamāja*)—The most important Father tantra in the Unexcelled Yoga tantra category. Its study and practice was a specialty of Marpa and later of Tsong Khapa.

evolution, evolutionary (S. *karma, karmika*)—Mental, verbal, or physical action which leads to life-affecting, eventually life-constituting, consequences. The modern materialistic worldview sees our present lives as results of biological evolution through the subtly encoded experiences of millions of previous representatives of our species. The Buddhist worldview sees our present lives as results of our own experiences from millions of previous lifetimes—subtly encoded in a spiritual gene we bring with us—combined with the physical genes we receive from our parents in a complex process of spiritual *and* biological evolution. Sanskrit *karma* (literally, creative action) conveys the laws whereby certain actions crystallize into patterns of being and thereby generate future life-forms. A modern person regards his hand with its opposed thumb as the result of genetic coding derived from millions of previous life-forms' survival behaviors together with random mutations preserved by the processes of natural selection. A Buddhist would view the hand as the result of spiritual genetic coding from his own countless millions of previous lives in which ethical actions such as giving, being just, tolerating, striving, contemplating, and understanding crystallized into patterns that engendered similar patterns in subsequent lives.

father-mother—*See* couple.

fierce deity—(1) Terrific buddha-forms that manifest the wisdom and compassion necessary to overwhelm the habitual fierceness of egotistical drives. (2) Terrific bodhisattvas who protect spiritual persons, defending them from those who would consume or obstruct them. (3) Wrathful, bloodthirsty worldly deities and spirits who have given themselves over to anger and hatred, thereby becoming demonic and harmful. Nonetheless, they have no hatred whatsoever in them, not even righteous hatred against evildoers. Their fierceness is tough love, tough compassion, like the fierceness of a mother who scolds her child to keep it from harm. The common translation, wrathful deities, is misleading as these deities are not filled with wrath. Fierce refers to their manifestations and makes no judgment about their mental state. *See also* dakini, Heruka.

five buddhas—*See* archetype-deity, clan.

five poisons—The five main negative emotional addictions that drive the cycle of samsara: delusion, hate, greed, pride, and envy.

five systems (S. *skandha*, heap, aggregate, or process)—The basic processes of the normal sentient being's body-mind complex consist of matter (form), sensations, conceptions, emotions, and consciousness. The scheme of the five systems is used contemplatively to allow the self-investigator to discover his or her reality of freedom from rigid self. *See also* body-mind complex.

five wisdoms—The primary energies or elements of the universe as understood by the enlightened mind. They are ultimate reality perfection, mirrorlike clarity, equalizing, discriminating, and all-accomplishing wisdoms; the colors blue, white, yellow, red, and green; the elements ether, water, earth, fire, and air; transmuted poisons of hate, delusion, pride, greed, and envy; and so forth. *See also* archetype-deity, clan, five systems, wisdom.

Four Noble Truths—The basic formula used by the Buddha to communicate his insight into the nature of suffering and the way to freedom from it. The truths are noble because they are true for a person who has become gentle by realizing selflessness and overcoming egotism. The truths are (1) that all delusion-driven life is suffering; (2) the causes of that suffering are misknowledge and evolution; (3) there is freedom from such suffering; and (4) the path to that freedom consists of a spiritual education in morality, meditation, and scientific wisdom. The first of these truths has attracted the most notice, but the third is the most important, being the Buddha's key achievement and his "good news." Many have observed that life is suffering, but few first liberated themselves and then taught others a practical and effective way to freedom. *See also* Buddhism.

fury-fire (S. *caṇḍī, caṇḍāli*, T. *gtum mo*)—The famous inner heat that Buddhist tantric adepts develop by focusing the heat normally produced in the digestive system, drawing it into the central nervous system, and using it to melt the inner neurotransmitters that intensify consciousness.

Gautama—*See* Shakyamuni.

Geluk order (T. Dge-lugs-pa)—The most recent of Tibet's major monastic orders, founded around 1400 by Tsong Khapa (1357–1419). Based on the older Kadam order founded by Atisha (982–1054), it is famed for its expansion of monasticism in Tibet, its scholarship, and its numerous great incarnations, including the Dalai Lamas.

gene—*See* spiritual gene.

Great Seal (S. *mahāmudrā*)—Ultimate reality as a consort in the enlightenment experience of union with infinite reality. *See also* mudra.

Guhyasamāja—*See* Esoteric Communion.

guru—The Sanskrit word for teacher. Literally, heavy, connoting the authority of the teacher in the conservative brahminical culture. The Tibetans translated it as lama, meaning unexcelled, indicating great authority but diminishing the sense of hierarchical superiority. *See also* lama.

Heruka—A Herculean, "blood-drinking" male buddha-deity, symbolizing the adamantine power of enlightenment to overwhelm all evil and negativity of the world. The critical fire of wisdom transmutes "blood"—the essential constitutive energy of the suffering-permeated life cycle—into the elixir-fuel of the dynamic liberation,

the power of compassion. *See also* dakini, fierce deity.

Hevajra—An important archetype-deity whose yoga is taught in a major Mother tantra of the Unexcelled Yoga tantra category; it was most favored by the Sakya order.

indestructible drop—*See* drop, soul.

Individual Vehicle (S. *Hīnayāna*)—A Universal Vehicle term for the foundational form of Buddhism, also called Individualistic or Monastic Buddhism. The term was originally derogatory, referring to the narrow-minded refusal of early Monastic Buddhists to accept the possibility that the Buddha also gave a universal, messianic teaching. In recent usage by Universalist civilizations, such as the Tibetan, it is descriptive and not derogatory, as the foundation of Monastic Buddhism is respectfully accepted. Thus it means a vehicle suitable for transporting the individual to freedom and enlightenment. *See* Buddhism.

Indra—The Vedic god of war, storm, and thunder, holder of the vajra-thunderbolt. In the Buddhist-Hindu period, he was king of the gods of the sense realm, ruling over a heavenly city atop the Indian analogue of Mount Olympus. He became a disciple, patron, and protector of the Buddha.

initiation (S. *abhiṣeka*, T. *dbang bskur ba*)—Literally, anointment, as in the coronation of a king or queen. The ritual acknowledgment of a being's assumption of a special transformation, blessing, authority, and responsibility. In Unexcelled Yoga tantra there are four main initiations, called vase, secret, wisdom-intuition, and word, that empower body, speech, mind, and the integration of all three to learn, practice, and realize all levels of the tantric path.

Jataka (S. *Jātaka*)—Stories of the Buddha's hundreds of former lives as a bodhisattva on his way to becoming a buddha.

Kadam order (T. Bka'gdams-pa)—A monastic order in Tibetan Buddhism, founded by Atisha (982–1054) and his main disciple, Dromtonpa. Based on the synthesis of Monastic, Messianic, and Apocalyptic Buddhisms of India, it focused on the messianic teaching of the spirit of enlightenment as love and compassion for all beings and was organized into a systematic path with renunciative, wisdom, and esoteric teachings. Later revived by Tsong Khapa, it was absorbed into the Geluk order after the early 1400s.

Kagyu order (T. Bka'rgyud-pa)—An important monastic order in Tibet, descended from Vajradhara Buddha through the great Indian adepts Tilopa and Naropa, to Marpa, Milarepa, and Gampopa, the Tibetan founders. Marpa, a layman, was the key translator who brought esoteric Indian teachings into Tibetan practice. Milarepa was the key practitioner who spent a lifetime integrating the teachings into his being. He is considered the first ordinary Tibetan (not already a buddha or bodhisattva reincarnation) to become a perfect buddha in a single lifetime. Gampopa, a monk and learned scholar of the Kadam curriculum, synthesized the yogic and tantric teachings of Marpa and Milarepa with the ethical and intellectual disciplines needed to establish an enduring institution.

Kalachakra Tantra (S. *Kālacakra Tantra*)—The *Time Machine Tantra* is one of the most important and elaborate of the Unexcelled Yoga tantras. It is one of the favorites of the Dalai Lamas, and the Namgyal monastery of the Potala Palace in Lhasa is renowned for its expertise in the arts associated with this tantra. Its vision of buddhahood is of an evolutionary time machine, an omnipresent force of wisdom and compassion in close contact with planetary beings throughout all the intricacies of their history.

karma—*See* evolution.

khatvanga (S. *khaṭvāṅga*)—A ceremonial staff carried by Mother tantra deities in particular, it is crowned by a carving of three human heads—fresh, dried, and a bare skull—symbolizing the conquest of the three poisons of lust, hate, and delusion. It is topped either by a vajra, symbol of compassion; or a trident, symbol of mastery over the threefold central channels of the yogic subtle nervous system.

lama (T. *blama*)—Spiritual mentor. Highly honored, the lama is the indispensable doorway to the practice and performance of tantra. The spiritual teacher in Tantric Buddhism serves most importantly as an icon, model, and example, a mental, verbal, and physical representation of the disciple's enlightenment potential. *See also* guru.

Land of Bliss—*See* Amitabha, buddhaverse, Sukhavati.

lord (S. *bhagavān*)—Fortunate Lord, an epithet of the Buddha. It conveys the intense respect in which he was held by his contemporaries.

magic-body (S. *māyādeha*)—The subtle body created on the third of the Perfection Stages, the stage of self-consecration. It is the highest, most esoteric, consciously created form of subtle body normally experienced by the dreamer in ordinary life, or by the ghostlike being in the subtle between states. It is essential in the acceleration of the evolutionary progress normally achieved by heroic deeds during many death-, between-, and life-sequences. It is paired with clear light as the male component of complete buddhahood in the tantric context.

Mahakala (S. *Mahākāla*)—A fierce deity who protects practitioners during their journey toward enlightenment. In myth he was a powerful demon who conquered even the greatest gods by means of a special boon from the supreme god Brahma. He was then subdued by the bodhisattvas Manjushri and Avalokiteshvara and subsequently devoted his powers to the service of the Dharma.

mahamudra (S. *mahāmudrā*)—See consort, Great Seal.

mahasiddha (S. *mahāsiddha*)—Great adept, the ideal tantric practitioner who has become a perfect buddha through the quick path of the tantras, yet remains in a coarse body for the benefit of sentient beings.

Mahayana (S. Mahāyāna)—*See* Buddhism.

Maitreya—Literally, loving one. A great bodhisattva presently residing in the Tushita Heaven, whence he descends to earth to benefit beings in many guises. In Buddhist mythology, he will manifest supreme buddha deeds, similar to those of Shakyamuni, on this earth sometime in the next thousand or tens of thousands of years. In the meantime, he is believed to exercise his compassion in myriad ways to benefit beings.

mandala (S. *maṇḍala*)—Literally, an essence-protecting environment. A mandala is a magical and sacred realm, created by the artistry of enlightened compassion in order to nurture beings' development toward enlightenment. Mandalas are the perfected environments of the buddhas, built upon the foundation of their perfect wisdom, just as the ordinary universe is built upon the foundation of ignorance. Mandalas are most familiar as geometrical paintings or drawings that look like floor plans of buildings or the orbits of planets. Actually they are three-dimensional perfected environments, mini-buddhaverses created by individuals to express their enlightenment, realms in which other beings can share the enlightened perspective. A tantric practitioner learns the mandalic architecture of a particular type of enlightenment when she is initiated into a tantric yoga practice; in the Creation Stage she develops the ability to visualize every detail of the total mandalic environment, to the degree where she can feel completely secure in its divine surrounding. Often mandalas have a central palace or mansion, with a highly complex and beautiful architecture, for the meditator's divine buddha-embodiment. Categorized by medium, there are painted, particle, architectural, body (visualized as manifest in parts of the coarse and subtle bodies), drop, and visualized mandalas. Categorized by residents, there are seed-syllable, symbol, and deity mandalas.

mandorla—A large halo painted behind a buddha or bodhisattva, encompassing the body and head haloes. It represents the spiritual aura or radiance.

Manjushri (S. Mañjuśrī)—The Bodhisattva of Wisdom. His most characteristic form is that of a youth, symbolizing that Buddhist wisdom is the clear knowledge of reality, critical and penetrating, not merely venerable resignation or heightened common sense accumulated from long experience. In his fierce archetype-deity form he is Yamantaka, the death-exterminator.

mantra (S. *mantra*)—Literally, saving the mind. A mantra is a creative sound expressing the deepest essence of things and understandings, so that its repetition can evoke a state of enlightenment or positive energy in a formulaic or even magical way. Some mantras resemble sentences and express a wish, vision, or affirmation, while others are one or a few syllables containing the germ of a deity, realm, or state of concentration. Mantras are the essence of poetic speech which does not merely describe substances and events, but consciously creates vision and meaning.

Mantrayana (S. Mantrayāna)—*See* Buddhism.

Messianic Buddhism—*See* Buddhism.

Milarepa (1040–1123)—The first Tibetan great adept, believed to have become a perfect buddha within his single lifetime. He was the disciple of the translator Marpa; his pupil Gampopa founded the Kagyu order. Milarepa was famous for singing profound spiritual teachings in lucid verses and for his mastery of the yoga of fury-fire, which enabled him to live comfortably naked in the Himalayan winter.

misknowledge (S. *avidyā*)—Ignorance as active wrong knowing—misperception or misconception—rather than mere failure to know. Such deliberate ignorance is the root of the samsaric life cycle and the primary cause of all suffering.

Monastic Buddhism—*See* Buddhism.

mudra (S. *mudrā*)—A sacred gesture symbolically expressing inner wisdom, or, in tantra, a female consort for yogic practices that harness sexual energies to the path. Some of the main gestures we see in Tibetan images are *abhaya,* the gesture of fearlessness, the right hand held in front with open palm raised up; *dana,* the gesture of giving, the right hand held open and downward; *dharmacakrapravartana,* the teaching gesture, each hand held with thumb and index fingers touching and the other three fingers upraised, the two hands touching each other in front of the heart center; *dhyāna,* contemplation gesture, either one or both hands held flat in the lap; *trisharana,* the Triple Refuge gesture, similar to the teaching gesture, with the emphasis on the three upraised fingers, representing the Buddha, Dharma, and Sangha; *tarjanī,* threatening gesture, with either hand held forward in a fist, the index and little fingers raised up; *varada,* boon-granting gesture, just like the giving gesture; and *vitarka,* analytic or fine discernment gesture, like a one-handed teaching gesture, one hand held up with thumb and index finger forming a circle, the other three fingers raised up. *See also* consort, couple, Great Seal.

Naropa—One of the great adepts of Indian Buddhist civilization, he lived in the tenth and eleventh centuries and attained the Great Seal after arduous studies with his mentor, Tilopa. Naropa used his superb intellect and education to write important tantric commentaries and practice manuals and in teaching the Tibetan translator Marpa and other important Indian, Nepali, and Tibetan adepts. He is a key figure in the transmission of the tantric sciences to the various Tibetan orders.

nirvana (S. *nirvāṇa*)—Supreme freedom from suffering, the goal of all Buddhist practice. It is attainable by all beings because it is the final reality of their condition. In some forms of Buddhism it is pictured as a state beyond the world, but in the Mahayana, or Universalist, Buddhism of Tibet and other East Asian Buddhist countries, it is not considered separate from the ordinary world. In fact, realization of nirvana transforms the ordinary relative world into an extraordinary perfect environment.

Nyingma order (T. Rnying-ma-pa)—One of the four orders of Tibetan Buddhism. Founded during the Tibetan empire with the establishment of Samye monastery in the eighth century by the abbot

Shantarakshita, the adept Padmasambhava, and the emperor Trisong Detsen, Samye was the first full Buddhist institution in Tibet. The Nyingma order emerged in the eleventh century when the other Tibetan orders began. It maintained its own distinct foundation, based on the older translations and teachings. (Its name means "older.") Its general teaching is the same as all Tibetan Buddhist schools. Its special teaching is the Great Perfection teaching of immanent enlightenment. In modern Tibet before the destruction, the Nyingma order had some 1,500 monastic communities with sophisticated programs of study and practice, and ministries in the surrounding society.

Perfection Stage—The second stage of the Unexcelled Yoga tantra follows the successful completion of the Creation Stage. After the practitioner stabilizes those visualizations, he is secure enough to begin rehearsing the death, between, and rebirth processes in order to accelerate his accumulation of merit and wisdom so as to gain buddhahood within a single or a few lifetimes. *See also* Creation Stage.

phenomenal reality—*See* reality.

psychonaut—A voyager into the soul, or Buddhist adept, who voluntarily abandons the pseudo-security of this planet of delusion, with its solid ground of ordinary, individuated suffering, to launch herself through the death dissolutions into the subtle between states. This exploration of the unconscious deepens her wisdom and expands her compassionate heroism as she serves universes of beings on the subtle level. She then returns to her ordinary embodiment to assist her contemporaries.

pure land—*See* Amitabha, buddhaverse, Sukhavati.

Pure Land Buddhism—Based on Indian sutras, this form of Buddhism developed in China and Japan as a religion whose devotees relied on the compassion of Amitabha to save them from further suffering in samsara after death. They hoped to gain rebirth in his blissful buddhaverse in order to learn there how to attain their own buddhahood.

Ratnasambhava—The transcendent buddha of the southern direction, lord of the jewel clan, representing transmutation of pride and stinginess into the equality wisdom, the color of gold, and the purification of the system of sensation. *See also* archetype-deity, clan.

reality (S. *dharmatā, satya, dharma*)—The actual condition of things. Enlightenment purports to be the perfect knowledge and awareness of that reality; the possibility of liberation from suffering is based on that truth: and the untruth of the ordinary condition of suffering. Buddhism recognizes two levels of reality or truth: the surface reality, which is relative and conventional, as opposed to the profound, ultimate, or absolute reality of nirvana or voidness, which exists just as it appears to exist, without any deception or change.

relative reality—*See* reality.

saha (S. *sahā*)—Literally, tolerable. The Buddhist name for our universe.

Sakya order (T. Sa-skya-pa)—One of the four orders of Tibetan Buddhism. It was founded with the establishment of Sakya monastery in 1073 and shares the same general Buddhist teaching as the other orders. Its special teachings are the *Hevajra Tantra* combined with a special method, "Path and Fruition."

Sakya Pandita (1182–1251)—One of the greatest of all Tibetan lamas, considered an incarnation of the Bodhisattva Manjushri. He wrote numerous important books, set the curriculum of study and practice for the Sakya monasteries on a sound footing, attained important realizations, and served his country by skillful negotiations with the Mongol emperors.

samadhi (S. *samādhi*)—Meditational practice and achievement. Usually defined as one-pointedness of mind, it can also refer to creative mind states after enlightenment, mental concentrations which produce special light rays and liberating environments for disciples.

Samantabhadra—The embodiment of benevolence, an important bodhisattva in the *Flower Garland Sutra*. As a buddha, he holds a central place in the contemplations of the Nyingma order.

samsara (S. *saṃsāra*)—The misknowledge-governed cycle of constant frustration and suffering, including death and rebirth.

Sangha—The community of Buddhist monks and nuns and, by extension, lay initiates and practitioners. *See also* Three Jewels.

seed-syllable (S. *bījamantra*)—A single syllable believed to contain the germ of a thing or a being from which it can magically be created by a deity or an enlightened being. Reciting mantric spells containing such seed-syllables is believed to have effects in the physical as well as spiritual worlds.

self-habit (S. *ātmagraha*, T. *bdag 'dzin*)—The unconscious sense of being an intrinsically real, self-sufficient, independent agent and perceiver in the midst of all one's circumstances and compulsions. This habit is considered the central addiction of the unenlightened personality, the root of all compulsiveness, confusion, and dissatisfaction.

Shakyamuni (S. Śākyamuni)—The Historical Buddha was born to the royal family of the Gautama clan in approximately 563 BCE, in the Shakya Republic, on the present border of India and Nepal. At twenty-nine years of age, Prince Siddhartha renounced his kingdom and departed on a six-year quest to discover reality. After many trials, he attained perfect enlightenment, and as a buddha was called Shakyamuni (the Shakya Sage). After teaching extensively for more than forty-five years, he attained parinirvana in approximately 483 BCE. The supreme emanation-body of our historical era, his life story is the paradigm of the Buddhist attainment of enlightenment.

Shambhala—An ancient kingdom somewhere north of Tibet and Mongolia, hidden magically under a force field until the future moment of the Buddhist apoca-

lypse. The king of Shambhala was believed to have requested the Kalachakra teaching from Shakyamuni, and it is widely practiced in his kingdom to this day. The Shambhala myth is the prototype for the idea of Shangri-la, which captured the Western imagination earlier in this century.

Shamvara, or ***Samvara*** (S. *Samvara*)—Literally, supreme bliss. The major Mother tantra among the Unexcelled Yoga tantras, believed to contain all the essential teachings of the female buddhas, the vajradakinis and vajrayoginis, most effective in mastering the clear light component of buddhahood.

Shingon order—The school of Japanese Buddhism founded by the great adept and teacher, Kukai, in the ninth century, based on Tantric Buddhism transmitted from India through China.

Shinto—The animistic, preliterate religion of Japan, oriented toward the worship of nature and tribal deities, codified in the nineteenth century into a formal cult centered on the imperial family.

Siddhartha Gautama—*See* Shakyamuni.

skull bowl (S. *kapāla*)—A symbolic implement of the fierce deities. It represents their insight into their own death and their transforming it into a means of liberation.

soul, indestructible drop (S. *jīva, aksarabindū*)—Though Buddhism denies the existence of any such fixed thing on the ultimate level, in relative reality, the deepest personal essence of a living being is what journeys from life to life, takes rebirth, and is finally enlightened. The Buddha's famous teaching of selflessness has often been translated in the past as soul-lessness, and used to confirm the Western sense that Buddhism is nihilistic and atheistic. The Buddha rejected any absolute, unchanging, fixed, intrinsically substantial, intrinsically identifiable soul, just as he rejected the same kind of self or ego. But relative, changing, relational, living, conventional entities—usefully termed ego, self, and soul—have never been denied in Buddhist psychology. Buddhism always rejected the Indian materialists who denied personal continuity and any sort of former or future lives. *See also* drop.

spiritual gene (S. *gotra*)—The seed of one's propensities, structures, affinities, and fortune developed from the evolutionary action of previous lives, carried as a subtle "drop" into the next life of a mammal. There it interacts with the physical genes from parents to determine the being's character in that life. It is a gene that constitutes the mind and attitudes of a being, just as the genes of father and mother structure a being's body. The Buddhist vision of conception is a beautiful moment in which the father's white drop meets the mother's red drop and the individual's blue drop enters their union. *See also* drop, soul.

stupa (S. *stūpa*, T. *mchod rten*)—A cairnlike monument erected to commemorate the presence and enshrine the relics of a deceased buddha. Shakyamuni gave instructions before his death that his remains were to be interred in such a funerary mount or monument. With square, triangular, round, and vertical forms symbolizing the primary elements, surmounted by the victory banners and parasols of enlightenment, stupas came to symbolize the Body of Truth, ultimate reality, the all-pervasive mind of all buddhas, hence the reality of the omnipresent immediacy of enlightened being in every atom and subatomic energy of the universe. In Tibet the people covered the landscape with stupas as reminders that enlightenment is the supreme reality, the heart of nature, and their own immediate freedom and security.

Sukhavati (S. Sukhāvatī)—Amitabha's Pure Land of Bliss, beyond as many universes as there are grains of sand in sixty-two Ganges riverbeds, is vividly described in the *Sukhavativyuha Sutra*. It is the heavenly home of the Bodhisattva Avalokiteshvara, and the prayed-for destination of Pure Land Buddhists. *See also* Amitabha, buddhaverse.

superficial reality—*See* reality.

sutra (S. *sūtra*)—Buddhist scripture, named after the string used to tie Indian loose-leaf books together.

thang ka—A portable scroll icon, usually of a buddha, bodhisattva, or deity, painted with mineral colors on fine cotton or silk and sewn into a brocade frame stretched on two end-sticks.

tantra (S. *tantra*)—A type of Buddhist (as well as Hindu and Jain) teaching that emphasizes spiritual technology and contemplative arts rather than philosophy. Sanskrit *tantra* refers to continuum and is related to the verb "to weave." In Buddhism, tantra is concerned with rebuilding the extraordinary realm of enlightenment with the energies of wisdom, after demolishing the ordinary world of suffering upheld by the energy of ignorance. It tends to be considered esoteric, as when taken out of context it can be misunderstood as denying the existence of the world of suffering. Rather, tantra can be viewed as the high technology needed to build an enlightened world by mobilizing great bliss in the form of creative imagination. The word *tantra* refers to the vehicle, to specific texts, and to systems of practice for developing that technology. There are four classes of tantra: Action, Performance, Yoga, and Unexcelled Yoga. The last is further divided into great, progressive, and ultimate yogas by the Nyingma order, and into Creation Stage and Perfection Stage by the other orders. There are Father and Mother tantras, so-called because they emphasize cultivation of magic-body and clear light respectively. *Esoteric Communion* is the paradigm of the former category, *Paramount Bliss* that of the latter.

Tara (S. Tārā)—The archangelic and archetype-deity bodhisattva representing the miraculous activities of all buddhas. In myth, she is born from Avalokiteshvara's tears of compassion or from her own vow to be enlightened and stay a woman. Her many emanations help beings overcome difficulties on the path to enlightenment. She and the Bodhisattva Avalokiteshvara are considered indivisible, each being the other's counterpart. While he manifests the concentrated compassion of all buddhas, she manifests the concentrated miraculous liberating activities of all buddhas. She is much more dynamic than he. As a buddha, she is the consort of Amoghasiddhi, the contemplative green buddha of the north, who symbolizes the all-accomplishing, or miracle-working, wisdom. There are innumerable manifestations of Tara, as many as beings require, but her most famous are the peaceful White Tara, who brings protection, long life, and peace; and the dynamic Green Tara, who overcomes obstacles and saves beings in dangerous circumstances.

tathagata (S. *tathāgata*)—Literally, one who has realized the ultimate reality of suchness. An epithet for buddhas. *See* archetype-deity, buddha.

Tendai order—The Japanese Buddhist order founded by Saicho in the ninth century, based on the Chinese T'ien T'ai school, itself based on the *Lotus Sutra* and the philosophy of the Universal Vehicle.

terrific deity—*See* fierce deity.

Theravada (S. Theravāda)—*See* Buddhism.

Three Bodies—*See* buddha-body.

Three Jewels—The Buddha, Dharma, and Sangha. *See* Buddhism.

Three Vehicles—*See* Buddhism.

transcendent buddhas—*See* archetype-deity, clan.

truth (S. *dharma*)—Usually a synonym of reality, though sometimes a statement that corresponds to or indicates that reality. *See* reality.

truth-body (S. *dharmakāya*)—*See* buddha-body.

Tsong Khapa (1357–1419)—One of the greatest Tibetan lamas, believed to be the third great incarnation of Manjushri (after Longchenpa and Sakya Pandita). His work set the curriculum for a vastly expanded monastic institution that industrialized Tibet's production of enlightened persons.

ultimate reality—*See* reality.

Unexcelled Yoga tantra—The most advanced of the four kinds of Buddhist tantras. *See* tantra.

Universal Vehicle—The Mahayana, or Messianic form of Buddhism, emphasizing the teaching of love and compassion, the inevitable implication of selfless wisdom. It provides a social teaching and a vehicle to carry all beings to enlightenment, expanding on the foundation of the Individual or Monastic Vehicle that carries beings one by one. *See also* Buddhism.

upāya—*See* art.

ushnisha (S. *uṣṇīṣa*)—The crown-protrusion on a buddha's head, symbolizing the cosmic openness of an enlightened being.

Vairochana (S. Vairocana)—Literally, shining one. One of the five transcendent buddhas who is the lord of the buddha clan and occupies the center in many popular tantras. He shares the eastern direction in the advanced Unexcelled Yoga tantras with Akshobhya. Vairochana represents the transmutation of hate or delusion into perfect reality (or mirrorlike) wisdom, and the purity of the consciousness or form systems. His color is blue or white. *See also* archetype-deity, clan.

vajra (T. *rdo-rje*, lord of stones)—An ultimately untranslatable Sanskrit word meaning diamond, adamantine, or thunderbolt, connoting immutability, unbreakability, and ultimate power. The vajra symbolized the supreme power of Indra in Vedic India and was used punitively by that god of war and storm. Universal Vehicle Buddhism transvalued it into a symbol of great compassion, the strongest power in the universe. In tantric art and ritual it symbolizes compassion as great bliss consciousness, with its companion bell representing the wisdom of the void, the male organ with the bell as the female, and the magic-body with the bell as the clear light.

Vajradhara—Holder of the Vajra, the teaching buddha in his tantric manifestation.

Vajrapani—Vajra-in-hand. This fierce blue bodhisattva attended Shakyamuni Buddha and remembered and transmitted all his magical, esoteric, tantric teachings.

Vajrasattva—One of the archetypal mild buddha-deities, sometimes considered the lord of a sixth buddha-clan, sometimes associated with Akshobhya, the lord of the vajra clan. In the broadest tantric terms, he is considered the archetypal male practitioner form adopted by the Buddha when he implements the esoteric tantric teachings. Therefore, any of the tantric buddha-deities can be called Vajrasattva.

Vajrayana (S. Vajrayāna)—*See* Buddhism, Esoteric Buddhism.

vehicle—*See* Buddhism.

wisdom (S. *prajñā*)—Wisdom is the most important mental power in Buddhism, as it is only wisdom that can bring about a being's liberation from suffering. It is defined as the perfect, experiential knowledge of the nature of reality, which is sheer relativity free of any instrinsically established persons or things. Wisdom can be personified as a goddess, the mother of all buddhas, or the female buddhas among the tantric archetype-deities, such as Vajrayogini. *See also* five wisdoms.

yab-yum—*See* couple.

Yama—The Indian god of death and justice, tamed by Manjushri and made into a Buddhist protector. He is the special protector of the Geluk order, as Tsong Khapa had a close personal connection with him.

Yamantaka (T. *shin rje shed*)—Literally, death-terminator. The fierce form Manjushri adopted to conquer Yama, the Indian god of death. Vajrabhairava, the diamond terrorist, is the most ferocious of these fierce forms, black Yamantaka the mildest, red Yamantaka medium fierce.

yoga—A yoking or harnessing of one's life to one's understanding or ideas, thus a method of implementing in life the positive principles of one's philosophy.

yogin—A yogi (male) or yogini (female) is a practitioner of Buddhist yoga, which "yokes" their life energies to knowledge and understanding.

SELECTED BIBLIOGRAPHY

For specialized monographs and articles, please see the endnotes for the essays in this catalogue.

BUDDHISM

Robinson, Richard H., and Willard L. Johnson. *The Buddhist Religion: A Historical Introduction.* 4th ed. Belmont: Wadsworth Publishing Company, 1997.

Snellgrove, David L., and Hugh L. Richardson. *A Cultural History of Tibet.* Boston and London: Shambhala, 1986.

Thurman, Robert A. F., trans. *The Tibetan Book of the Dead.* New York: Bantam Books, 1994.

Thurman, Robert A. F. *Essential Tibetan Buddhism.* San Francisco: Harper, 1995.

Yamasaki Taiko. *Shingon: Japanese Esoteric Buddhism.* Translated and adapted by Richard Peterson and Cynthia Peterson. Boston: Shambhala, 1988.

BUDDHIST ART

Brauen, Martin. *Mandala.* (trans. Martin Wilson) Boston: Shambhala, 1997.

bSodnams rGyamtsho. *The Ngor Mandalas of Tibet: Listing of the Mandala Deities.* Revised by Musashi Tachiaka, Shunzo Ondada, Keiya Noguchi, and Kimiaki Tanaka. Bibliotheca Codicum Asiaticorum. Tokyo: Centre for East Asian Studies, 1991.

Chūgoku Sekketsu: Ansei Yurinkutsu (The Grotto Art of China: The Yulin caves at Anxi). Tokyo: Heibonsha; Beijing: Wenwu Chubanshae, 1990.

Dahmen-Dallapiccola, Anna Libera, and Stephanie Zingel-Avé Lallemant, eds. *The Stúpa: Its Religious, Historical, and Archaeological Significance.* Wiesbaden: Steiner, 1980.

Goepper, Roger, and Jaroslav Poncar. *Alchi: Ladakh's Hidden Buddhist Sanctuary.* Boston: Shambhala, 1996.

Gomez, Luís O., and Hiram W. Woodward, Jr., eds. *Barabudur: History and Significance of a Buddhist Monument.* Berkeley and Los Angeles: University of California Press, 1981.

Haruki Kageyama. *The Arts of Shinto.* Translated and adapted by Christine Guth. New York: Weatherhill, 1973.

Huntington, Susan L., and John C. Huntington. *Leaves from the Bodhi Tree: The Art of Pala India.* Dayton, Ohio: Dayton Art Institute, 1990.

Ishida Hisatoyo. *Esoteric Buddhist Painting.* Translated and adapted by E. Dale Saunders. Tokyo, New York, and San Francisco: Kodansha International and Shibundo, 1987.

Jackson, David P. *A History of Tibetan Painting: The Great Tibetan Painters and Their Traditions.* Vienna: Verlag der Österreichischen Akademie der Wissenschaften, 1996.

Klimburg-Salter, Deborah. *The Silk Road and the Diamond Path: Esoteric Buddhist Art on the Trans-Himalayan Trade Routes.* Los Angeles: University of California/Los Angeles Art Council, 1982.

Morse, Anne Nishimura, and Samuel Cromwell Morse. *Object as Insight: Japanese Buddhist Art and Ritual.* Katanoh and New York: Katanoh Museum of Art, 1995.

Murase Miyeko, with Gratia Williams Nakahashi and Stephanie Wade. *Jewel Rivers: Japanese Art from the Burke Collection.* Richmond: Virginia Museum of Fine Arts in cooperation with the Mary and Jackson Burke Foundation, 1995.

Pal, Pratapaditya. *Tibetan Painting: A Study of Tibetan Thangkas, Eleventh to Nineteenth Centuries.* Basel: Ravi Kumar, 1984.

Pal, Pratapaditya, with Ian Alsop, Heather Stoddard, and Valrae Reynolds. *Art of the Himalayas: Treasures from Nepal and Tibet.* New York: American Federation of Arts, 1991.

Raghu Vira and Lokesh Chandra. *Tibetan Mandalas: Vajravali and Tantra-Samuccaya.* New Delhi: International Academy of Indian Culture, 1995.

Rhie, Marilyn, and Robert A. F. Thurman. *Wisdom and Compassion: The Sacred Art of Tibet.* Expanded ed. New York: Tibet House, 1996.

Rosenfield, John, and Elizabeth ten Grotenhuis. *Journey of the Three Jewels: Japanese Buddhist Paintings from Western Collections.* New York: The Asia Society, 1979.

Singer, Jane Casey, and Philip Denwood, eds. *Tibetan Arts: Towards a Definition of Style.* London: Laurence King in association with Alan Marcuson, 1997.

Weidner, Marsha, ed. *Latter Day of the Law: Images of Chinese Buddhism, 850–1850.* Laurence, Kansas: Spencer Museum of Art; Honolulu: University of Hawaii Press, 1994.

RELATED PUBLICATIONS

Bryant, Barry. *The Wheel of Time Sand Mandala: Visual Scripture of Tibetan Buddhism.* New York: HarperCollins, 1992.

Gold, Peter. *Navajo & Tibetan Sacred Wisdom: The Circle of the Spirit.* Rochester, Vt.: Inner Traditions, 1994.

Jung, C. G. *Mandala Symbolism.* Translated by R.F.C. Hull. Princeton: Princeton University Press, 1973.

INDEX